UNDERSTANDING YO
SCIENCE ASPIRATIONS

Understanding Young People's Science Aspirations offers new evidence and understanding about how young people develop their aspirations for education, learning and, ultimately, careers in science. Integrating new findings from a major research study with a wide-ranging review of the existing international literature, it brings a distinctive sociological analytic lens to the field of science education.

The book offers an explanation of how some young people become dedicated to following science and what might be done to increase and broaden this population, exploring the need for increased scientific literacy among citizens to enable them to exercise agency and lead a life underpinned by informed decisions about their own health and their environment. Key issues considered include:

- why we should study young people's science aspirations;
- the role of families, social class and science capital in career choice;
- the links between ethnicity, gender and science aspirations;
- the implications for research, policy and practice.

Set in the context of international policy concerns about the urgent need to improve, increase and diversify participation in post-16 science, this key text considers how we must encourage a supply of appropriately qualified future scientists and workers in STEM industries and ensure a high level of scientific literacy in society. It is a crucial read for all training and practising science teachers, education researchers and academics, as well as anyone invested in the desire to help fulfil young people's science aspirations.

Louise Archer is Professor of Sociology of Education at King's College London, UK.

Jennifer DeWitt is Research Fellow at King's College London, UK.

UNDERSTANDING YOUNG PEOPLE'S SCIENCE ASPIRATIONS

How students form ideas about 'becoming a scientist'

Louise Archer and Jennifer DeWitt

Routledge
Taylor & Francis Group

LONDON AND NEW YORK

First published 2017
by Routledge
2 Park Square, Milton Park, Abingdon, Oxon OX14 4RN

and by Routledge
711 Third Avenue, New York, NY 10017

Routledge is an imprint of the Taylor & Francis Group, an informa business

British Library Cataloguing in Publication Data
A catalogue record for this book is available from the British Library

Library of Congress Cataloging in Publication Data
Names: Archer, Louise, 1973- | DeWitt, Jennifer (Jennifer Eileen)
Title: Understanding young people's science aspirations : how
students form ideas about "becoming a scientist" / Louise Archer and
Jennifer DeWitt.
Description: Abingdon, Oxon; New York, NY: Routledge, 2016.
Identifiers: LCCN 2016009920 | ISBN 9781138793576 (hardback) |
ISBN 9781138793583 (pbk.) | ISBN 9781315761077 (ebook)
Subjects: LCSH: Science—Study and teaching—Social aspects.
Classification: LCC Q181. A6935 2016 | DDC 507.1—dc23
LC record available at https://lccn.loc.gov/2016009920

ISBN: 9781138793576 (hbk)
ISBN: 9781138793583 (pbk)
ISBN: 9781315761077 (ebk)

Typeset in Bembo
by Keystroke, Neville Lodge, Tettenhall, Wolverhampton

For Barnaby, Jamie and Martha

CONTENTS

FIGURES AND TABLES

Figures

Tables

ACKNOWLEDGEMENTS

We would like to thank everyone who helped us with the production of this book. At the time of the submission of this manuscript, it has been seven years since we first embarked on the ASPIRES project. Over this time we have received valuable support, engagement, discussion and feedback from a wide range of friends and colleagues regarding the ideas and analyses that we have brought together here. Indeed, we are unlikely to be able to do justice to all of you!

The data that we draw on were collected as part of a research project exploring children's science and career aspirations from age 10 to 14, which was funded by the Economic and Social Research Council (RES-179-25-0008) as part of the Targeted Initiative on Science and Mathematics Education (TISME), a research programme funded by the ESRC in partnership with the Institute of Physics, Gatsby Charitable Foundation and the Association for Science Education. The ASPIRES surveys were conducted with the assistance of the NFER. We extend our thanks to all members of the KCL project team who were involved over the five years of the project, including Jonathan Osborne, Beatrice Willis, Billy Wong and Justin Dillon. We also want to thank all the researchers who have assisted with data collection, including Annalisa Fagan, Billy Wong, Sophie Kelsall Greener and Johanna Woydack. Thanks also to the members of the ASPIRES advisory group for their useful feedback and input.

Particular thanks must also go to Emily MacLeod for her invaluable help in compiling references and formatting the book – it is very much appreciated! We thank our King's College London colleagues for their ongoing support and interest during the writing of the book, especially Becky Francis and our fantastic colleagues in the Science and Technology Education Group (STEG) – you know who you all are!

Without doubt our greatest thanks go to the parents and young people who so kindly agreed to share their views, experiences and lives with us throughout the project. We thank the schools and teachers who generously allowed us access to their students for the three surveys and the interviews. And we give particular thanks to our interview participants – it has been a privilege to work with you over the years.

Some of the data and analyses we report are drawn from previously published articles in *American Educational Research Journal*, *International Journal of Science Education*, *International Journal of Science and Mathematics Education*, *Journal of Education Policy*, *Pedagogy, Culture and Society*, *Journal of Research in Science Teaching*, *Research in Science Education* and *Science Education*; we thank the publishers for granting us permission to reproduce material.

We are grateful to Routledge and Sarah Tuckwell for supporting us through the production of the book and for their patience and understanding when the deadline needed to be extended due to Jen's maternity leave.

Finally, thanks to our wonderful family and friends for their ongoing love and support – and for enabling us to write this book.

Louise Archer and Jennifer DeWitt

1

WHY STUDY YOUNG PEOPLE'S SCIENCE ASPIRATIONS?

Why is science participation an issue?

Science participation occupies a distinctive and prominent position within international policy discourse. Governments and policy-makers across Western developed nations are highly concerned that more needs to be done to improve – to increase and widen – participation in post-compulsory Science, Technology, Engineering and Mathematics (STEM) at all levels (e.g. ACOLA, 2013; Adler-Nissen et al., 2012; CBI, 2012; HM Treasury, 2011; House of Lords, 2012; Perkins, 2013; US President's Council of Advisors on Science and Technology, 2010[1]). This is particularly the case for the physical sciences, where participation rates remain below desired levels and the profile of a 'typical' graduate remains White, male and middle class (e.g. AAUW, 2010; Smith, 2010a, 2010b, 2011). It is a point of ongoing puzzlement and frustration that these patterns persist and that the figures largely appear to be resistant to the decades of interventions that have been undertaken to try to broaden the profile of those pursuing science at university and beyond. For instance, in the UK, initiatives aimed at increasing and/or widening the profile of STEM graduates appear to have had little lasting impact on higher education participation rates (Smith, 2010a; Smith and Gorard, 2011; see also Royal Society, 2008a, 2008b). Yet, internationally considerable energy and resource continues to be invested in improving STEM participation via a myriad of local and high-profile national programmes, coalitions and campaigns (e.g. Change the Equation in the US,[2] the 'Your Life' campaign in the UK,[3] and the Australian government's allocation of $54.0 million in the 2012–13 Budget for the four year 'Mathematics and science—increasing participation in schools and universities' programme).[4] In short, the question of how we might improve STEM participation remains a key national and international policy concern – although, as we discuss next, there are different, competing rationales given for why STEM participation needs to be urgently addressed.

Broadly speaking, the rationale for increasing science participation is framed as an imperative for supplying the science 'pipeline' (the future STEM professionals required by the economy) or for improving public scientific literacy for social justice ends. As we discuss later in this book, while the two rationales are often cited together as complementary reasons for the need to improve STEM participation, they do not necessarily fit easily together, either conceptually or in practice, and can conflict with one another.

Unsurprisingly, it is the economic, 'pipeline' rationale that achieves most prominence within national policy discourse. From this perspective, STEM industries are understood as being vital elements of the current and future national economy (e.g. BIS, 2009; CBI, 2010, 2012; House of Lords, 2012). For example, a report by the UK Council for Industry and Higher Education (CIHE, 2009) states that:

> the workforce of the future will increasingly require higher-level skills as structural adjustments in the economy force businesses to move up the value chain. These jobs of the future will increasingly require people with the capabilities that a STEM qualification provides.

The UK Commission for Employment and Skills (UKCES, 2012) predicts that by 2020, while many other fields are expected to shrink, there will be a 13% expansion in the demand for science, engineering and technology professionals in the UK. Some have argued that there is a lack of definitive and reliable data on the supply and demand of STEM graduates and postgraduates (e.g. House of Lords, 2012), and it is contested as to how many future scientists the economy actually needs (e.g. Lowell et al., 2009; Xie and Killewald, 2012), although it is generally agreed that predicted STEM skills gaps in key areas are a valid concern (e.g. House of Lords, 2012; Royal Academy of Engineering, 2012). The widespread fear is that a failure to produce sufficient numbers of adequately qualified/skilled STEM workers will compromise national economic competitiveness (CBI, 2010; Royal Society, 2008a, 2008b). Indeed, the Confederation of British Industry[5] (CBI, 2012) reports that just under half of employers currently have (and expect further) difficultly recruiting employees with the STEM skills and knowledge that they require. These issues need to be understood in context: for instance, in the UK, the overall number of STEM graduates is increasing – but this is largely because the overall number of graduates is increasing. Indeed the percentage of STEM graduates decreased slightly from just over 43% in 2002–3 to just under 42% in 2009–10 (House of Lords, 2012). Moreover, rates of participation in 'core' STEM subjects (e.g. mathematics, physics) constitute only a small proportion of overall STEM participation rates. As Smith (2010a, 2010b) explains, the problem is not that undergraduates are not studying science per se; rather, the issue lies with uneven rates of participation between different STEM subject areas.

Despite its dominance in policy discourse, the economic, 'pipeline' rationale is not the only reason that is given for trying to improve STEM participation. Indeed, some would argue that the pipeline discourse is neither the most important nor the most useful rationale for improving STEM participation. The second discourse that we would like to consider here is the 'public scientific literacy' rationale. This perspective argues that STEM participation needs to be *widened* (not just increased) for reasons of social equity. In other words, science is understood as being a public good, such that achieving equitably spread, high levels of scientific literacy (Durant, 1993) across the population is vital for the creation of a 'good society' (e.g. Millar, 1996; Millar and Osborne, 1998; Osborne, 2007). From this perspective, it is a matter of social justice that all citizens should be able to understand STEM (be STEM 'literate' and be sufficiently informed about, and have the opportunity to inform, STEM developments in society). In other words, all citizens should be able to understand, participate in and shape scientific developments in society. Additionally, because analysis suggests that some STEM qualifications can carry a wage premium, enabling those who possess them to access favourable (high pay and status) jobs (e.g. Greenwood et al., 2011), it is important that everyone has an equal opportunity to access and participate in STEM, irrespective of their social background. Another important aspect of the equity rationale is that STEM education and industries need to be inclusive of, and informed/shaped by the interests, needs and talents of, a representative workforce. As we have written elsewhere (Archer et al., 2015), we believe that science is a key form of symbolic capital which can facilitate agency and the re/production of relations of subordination and/or privilege (Bourdieu, 2010). Currently the 'goods' of science participation are inequitably spread across society (Archer et al., 2012b; Gorard and See, 2009), so we consider it a social justice imperative that we try to find ways to disrupt (and make more equitable) current patterns of participation.

Who participates and who does not?

In the UK, as in many Western developed nations, participation in post-16 science, technology, engineering and mathematics varies considerably by gender, ethnicity and social class (Royal Society, 2008b). In the physical sciences, engineering and mathematics, women, working-class students and those from particular minority ethnic backgrounds (e.g. Black Caribbean and Pakistani/Bangladeshi) remain starkly under-represented at degree level (Smith, 2010a, 2010b, 2011) and in the wider workforce, with statistics suggesting that women make up around 14% of the UK STEM workforce,[6] and around a quarter of the STEM workforce in the US.[7] These trends are also very noticeable in physics at A level (IOP, 2012). It has also been noted that England has one of the worst gender profiles in the world in relation to participation in engineering (Perkins, 2013[8]).

Since the 1970s, there have been improvements in gender equity within science, with greater numbers of women and girls now taking STEM qualifications, entering STEM careers and contributing to the wealth of STEM knowledge and research in many Western nations (e.g. AAUW, 2010). Indeed, it has been noted that there are few, if any, gender differences in attainment in school science (Haworth et al., 2008; Royal Society, 2008b; Smith, 2011) and mathematics (Boaler and Sengupta-Irving, 2006). However, despite these advances, there are still persistent gender inequalities in terms of students' *attitudes* to science/mathematics and their patterns of *participation* in post-16 science/mathematics.

Patterns of participation with regard to social class are similarly entrenched – although they tend to command less policy and public attention. As Gorard and See (2009) discuss, students from poorer families are less likely to study science subjects post-16 compared to many other subjects, and those who do are less likely to obtain grades high enough to enable further study of the subject.

'Race'/ethnicity also correlates with notable patterns of participation in science. For example, work by Elias et al. (2006) and Jones and Elias (2005) found that, among students eligible to study physics at degree level (i.e. those with relevant qualifications/grades to be eligible for entry to a physics degree programme), British students from Black Caribbean, Black African, Pakistani and Bangladeshi backgrounds were heavily under-represented, whereas British Chinese and Indian students were proportionally over-represented. Their analysis suggests that while differential attainment may play a part in producing patterns of participation, it does not fully explain the situation, as such patterns are still evident even among similarly qualified students.

As we discuss in this book, evidence from our ASPIRES study suggests that identities and inequalities of gender, social class and ethnicity play an important role in shaping the extent to which young people see science as being 'for me', or not.

Is science 'special'?

Writing a book about science participation and young people's science aspirations inevitably raises the question: but what's so special about science? Indeed, a number of subject areas (Modern Foreign Languages, MFL, being an obvious example) might lay claim to a similar 'crisis' in participation, with uneven patterns of pre- and post-16 participation and with parallel claims from employers that there are insufficient numbers of appropriately qualified candidates to fulfil their needs and requirements (e.g. Taylor and Marsden, 2012). In this respect, science is not particularly different or special. However, we would suggest that science is *distinctive* in terms of the level of policy/government and industry interest and investment in STEM participation. Moreover, while we do not necessarily believe that, intrinsically, science is any more or less valuable than any other subject, we would suggest that the current exchange value of STEM qualifications in the labour market again marks the field out as distinctive and worthy of further investigation, not least in light of our concerns with social in/equality. The distinctiveness of science is also underlined by its status as one of the 'core' subject areas; the more restrictive entry qualifications required for some science A levels (notably physics); and the relatively high social status of science subjects within society. Moreover, there is a notable strength and prevalence of concern that, compared to other school subjects, science is failing to engage young people (Jenkins and Nelson, 2005; Lyons, 2006; Osborne and Collins, 2001; Sjøberg and Schreiner, 2005), again suggesting something distinctive about science. Finally, in the UK, science is treated somewhat uniquely within the English education system in terms of how it is organised and structured at GCSE level: science is the only subject area to be stratified into core ('Double Award') and extended ('Triple Award') option routes.[9] In all these respects, we would argue that science is distinctive and provides a particularly interesting case study for sociological examination.

Our focus on 'science', rather than 'STEM', also requires justification. In essence, our focus on science is largely pragmatic, an attempt to restrict our area of inquiry within manageable parameters. We certainly feel that the issues around participation in technology, engineering and mathematics are equally important and pressing as they are for science. Moreover, we suggest that many of the issues we raise and the processes and factors that we identify as influencing young people's aspirations will, more than likely, have parallels with young people's views and aspirations in relation to technology, engineering and mathematics. That said, where we have data relating to these other areas, these are reported.

Our use of the term 'science' also deserves some explanation and clarification. When working with our younger cohorts in particular, we deliberately used the term science for pragmatic reasons, because it is the term that most primary school students are familiar with, as these lessons tend to be called 'Science' at school. However, at secondary school level, students may be more aware of being taught separate areas of science (usually biology, chemistry and physics). Hence, with older students, but particularly among our Year 9 cohort, we did probe these distinctions in more detail. We also conducted discussions with Year 6 and Year 8 groups to inform the development of survey items and interview instruments, and to explore what the young people understood by the term 'science'. For instance, students who took part in the four Year 8 discussion groups (two groups of girls and two groups of boys) explained that, for them, 'science' generally brought to mind school science and topics within school science (e.g. space, chemicals, human body). They also thought of practicals or experiments, as well as 'explosions'. Although they could generally distinguish among biology, chemistry and physics, these distinctions were not yet clear cut and, when answering questions about 'science', they tended to blur the boundaries between the sciences, rather than to think about a particular subject area – or even topic – within science. Similar tendencies were found in discussion groups with Year 6 students, except they were less likely to be familiar with the subject areas of biology, chemistry and physics.

Why focus on aspirations?

In this book we discuss our five-year research project, the ASPIRES study, in which we sought to better understand how young people form their science and career aspirations between the ages of 10 and 14. As we have discussed in a number of our papers and related writing (e.g. Archer, 2014; Archer et al., 2014c), we understand aspirations as expressions of people's hopes or ambitions. As Brannen and Nilsen (2007, p. 155) discuss, aspirations can range from vague and uncertain ideas about the future through to 'more concrete and achievable' plans. In other words, young people's aspirations can vary considerably:

> From intensely held goals and desires to looser, more nebulous interests; from 'high' or lofty ambitions to more prosaic, mundane or realistic expectations; from 'already known' and concrete expectations to fragile dreams that are constantly mediated and shaped by external constraints.
>
> *(Archer et al., 2010b, p. 78)*

However, the question might reasonably be asked – why focus on *aspirations*? After all, it is doubtful that many readers of this book aspired, as children, to the precise job/s that they have ended up in! So if children's aspirations do not predict their future outcomes, what value is there in studying them? We suggest there are three main reasons why a focus on aspirations is useful.

First, while not predictive, childhood aspirations can give a reasonably good approximation of the general type of career path that young people go on to take in the future (Trice, 1991b; Trice and McClellan, 1993). For instance, Croll (2008) undertook a longitudinal analysis of data from the British Household Panel Survey, finding that approximately half of those young people who expressed a particular aspiration at age 15 were actually in a similar type of occupation when they were surveyed again 10 to 15 years later. Evidence from the US further suggests that this link, between aspirations and outcomes, may be particularly salient in the case of science. Tai et al. (2006) analysed longitudinal data from the National Education Longitudinal Survey (NELS) of 1988, which began with a survey of 24,599 8th graders (ages 13–14 in 1988), followed by a further four follow-up surveys conducted over the subsequent 12 years. Their analysis found that a young person who aspires to a career in science at age 14 is almost three and a half times more likely to end up taking a degree in the physical sciences or engineering than a peer without such aspirations. This effect was even more pronounced for those who both aspired to a science career and attained highly in mathematics at age 14, with 51% of these students going on to take a STEM-related degree. As we discuss in Chapter 2, our ASPIRES data would also appear to suggest that children's aspirations seem to remain relatively stable, at the level of broad, general categories of aspiration, over the 10–14 age period.

Second, from a sociological perspective, we believe that aspirations can provide a useful 'tool' for researchers who want to understand young people's lives and identities. This is because we understand aspirations as not simply personal attitudes or views, but as socially constructed phenomena that are shaped by young people's social and cultural histories and locations. That is, the future options that a young person might see as being possible (or impossible) and desirable (or undesirable) 'for me' will be influenced by their experiences, their background, how they have been brought up and their sense of who they are – all of which will vary by axes such as gender, social class and ethnicity. In short, we think that aspirations can tell us about people's social identities and locations. This view, of aspirations as socially constructed phenomena, is also borne out by evidence of aspirations being strongly socially patterned, that is, varying in predictable ways within and between particular social groups, for instance in terms of gender (e.g. OECD, 2012a), ethnicity (e.g. Archer and Francis, 2007) and social class (e.g. Archer et al., 2010a).

Third, the concept of 'aspiration' is often invoked within education policy discourse and forms a focal point within a raft of interventions that seek to improve young people's educational participation and engagement. For instance, over the last decade it has been very common for successive UK governments to highlight how a 'poverty of aspiration' is holding back the educational achievement and participation of working-class and (some) minority ethnic communities (e.g. DfE, 2010; DfES, 2003, 2004, 2005). This concern with low aspirations has also been echoed in the US, for instance in George W. Bush's (2000)[10] pronouncement that 'we cannot afford to have an America segregated by class, by race, or by aspiration'. This persistent policy concern with the 'problem of low aspirations' (Strand, 2007) has been mirrored by a proliferation of initiatives aimed at 'raising' young people's aspirations (particularly those from socially disadvantaged backgrounds) in order to improve their attainment, participation and/or life chances. Such schemes have included government-sponsored national programmes, such as *Aiming High* and *Aim Higher*[11] in the UK, and independent initiatives organised by countless charities and NGOs in the UK,[12] US[13] and beyond.

We should also add a note here, for the purpose of clarity, to explain what we mean by the term 'science aspirations'. We use this term quite specifically to refer to careers in science (e.g. working as a scientist) which are allied to the natural and physical sciences. We use the term 'STEM careers' (and the even broader terminology of science/STEM-related careers) to refer to jobs that more broadly relate to engineering, mathematics, technology and medicine. For instance, while we see medicine (and related careers, such as a vet) as STEM careers, we do not categorise them as 'science careers' per se. This is driven in large part by the distinction that many students seem to make between science and medicine. For instance, in Year 6 (as evidenced by focus groups and other interviews and the Y6 survey), students were asked about what they consider 'science' to be. The vast majority explained science through reference to aspects of the physical sciences (e.g. chemicals, space, experiments) but far fewer grouped it with medicine. Indeed, it was only as students moved through secondary school that they seemed to become more aware that science is related to medicine and that medical careers require the study of science (a fact that 'surprises' some students). Moreover, interviews throughout the study indicate that students do not tend to construct the term 'scientist' to include doctors (and other medical careers).

Key concepts: identity, intersectionality and science capital

Perhaps one of the distinctive features of our approach is the sociological lens that we bring to bear on the study. In particular, we are interested in both people's identities (the sense they have of themselves, how they are seen by others, and the sense that people have of how others see them) and their structural locations (in particular, how wider inequalities such as those related to gender, social class and ethnicity shape their lives, sense of self, aspirations, life chances and so on). As we set out next, we draw predominantly on two bodies of sociological work: critical theorisations of identity and Pierre Bourdieu's theory of social reproduction. We feel that the combination of these conceptual lenses enables us to attend to both agency and structure. That is, they provide tools for us to explore how people construct, or create, their identities and how they make 'choices', while also paying attention to the ways in which people's thoughts and actions are shaped by conditions that are not of their own choosing.

Theorising identity

Our approach draws on 'critical' sociological theories – in other words, theories that are primarily concerned with critiquing inequitable power relations in society. In particular, our understanding of identity draws on work from feminist post-structuralists, such as Judith Butler, and postcolonial theorists, such as Stuart Hall. These approaches share in common a conceptualisation in which identity is not fixed, but rather is something that is fluid and 'always in process' (Hall, 1990, p. 222). That is, identity is not something that you 'have' or 'are', it is something that you are constantly 'doing' (and re-doing). As Spivak (1988) puts it, identity is not a full stop – it is an ongoing sentence.

From this perspective, identity is produced within and through discourse (Anthias, 2001; Burman and Parker, 1993; Gee, 1996) and is structured by relations of power (Foucault, 1978). Social structures (e.g. of gender, class, ethnicity) play an important role in shaping the identities, choices and aspirations that people perceive as possible and desirable ('for me'). From this perspective, identity is understood as the ongoing articulation of complex and shifting subject positions within wider relations of power and structures of privilege/subordination (Anthias, 2001).

We find Butler's (1990, 1993) theorisations of gender as 'performance' particularly useful. Butler is primarily concerned with conceptualising gender but, as discussed below (in the section on Intersectionality), we feel that her concepts extend across different social axes. For Butler (1990), gender is an inherently relational construct. That is, masculinity and femininity do not 'exist' independently – they only make sense in relation to one another. Moreover, Butler argues that gender is *performative*. In other words, gender is not the 'result' of a person's sex and does not emanate 'naturally' from particular (sexed, racialised, classed) bodies. Instead, Butler conceptualises gender as a socially constructed performance that is produced through discursive and bodily 'acts'. In this respect, gender is not something you 'are' or 'have' but rather is something that you 'do' (perform) and continually re-do. By separating gender from sexed bodies, Butler argues that gender is actually an 'illusion' (Butler, 1990, pp. 185–186), albeit a very powerful illusion. This illusion is created constantly through what people say and do (i.e. through verbal and bodily performances). This conceptualisation of gender as a performance – something that you 'do' – is conveyed by the terminology 'doing boy' and 'doing girl'.

Similarly, we understand social class and 'race'/ethnicity as also being socially constructed and forever 'in process'. As with gender, class and ethnicity are also 'fictions', not the natural products of particular bodies or biology, although – as with gender – ethnicity and social class also entail very real, material consequences (Hall, 1990, 1992, 1996). As Anthias and Yuval-Davis (1992) powerfully explain, 'ethnic groups' are not simply givens. The boundaries of ethnicity are continually shifting and contested – notions of 'belonging' and categorisation being fiercely debatable. Indeed, some suggest that ethnic groups might be better understood as ethnic collectivities, which are forever in the process of 'becoming'. Anderson (1992, p. 6) describes ethnic collectivities as 'imagined communities', which may be organised around notions of common origin, but which are constantly shifting and negotiated. These groupings are socially and historically located (and hence the boundaries and meanings associated with them shift across time and space) and are inflected by gender and social class (Anthias and Yuval-Davis, 1992).

Debates around social class and classed identity have developed along similar lines. Although some sociologists have controversially claimed that social class is 'dead' (Pakulski and Waters, 1996), arguably social-class analysis is as 'alive' as it ever was. Alongside more classical sociological interest in defining measures to ascertain people's social class and/or socio-economic status (e.g. Goldthorpe, 1996; ONS, 2001), there has been a growth in cultural class analysis (e.g. Bennett and Hogarth, 2009; Savage, 2000; Savage et al., 2013). This perspective understands that many people may not self-consciously identify themselves in class terms, but social class still has a profound effect on their lives (Savage, 2000). The cultural class analysis approach conceptualises class identity as performed through 'taste' and cultural consumption – with the boundaries of class being hotly contested. Our own understanding of class is very much influenced by this work, and particularly the underpinning theoretical framework in the form of the sociology of Pierre Bourdieu, which is further elaborated later in this chapter.

Science identity

In extending the notion of identity to the topic of young people's science aspirations and their identification (or not!) with science, we have found the concept of 'science identity' useful. In particular, we have drawn on Carlone and Johnson's (2007) explication, in which they conceptualise science identity as having two key dimensions: (i) an individual's sense of self in relation to science and the extent to which someone considers (or, as we would understand it, *performs*) him/herself as interested in and/or competent at science, and (ii) the extent to which they are recognised by others as being talented/good at science and/or having potential in science (or, as we would put it, the extent to which others regard the individual's performances as being authentic and congruent with the dominant context within which they are enacted). In other words, Carlone and Johnson propose that science identity captures the extent to which a person both sees themselves and is recognised by others as being a 'science person'. Research has found that a student's science identity can substantially help (or hinder) their ability to learn science and participate in school science (Calabrese Barton and Tan, 2010). Where there are tensions, for instance between a student's sense of self and the ways in which they are seen by others, this may constrain their science learning and participation (e.g. Brickhouse et al., 2000; Carlone, 2004). In this book, we integrate the notion of science identity with our conceptual position on identity as performance and identity as intersection (see next section) in order to explore the ways in which young people are able to perform themselves as 'a science person' (and to be recognised as such by others), or not. We also use the concept to consider what sorts of identity positions are constructed, valued and made possible by science – for instance, examining how the 'brainy' image of scientists can make it difficult for some students to recognise and perform themselves as a 'science person'.

Intersectionality

As discussed above, our theoretical approach foregrounds the relationship between identities and inequalities of 'race'/ethnicity, gender and social class. In order to keep an analytic hold on all these axes at once, we draw on intersectionality theory (e.g. Collins, 2000; Crenshaw, 1989). Intersectionality theory proposes that social divisions are not separate phenomena, but are intrinsically interlinked. That is, the meaning of one cannot be divorced from the others. A person's identity is performed and constituted within a nexus of multiple, intersecting social relations (Collins, 2000) and it is the complex combination of these relations of power, privilege and subordination which needs to be grasped and addressed by the researcher. The intersectional approach differs from an additive model in which each axis is viewed as a discrete 'thing' (e.g. a gender identity; a class identity; an ethnic identity; a set of relations which is similar for all those within the category) which can be 'added' together (e.g. an individual might have three separate identities, relating respectively to their gender, ethnicity and social class). In contrast, an intersectional approach understands the very nature of each set of social relations as interacting with, and mediated by, other social axes of inequality. In this formulation, there is no single ethnic identity that is not also gendered and classed; no form of femininity that is not also at once racialised and classed; and no class identity that is not inherently racialised and gendered (see also Archer and Francis, 2007). Applying this perspective to science, we thus understand young people's science identities as mediated by 'race'/ethnicity, social class and gender (e.g. Calabrese Barton and Brickhouse, 2006), which shape the extent to which science aspirations are perceived as possible and desirable ('for me').

'Science capital': using and extending Bourdieu's concepts

The final main conceptual lens that we bring to bear on our understanding of young people's science aspirations comes from Bourdieu's theory of practice (e.g. Bourdieu, 1984, 2001; Bourdieu and Passeron, 1990). Bourdieu's work is concerned with understanding the reproduction of social inequalities in society. He proposes that relations of privilege and domination are produced through the interaction of *habitus*, *capital* and *field*. Habitus, Bourdieu argues, comprises an inner matrix of dispositions – acquired through socialisation – that shapes how an individual operates in the social world. Habitus provides a practical 'feel' for the world, framing ways of thinking, feeling and being, such as taken-for-granted notions of 'who we are' and 'what we do' and what is 'usual' for 'us'. For instance, various studies have shown how habitus can shape the extent to which higher education is seen as an expected, 'automatic' post-16 route or as 'not for the likes of us' (Archer et al., 2003; Reay et al., 2005).

As discussed in Archer et al. (2012a), we extended this notion of individual habitus to the family ('family habitus'):

> to explore the extent to which families construct a collective relationship with science and the extent to which this is shaped by their possession of particular sorts of economic, social and cultural capital. In particular, we examine participants' accounts of how science is 'woven' into un/conscious family life (or not).

Capital refers to the resources that a person has at their disposal. These resources can be economic, cultural, social and/or symbolic. The value of capital is not fixed but is determined by the field (context, setting) within which they are operating. For instance, a particular resource may carry a high value within one field but not another. This is because field governs the 'rules of the game', determining the value of particular forms of capital within a given context. As Bourdieu and Wacquant (1992, p. 101) discuss, 'capital does not exist and function except in relation to a field'. In short, as Bourdieu explains, it is the interaction of habitus with capital within the context of the field that produces social relations of advantage and disadvantage.

Bourdieu proposes his ideas as 'open concepts designed to guide empirical work' (Bourdieu, 1990, p. 107) and during the course of the ASPIRES project we extended Bourdieu's concept of capital into the notion of 'science capital'. As we discuss in Archer et al. (2013), we use science capital as a conceptual tool for understanding patterns in the formation and production of children's science aspirations.

> science capital is not a separate 'type' of capital but rather a conceptual device for collating various types of . . . social and cultural capital that specifically relate to science – notably those which have the potential to generate use or exchange value for individuals or groups to support and enhance their attainment, engagement and/or participation in science.

As we have further developed elsewhere (Archer et al., 2015), we conceptualise science capital as primarily encompassing science-related forms of social capital (e.g. science-related social networks; knowing people who have science knowledge and/or science-related jobs) and science-related cultural capital (science-related qualifications, scientific literacy; understanding about how science works, and so on). Other forms of capital might also be deployed to generate science capital. For instance, economic capital (money) might be used to purchase STEM resources and opportunities (e.g. science kits, tutoring, visits to science centres and events).

We propose that the symbolic and exchange value of science capital will depend on the field; for example, the science capital possessed and produced by young people from socially disadvantaged backgrounds may not be valued highly within school science contexts. That is, while such knowledge may have local 'use value' (be valued by those who possess it and be useful for a range of reasons), it may not necessarily have 'exchange value' (e.g. be easily translatable into social advantage in the context of school science). An example might be of a working-class young woman who has developed an interest in and a practical competence around using chemicals to dye hair, but whose knowledge, interest and expertise are not harnessed or built on within school science and do not 'translate' into either science attainment, identity or further participation.

We thus see a key goal for critical science education as being to find ways to change dominant relations within the field, in order to better support and enable a wider diversity of students to engage with science. This project very much follows the lead of scholars such as Angela Calabrese Barton and colleagues (e.g. Basu et al., 2011; Calabrese Barton and Tan, 2010) who argue that democratic science education needs to find ways to leverage and value young people's different 'funds of knowledge' within mainstream contexts.

The ASPIRES study

The ASPIRES study was a five-year investigation of children's science and career aspirations, from age 10 to 14. It was funded by the UK's Economic and Social Research Council (grant number: RES-179-25-0008) as part of its Targeted Initiative on Science and Mathematics Education (TISME). In order to generate both a breadth and depth of data, we used mixed methods, namely an online survey (comprising in total over 18,000 responses) and longitudinal, in-depth individual interviews conducted with a sample of parents and young people. The survey and interviews were conducted at three time points: Phase 1 was conducted at the end of primary school (age 10/11, Year 6); Phase 2 was undertaken two years later, when students reached the second year of secondary school (age 12/13, Year 8); the final phase was administered when students reached age 13/14, in Year 9.

Surveys with students from age 10 to 14

We conducted three largely representative surveys over the course of the project. In Phase 1, the survey was completed by 9,319[14] students in England, who were recruited from 279 primary schools (248 state schools and 31 independent). This sample represented all regions of the country and was roughly proportional to the overall national distribution of schools in England by attainment and proportion of students eligible for free school meals. The second phase of the survey was conducted two years later (2011/12), when participants were in Year 8 (age 12/13 years). Some 5,634[15] Year 8 students from 69 secondary schools (58 maintained and 11 independent schools) completed the Phase 2 questionnaire between September and December 2011. The third phase was administered one year later, when students were in Year 9 (age 13/14 years) – 4,600 students from 147 schools completed the questionnaire in Year 9 between February and May 2013, of whom 1,043 had also completed the survey in Year 6. Again, schools in both Phases 2 and 3 represented all nine Government Office Regions in England and comprised a range of attainments at Key Stage 3 science (from 2008) and a range of free school meals (FSM) eligibility. Of the 4,600 students who participated in Survey 3, 2,038 (44.4%) were male and 2,550 (55.4%) were female (12 students did not provide their gender). A total of 4,438 (96.5%) attended state schools and 162 (3.5%) attended independent schools.

Full details of the survey and its methods, analyses and findings are discussed in separate publications (DeWitt and Archer, 2015; DeWitt et al., 2011, 2013b, 2014), but here we present a summary of the key features. We collected a range of demographic data (including measures of cultural capital)[16] on the surveys. The majority of questions used a Likert scale to elicit attitudinal responses. Each of the surveys focused largely on the same key topic areas, in order to allow for data comparison, although some questions were added or adjusted between the different phases, to reflect changes, such as between primary and secondary school (Y6 and Y8 surveys). We asked students about a wide range of topics, including: their aspirations in science; attitudes towards school science; self-concept in science; images of scientists; participation in science-related activities outside of school; parental expectations; parental school involvement; parental attitudes towards science; and peer attitudes towards school and towards school science. Aspirations, subject choices and post-16 plans were explored more deeply in the Year 8 and 9 surveys, reflecting the growing maturity of the participants and the increasing relevance of these aspects of their lives. For instance, in the second survey items were added about students' perceptions of their science teachers, the perceived usefulness of studying science and future subject choice (post-compulsory).

The development and validation of the survey instrument are described more fully elsewhere (e.g. DeWitt et al., 2011), as are key findings from all three surveys (DeWitt and Archer, 2015; DeWitt et al., 2013b, 2014), which provides further detail on the reliability and validity of the survey instrument, as well as the specific items. But, to summarise, first, reliability and validity analyses were conducted using principal components analysis and Cronbach's alpha to determine internal consistency and unidimensionality of scales. These analyses revealed similar components in each of the three surveys, with acceptable to good Cronbach's alpha values. Next, the composite variables (components) that emerged from the first set of analyses were utilised to explore patterns in children's responses, including by gender, ethnicity, social class and cultural capital. More specifically, student responses to the items in each of the components identified by the principal components analysis were scored (e.g. strongly agree = 5, agree = 4, strongly disagree = 1 and so forth) and summed across items to create composite variables. These variables were used in descriptive and multivariate analyses to form an overview of the data.

Following these initial analyses, we conducted multi-level modelling (MLM) analyses, which investigated factors that may be related to children's aspirations in science (or other outcomes of interest). MLM analyses are similar to regression analyses in that they identify variables that account for significant proportions of variance in an outcome variable. For instance, in our work they are used to identify which combination of independent variables (e.g. gender, parental attitudes to science) best explains the variation in students' aspirations in science. The advantage of multi-level models is that they take into account that students' responses are grouped by school (i.e. that students' responses within a school tend to be similar to a degree, due to sharing the same environment), and therefore they use a more accurate measure of standard error than standard regression models. As a consequence, it is less likely that independent variables will be included in the final model that are not significantly and sufficiently related to the outcome, thus increasing the accuracy of the model.

Interviews with students and parents

While the surveys provide a broad-brush picture of the developing and changing aspirations of a large cohort of students, we also wanted to explore young people's views, experiences and aspirations in greater depth. To this end we longitudinally tracked a subsample of students via individual interviews. We also interviewed their parents, where possible, to help contextualise and provide another dimension to the analysis.

In the first phase of the qualitative research we conducted 170 interviews with 78 parents and 92 children aged 10/11 (Year 6). Participants were drawn from 11 schools in England (nine state and two independent schools). Potential schools were purposively sampled from the list of 279 schools that responded to the Phase 1 survey as part of the wider study to represent a range of geographic and social/economic contexts, including multi-ethnic urban, suburban and rural schools. Schools were provided with information letters about the project and were asked to distribute consent forms to all parents in the year group. All those who agreed to take part were interviewed. Students came from a broad range of socio-economic classes and ethnic backgrounds. For Phase 2 we managed to follow up 85 of these pupils when they were in Year 8 (37 boys and 48 girls), and in Phase 3 (Year 9) we managed to re-interview 83 students and 74 parents. These students now attended 41 secondary schools in nine areas of England and Wales.

Interviews lasted between 30 minutes and 1 hour (for students) and up to 1.5 hours (with parents). The majority of interviews with parents and students were conducted by both of us (Jen and Louise) but we were also assisted by a team of additional researchers (Beatrice Willis, Billy Wong, Sophie Kelsall Greener, Annalisa Fagan and Johanna Woydack) for some of the student and a number of the parent interviews. The majority of interviews were conducted by Jen DeWitt. All but one of the interviewers are White middle-class women (with English, American and French national backgrounds) and Billy is a British-Chinese male. Interviewees were invited to choose their own pseudonyms; hence the majority of the pseudonyms used in this book reflect the personal choices of interviewees.

As with the surveys, the majority of the areas we asked interviewees about remained fairly constant over time, in order to allow for comparison of data across interview points. But some areas of questioning were adapted to reflect changes in the young people's experiences, the differential organisation of school science across year groups, and to enable greater probing of salient key areas (such as Year 9 option choices). Interview topic areas included: students' constructions of self (in and out of school, interests, learner identity, self-efficacy); experiences of school; experiences of and views on school science; teachers and other subjects; aspirations and the future; formation of aspirations; influences on choices, processes of decision-making; imagined future subject choices; gendered constructions of self and others; extra-curricular activities; images of scientists; achievement and popularity; perceptions of the usefulness of science. Brief fieldnotes were also taken after each interview to record the interview context, key non-verbal occurrences and other physical/behavioural points relating to interviewees (e.g. fidgeting, nervousness, confidence).

All interviews were digitally audio-recorded and transcribed. In line with the study's conceptual approach, data were analysed using a discourse analytic approach (Burman and Parker, 1993). As Alldred and Burman (2005) discuss, this form of analysis differs from more general approaches to discourse analysis (Wilkinson and Kitzinger, 1995) in that it does not attempt a close, 'micro' analysis of the text, but rather focuses on looking for patterns in participants' talk (discourses). This approach is centrally concerned with the organisation of power within people's talk and tries to pull out the social implications of particular constructions – for instance examining what a person's talk is 'doing'.

In analysing the qualitative data, we collated the transcripts into 'student' and 'parent' groupings. All interviews pertaining to a particular student or parent were grouped together, to enable a longitudinal 'picture' of the individual over time. A summary grid was produced for each individual, detailing their demographics and responses to key questions/areas of interest over the three time points (e.g. 'aspirations, Y6–Y9'). Using the grid as a guide, and moving between the grid and the original transcripts, data were initially coded by at least two researchers and organised using the NVivo software package into key themes and responses to questions. Categorisations produced by either Louise or Jen were checked by the other author to ensure that these also fitted with her reading of the data. Potential relationships were tested and refined through successive phases of coding and analysis, iteratively testing out emergent themes across the data-set to establish 'strength' and prevalence (Miles and Huberman, 1994). Moving between the thematically coded data and the individual participant grids, we sought to identify patterns within participants' talk relating to key areas of interest – as exemplified by the different chapters in the book. Data were also subjected to a theoretically informed analysis (in line with our conceptual framework, as outlined earlier in the chapter), for instance to tease out interactions of habitus, capital and field in the production of aspirations (e.g. Chapter 5), or to identify racialised, gendered and classed identity performances, which were then explored in relation to the particular theme in question, such as gendered (Chapter 6) and racialised (Chapter 7) patterns of science aspiration, or students' views of scientists (Chapter 4).

Summary

In this chapter we have outlined why science participation continues to be an issue worthy of academic exploration. We have summarised the key issues for improving participation, discussing unequal patterns in STEM participation. We have argued that science is not inherently 'special' and deserving of special treatment, but it does constitute a distinctive and hence interesting area for analysis. We made a case for why the study of aspirations is potentially valuable and useful – even though they do not provide a detailed prediction of a young person's future pathways. We also set out the conceptual framework for our study and book, drawing on critical sociological theorisations of identity as performance, adopting an intersectional lens and using Bourdieu's theory of social reproduction – and extending this through the notions of *family habitus* and *science capital.* Finally, we provided some detail regarding the main data-sets that we draw on in the book, namely the surveys conducted with over 18,000 young people at the ages of 10/11, 12/13 and 13/14, and the longitudinal interviews conducted over the same time points/period with 83 students and 74 parents.

Notes

1 See www.whitehouse.gov/administration/eop/ostp/pcast/docsreports (accessed 28/1/16).
2 www.changetheequation.org/ (accessed 21/12/15).
3 http://yourlife.org.uk/about/ (accessed 21/12/15).
4 www.aph.gov.au/About_Parliament/Parliamentary_Departments/Parliamentary_Library/pubs/rp/BudgetReview201213/Mathematics (accessed 21/12/15).
5 The CBI is a leading UK independent employer's organisation.
6 www.wisecampaign.org.uk/resources/2015/09/women-in-the-stem-workforce (accessed 21/12/15).
7 www.whitehouse.gov/sites/default/files/microsites/ostp/stem_factsheet_2013_07232013.pdf (accessed 21/12/15).
8 www.gov.uk/government/uploads/system/uploads/attachment_data/file/254885/bis-13-1269-professor-john-perkins-review-of-engineering-skills.pdf (accessed 21/12/15).
9 There is currently a wide array of science qualifications that can be taken at Key Stage 4 (KS4), when national examinations (GCSEs) are taken by students who are 16 years old. The different options have undergone various changes, in format, content and nomenclature, over the last decade, and include statutory and non-statutory elements, spanning from the more traditionally academic (e.g. the equivalent of two GCSEs in all three sciences, called Double Award or Core and/or Additional Science GCSEs; GCSEs in all three single sciences, often referred to as 'Triple Science'; Further Additional Science; GCSE Single Award in Combined Science, and more) to more applied and vocational options (e.g. GCSE Additional Applied Science; GNVQ Science, BTEC Firsts in Applied Science, and OCR Nationals).
10 G.W. Bush (2000) Speech delivered at the NAACP 91st annual convention, Monday, 10 July 2000. Published at www.washingtonpost.com/wp-srv/onpolitics/elections/bushtext071000.htm (accessed 25/7/2014).
11 www.education.gov.uk/publications/standard/publicationDetail/Page1/PU214; www.aimhigher.ac.uk/sites/practitioner/home/ (accessed 22/2/16).
12 For instance, at the time of writing, the introductory web page of educational charity 'Young Enterprise' states: 'We believe that developing strong aspirations is key to boosting employability and entrepreneurship', www.young-enterprise.org.uk (accessed 1/9/12).
13 http://highaspirationskc.org/about/ (accessed 22/2/16).
14 Of the students who completed the survey, there were 50.6% boys, 49.3% girls; 846 (9.1%) in private schools, 8,473 (90.9%) in state schools; 74.9% White, 8.9% Asian (Indian, Pakistani, Bangladeshi heritage), 7.5% Black (Black African, Black Caribbean), 1.4% Far Eastern, 7.8% mixed or other.
15 Of the 5,634 students who participated in Survey 2, 2,251 (40.0%) were boys and 3,358 (59.6%) were girls (25 students did not provide their gender). Some 5,226 (93%) attended state schools and 408 (7%) attended independent schools; 711 of the 5,634 students who completed Survey 2 also completed Survey 1.
16 Cultural capital was determined by responses to items such as parental university attendance (and leaving school before age 16), approximate number of books in the home and frequency of museum visitation. These items were used to provide an overall indication of level of cultural capital, which was grouped into: very low, low, medium, high or very high.

2

WHAT DO YOUNG PEOPLE TODAY ASPIRE TO?

As outlined in Chapter 1, the ASPIRES project is based on the premise that aspirations are an interesting and important focus for study. First, aspirations can, in some cases, provide a probabilistic indication of a young person's future occupation (Trice, 1991a, 1991b; Trice and McClellan, 1993). Some researchers have also suggested that 'high' aspirations might contribute to building resilience among young people from disadvantaged backgrounds (e.g. Flouri and Panourgia, 2012). However, we would urge caution around this assertion, as others (Croll, 2008; Gorard et al., 2012; Yates et al., 2011) have drawn attention to the potentially negative outcomes for young people from disadvantaged backgrounds who aspire highly but lack the academic attainment and capital to achieve their ambitions.

Second, aspirations constitute a clear focus of concern within education policy, which continues to be dominated by discourses around 'raising aspirations', despite repeated critiques from educational research, notably showing that young people from working-class and/or minority ethnic backgrounds often do hold high aspirations (e.g. Archer and Francis, 2007; Archer et al., 2003; Croll, 2008; Kintrea et al., 2011; Strand and Winston, 2008).

Third, and finally, in our work we view aspirations as being of sociological interest – as indicative, socially constructed phenomena that provide a means for examining the interplay between agency and social structures within young people's lives. From an equity perspective, there is an interest in exploring and explaining gendered (OECD, 2012b), classed and/or racialised (e.g. Archer and Francis, 2007) patterns in young people's aspirations. In this chapter we draw on a Bourdieusian analytic lens: we understand an individual's sense of their own future not merely as being a personal cognition, but as formed through their relationship with the wider social context, including fields of home and schooling. In line with Bourdieu, we also consider the habitus of the participants in our study, which provides a practical 'feel' for the world and is shaped by a person's upbringing and social location. As Reay (2004) explains, habitus can be understood as an internal matrix of dispositions, shaping how an individual understands and engages with the social world. For instance, Reay et al. (2005) show how differently classed and racialised habitus can shape students' perceptions of going to university either as an 'automatic', taken-for-granted assumption or as 'not for the likes of us'. Habitus does not operate alone; it interacts with capital (resources – which can be economic, cultural, social or symbolic). As Bourdieu argues, interactions of habitus and capital within fields, such as the education system, have profound effects on people's life chances and their perceptions of the future.

Our work also builds on previous research on young people's aspirations, including a number of highly informative quantitative analyses of large national longitudinal data-sets, such as the British Household Panel Survey (BHPS) (e.g. Croll, 2008; Croll et al., 2011), the Longitudinal Study of Young People in England (LSYPE) (e.g. Attwood and Croll, 2011; Gutman and Schoon, 2012), the National Child Development Study (e.g. Schoon, 2001) and the Youth Cohort Study (e.g. Yates et al., 2011). There have also been insightful smaller, in-depth qualitative studies looking at young people's aspirations, for instance among urban youth (e.g. Archer et al., 2010b; Ball et al., 2000; Francis, 2000b), minority ethnic pupils (e.g. Archer and Francis, 2007; Wong, 2012) and young women (e.g. Fuller, 2009). Croll (2008) notes that young people surveyed by the BHPS in the 1990s (at age 15) were occupationally ambitious (with most aspiring to professional and technical/managerial careers). Our samples of contemporary youth are not only younger but also constitute a different generation from that examined by Croll (2008), raising the questions: are contemporary young people in England also part of the 'Ambitious Generation' (Schneider and Stevenson, 1999), or are they more circumspect given their social location in the current 'age of austerity' and the global recession taking place during most of this study?

In sum, this chapter explores what young people aspire to in early secondary school. It outlines the main aspirations and sources of these aspirations as expressed by young people in the last year of primary school (Year 6, age 10/11) and the second (Y8, age 12/13) and third (Y9, age 13/14) years of secondary school. Although the ASPIRES project ostensibly focused on aspirations in science, the aspirations of our participants were not limited to science or STEM-related careers. Nevertheless, some of the issues surrounding the formation and development of aspirations are exacerbated in the case of science, a point we will return to later in the chapter.

Overview of aspirations

The study gathered data on young people's stated aspirations in several ways – through open-ended (free-response) and closed (Likert-type) questions on the survey and via in-depth, probed questions within the interviews. Most of the survey data reported in this chapter are based on descriptive statistics and are used to provide a broad overview of aspirations. The interview data were initially coded and sorted (e.g. by key topic areas, themes and responses to particular questions). The coded extracts were then searched to identify patterns of aspirations, which were then tested and refined through successive phases of coding and analysis, iteratively testing out emergent themes across the data-set to establish 'strength' and prevalence (Miles and Huberman, 1994). These coded themes were then subjected to a more theoretically informed analysis (in line with our Bourdieusian conceptual framework) to identify interplays of habitus and capital within the development of children's aspirations. Where possible, we also sought to identify practices of power and gendered, classed and racialised patterns within respondents' talk, relating these to reported sources of aspirations (to identify how different patterns of aspiration, as identified within respondents' talk, might be related to differential social locations, practices and resources).

As might be expected (due to differences in sampling and the way questions are asked), these different sources produced slightly different forms of response, but, comparing across the different forms of data, a common pattern emerges in terms of the most popular aspirations, with careers in sports, teaching, medicine and the arts being among the most popular aspirations over the years, with business and law also emerging as highly popular in Year 8 and continuing into Year 9. Figures 2.1 to 2.3 summarise young people's responses to questions about preferred aspirations.

Looking at the coded free responses on all three surveys (see also Figure 2.1),[1] the five most popular aspirations in Year 6 were sports (9.0%), performing arts (7.3%), teacher (5.3%), doctor (4.5%) and vet (3.7%). In Year 8, the top five were performing arts (13.5%), doctor (6.9%), business (6.3%), sports (6.2%) and

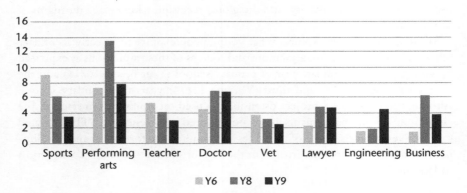

FIGURE 2.1 Percentage of aspirations expressed (free response)

Note: This graph portrays the percentage of all aspirations expressed (within each year group) that fell into these particular categories. Sports and performing arts may be particularly high because those categories comprised a number of jobs (e.g. football, cricket, rugby under 'Sports' and dancer, singer, pop star, musician, actor under 'Performing arts').

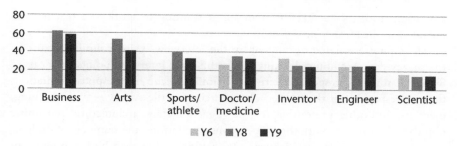

FIGURE 2.2   Percentage of students aspiring to jobs (restricted choice)

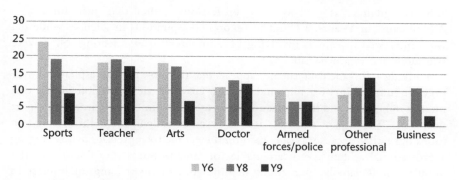

FIGURE 2.3   Top aspirations expressed in interviews (number of students)

lawyer (4.5%) (with teacher at 4.1%). In Year 9, the top five were performing arts (7.8%), doctor (6.8%), lawyer (4.7%), engineer (4.5%) and business (3.8%). While some of these patterns may seem surprising (e.g. the spike in aspirations for performing arts in Year 8), this is partly due to the way students responded to the question. For instance, in Year 8, students often named more than one performing arts aspiration (i.e. singer, actor, dancer). Moreover, the categories of sports and performing arts comprised a number of different occupational aspirations. It is also noteworthy that a wider range of aspirations were expressed in later surveys (Y8 and especially Y9). Finally, despite popular concern that many boys want to be footballers,[2] the percentage expressing this aspiration dropped precipitously over time, with football not even featuring in the top 20 on the Year 9 survey. Moreover, the proportion of aspirations in other sports also declined sharply by Year 9.

The Year 8 and 9 surveys also presented students with a list of possible options for jobs/careers and asked them to rate their interest in each of them. Students could express interest (by agreeing/disagreeing) in all of the careers – or none of them. As reflected in Figure 2.2, most (around 60%) agreed/strongly agreed that they would like a career in business, but arts, sports and medicine (and teacher in Year 9 – with 33.5% of students expressing interest) were all highly popular aspirations too. (Note that the item about wanting to work as a teacher was included in the Year 9 survey only.)

The aspirations stated by students in the interviews paint a similar picture to the survey data – although looking across the three interview points (in Years 6, 8 and 9), students' responses were more similar to the free-response aspirations than to responses on the limited choice items on the survey – with teaching, medicine and other professions (e.g. law, accountancy, architecture) remaining popular over time. As with the free-response aspirations, the numbers of students interested in sports decreased over time. Business appears to be less popular in Year 9 than in Year 8, but this trend may be due to students becoming more specific in their aspirations (i.e. expressing interest in marketing, advertising and accountancy, as well as other professions, rather than just 'business'). Additionally, in Year 9, 12 students expressed aspirations in science, while ten were interested in careers involving IT/computers or engineering. Nine were also interested in journalism.

Looking across the data, then, it appears that the most popular aspirations over time are in medicine, teaching and the arts. However, it is also noteworthy that interest in business and the professions increases over time, while interest in sport decreases. We suspect that this is not because students have lost interest in sport, but rather because, as they mature, they come to appreciate that becoming a professional athlete is not attainable for anyone but a tiny fraction of the population. Relatedly, our count of nine students expressing an interest in sports in Year 9 includes those expressing an interest in becoming a PE teacher (n = 2) or personal trainer, and no student expressed becoming a professional athlete as their sole aspiration.

It is also notable that, in both the quantitative and the qualitative phases of the study, most children expressed an occupational aspiration. Only four students in Year 8 and four in Year 9 were unable to do so. As Flouri and Panourgia (2012, p. 14) discuss in their research with primary school children: 'we note that even at this young age the great majority of the children stated a career rather than a life aspiration, which suggests that career aspirations (or what they may be proxy measures for) may be important'.

A 'poverty of aspiration'?

In line with findings from Croll (2008) as well as other research (e.g. Gorard et al., 2012; Kintrea et al., 2011), young people in our study generally expressed 'high' aspirations. There was little evidence of a 'poverty of aspiration', with young people from all social-class backgrounds expressing broadly comparable aspirations (although it should be noted that the sample did contain proportionally more students categorised as having high/very high cultural capital than those having low/very low cultural capital). As found by Croll (2008), professional, managerial and technical careers were the most popular as aspired to by the majority of young people in our study. Very few aspired to skilled manual and even fewer to unskilled manual jobs. It was also notable that most students aspired to make a lot of money in the future (close to 90% in Years 8 and 9 agreed it was fairly or very important to them personally), and 64.8% of Year 6 pupils and 51.1% of Year 8 pupils agreed that it was fairly or very important to them to 'become famous' in the future. (This question was not asked in the Year 9 survey.) In other words, we would suggest that, in general, the young people in our study can also be regarded as part of the 'Ambitious Generation' and are not suffering unduly from 'low aspirations'.

However, whereas Croll (2008) found a widespread notion of meritocracy and a general confidence that 'most young people believed that they could get what they want through effort', the young people in our study appeared somewhat more circumspect and unsure. While 34 students (out of 71 Y8 interviewees who expressed a codeable view on the likelihood of being able to achieve their aspirations) felt reasonably confident, almost the same number (37 young people) expressed a degree of uncertainty – 19 felt unsure and believed that successfully achieving their aspirations would depend on their own achievement and/or effort (of which they felt uncertain). A further 18 students expressed a more general (unspecified) uncertainty (often articulating their chances of achieving their aspiration as '50/50' and suggesting that they did not know if they might change their mind in future). The uncertain/precarious labour market and the recession were explicitly mentioned by five students, along with HE fees/lack of places (n = 2). A similar pattern emerged from the Year 9 interviews, with 30 (of 63 expressing a codeable view) feeling confident about achieving their aspirations, while 33 were less certain. Of that 33, 16 believed that their goals were 'probably' attainable, depending on their degree of effort and attainment, and 17 expressed a more general uncertainty. Additionally, while only two of the Year 9 interviewees mentioned the recession in relation to their aspirations, 14 brought up the issue of costs of HE as being something that could – or probably would – prevent them from going to university. Taken together, this pattern of responses suggests that young people today, while ambitious, may be somewhat less confident that they will achieve their goals than their counterparts in 1995.

In one sense, the young people in our study might be said to be more realistic than their predecessors. As Croll (2008), among others, comments: 'The availability of jobs in higher socio-economic-status occupations is not going to keep up with the ambitions of the young people' (p. 254). Referring to Brown and Hesketh's (2004) notion of market 'congestion', Croll's analysis shows how ambitious young people from less advantaged backgrounds are 'less likely to be educationally equipped to realise their ambitions' (p. 255), and that young people's professional ambitions are not borne out in reality. Comparing ambitions at age 15 with later outcomes among the BHPS sample at age 20–25, Croll found that while 14.1% aspired to professional jobs at 15, only 5.0% of the BHPS sample had such jobs in the late 1990s. In contrast, while only 3.5% of young people aspired to partly or unskilled jobs at age 15, by adulthood 22.0% of the sample were in these professions.

In addition to the particular aspirations expressed, pupils in our survey also showed a clear interest in attaining a good 'quality' of working life and many expressed altruistic aspirations, such as 'to make a difference in the world' (77.9% of Y8 and 76.6% of Y9 students agreed this would be fairly or very important to them). Their aspirations were not solely focused on achieving personal fame, status or wealth. About 95.6% of Year 8 pupils agreed that it would be important for them to have time for family in the future, and 90.3% (86.9% at Y9) aspired to 'help others'; 91.2% (79.4% at Y9) felt it was important to 'please my family', and most (90.6%) wanted a job that would enable them to have time for hobbies and other interests.[3]

Parental aspirations

Parental aspirations for their children (as perceived by children) also appeared to be high, countering popular policy notions about cultures of low aspirations. Overall, students generally reported strong parental encouragement and support for their aspirations and future success. For instance, in the Year 9 survey, 73.7 % of pupils (77.3% in Y8) agreed/strongly agreed that their parents want them to make a lot of money when they grow up; 96.8% (97.5% in Y8) agreed/ strongly agreed that their parents want them to get a good job in the future, and 95.4% (95.1% in Y8) agreed/strongly agreed that it is important to their parents that their child achieves well in school. About 65% (down from 72.1% in Y8) said that their parents expect them to go to university, a figure that to some extent reflects the UK's relatively high rates of post-16 participation (OECD, 2012b) but which exceeds actual current rates of university participation, suggesting that aspirations do not wholly match outcomes.

Within these overall patterns, closer inspection reveals some key differences among subgroups. For instance, children with higher levels of cultural capital are more likely to report parental expectations of university attendance. Indeed, 87.7% of Year 9 children with very high levels of cultural capital agreed that their parents expect them to attend university, while 52.0% of those with low levels report the same expectations (and 37.4% of those with very low cultural capital). This tendency is mirrored in the scores on a composite variable about parental aspirations more broadly (comprising items about parental expectations of university attendance, of making money and having a good job when in adulthood and of getting good marks in school). As cultural capital increased, so too did scores on this variable, a statistically significant relationship (ANOVA; $F(4, 4595) = 54.480$, $p < 0.001$).

These patterns were mirrored in the qualitative data as well. For instance, most parents interviewed believed that their children's aspirations were achievable, as long as the children were willing to put in the work or put their minds to it. Indeed, some parents felt that their children knew more about how to achieve their aspirations than they did:

[Neb] also said to me this week 'I see that MI5 is advertising for astro-physicists'. I said 'Really?' He said 'Yeah, apparently they used physicists in MI5'. He said 'I think that's what I'd like to do'. I said 'Okay'.

(Ruth, White, upper-middle-class mother)

Parents also believed that, for most children, attending university was both attainable and important ('So but definitely they will have to. You have to go to university, can't finish A Level and stop like that.' [John, Black, working-class father]). At the same time, parents were also keenly aware of the pressures their children would face upon entering the job market, with many parents, particularly those with lower socio-economic status, expressing sentiments that 'it's not an easy world out there'. These pressures may indeed mean that some children, particularly those with lower levels of cultural capital, are not able to achieve their ambitions, a feeling poignantly expressed by Football Master's mother about her son's aspiration to become a vet:

Yeah, so I hate to say I think it's possibly a pipe dream, because, and I don't think I'd ever say to him oh it's not going to happen, you know but I don't, I personally don't think it will happen.

(Laura, White, lower-middle-class mother)

Moreover, although parents strongly supported their children's aspirations and dreams for the future, the interview data also reflected the way in which some parents, again particularly those with less economic and social capital, felt they lacked particular knowledge to potentially help support their children's choices. For instance, Charlie's mother was not certain what courses were necessary to become a lawyer (her daughter's aspiration) and certainly did not know any lawyers personally.

Nevertheless, young people's general perceptions of high parental aspirations are an encouraging sign for their futures, especially among those from more disadvantaged backgrounds. As Schoon and colleagues (2004) suggest, socio-economic adversity is a significant risk factor for educational failure but high parental aspirations are significantly associated with educational resilience among disadvantaged families. However, as Schoon and colleagues also discuss, the effect of parental aspirations can also be context specific. Hence, we remain cautious as to the extent to which children's own high aspirations and perceptions of high parental aspirations and support will translate into social mobility for all in our study, particularly as they are tempered by access to cultural, social and economic capital. We theorise further around issues related to family influences on aspirations – and attainment of those aspirations – in Chapter 5.

Gendered, classed and racialised patterns

We also found some evidence, particularly within the survey, of gendered, classed and racialised patterns within certain pupil aspirations. For instance, girls were much more likely than boys to aspire to arts careers (50.2% of Y9 girls and 29.1% of Y9 boys aspired to careers in the arts), and boys were disproportionately likely to agree that they were interested in careers in engineering (44.3% of Y9 boys, and 10.6% of Y9 girls; see also OECD, 2012b). Additionally, a principal components analysis of the Year 9 survey data indicated that items about future jobs in which they might be interested (e.g. 'When I grow up, I would like to work in sports') grouped into two components which could be described as 'traditionally feminine' and 'traditionally masculine' occupations. The 'traditionally feminine' occupations included hair/beauty, the arts, teaching/work with children and designer, while the 'traditionally masculine' component incorporated trades, engineering, inventor, business, law and sports/professional athlete. Not surprisingly, multivariate analyses (ANOVAs) reflected that the mean of boys on the 'traditionally masculine' component (18.66 out of a possible 30) was significantly higher than that of girls (14.73) ($F(1, 4586) = 920.47, p < 0.0001$). Likewise, the girls' mean on the 'traditionally feminine' component (12.27 out of a possible 20) was significantly higher than that of boys (9.38) ($F(1, 4586) = 862.88, p < 0.0001$). These findings are also reinforced by multi-level modelling analyses of these components (or composite variables), which reflected that gender had a very large effect size of 0.85 in the model of the 'traditionally masculine' composite variable, and an effect size of 0.81 in the model of the 'traditionally feminine' composite variable.

There were also classed patterns across aspirations, with more privileged children (i.e. those with the highest levels of cultural capital) being more likely to aspire to professional careers, particularly in medicine and science. For instance, Year 9 pupils with very high cultural capital were noticeably more likely to aspire to become a doctor than those with very low cultural capital: 44.4% of those with very high cultural capital agreed/strongly agreed that they would like to become a doctor or work in medicine, as compared with only 23.7% of those with very low cultural capital. Likewise, of those Year 9 students with very low cultural capital, only 10.1% agreed/strongly agreed they would like to become a scientist, compared to 25.1% of those with very high cultural capital.

Looking at our aspirations survey data in terms of ethnicity, minority ethnic groups were generally more likely to aspire to work as a doctor/in medicine, compared with White students. By ethnicity, the percentage of Year 9 students agreeing/strongly agreeing that they would like to work as a doctor or in medicine were: Black, 51.1%; Asian, 55.6%; Chinese, 43.2% and White, 29.9%. Asian students were the most likely to aspire to work as a scientist, with 23.0% agreeing/strongly agreeing that they would like to become a scientist, in comparison with 21.2% of Chinese students, 16.2% of Black students and 12.8% of White students.

In contrast with medicine and science, business was a generally popular career aspiration across most groups of students (with high proportions of boys and girls aspiring to business, as well as 51.1% of those with very low cultural capital and 59.6% of those with very high cultural capital agreeing/strongly agreeing they

would like to work in business). Black students seemed particularly inte.
with 72.2% of Black students in our Year 9 sample agreeing/strongly agree.
that they would like to work in business (compared to 64.7% of Asian students
and 55.3% of White students).

Dorr and Lesser's (1980) review found that although children develop more
extensive and detailed knowledge about occupations as they grow older, a pattern
also reflected in students' replies to a free-response question about aspirations
reported previously, earlier gendered and cultural stereotypes tend not to change
over time. Subsequent research also indicates that boys may remain more gender
stereotyped in their career choices than girls (Francis, 2000a, 2000b; Helwig,
1998a, 1998b). Our analyses suggest that, by early secondary school, children are
already sensitive to, and situating themselves within, quite complex gendered,
classed and racialised identities and inequalities, which render particular jobs as
more possible and desirable than others. (Note that although the percentages
reported above are from our Year 9 survey, very similar patterns were apparent
in the Year 8 survey data.) Indeed, we would suggest that students' aspirations
are already strongly socially structured.

We now move on to consider the sources of children's aspirations, drawing
in particular on interview data.

Sources of aspirations

Students who were interviewed were asked in detail about their aspirations, the
reasons for their interest, how these ideas developed and what had influenced
their ideas. We also asked if they already knew anyone working in this, or a
similar, line of work and probed their knowledge of progression routes into job
fields and whether they engaged in any related activities. We then cross-analysed
'sources' of aspirations by the various 'types' and categories of aspiration (e.g.
teaching, sports, business) to explore whether there were any discernible patterns.
The findings are detailed in Table 2.1.

Both home and school appear to be key influencers/shapers of aspirations of
Year 9 students. Families and home contexts are particularly influential, with 19
students (out of 83) aspiring to the same job as a family member and 15 aspiring
to the same job as a family friend or neighbour. These are more often children
from professional/managerial backgrounds, aspiring to careers in medicine,
teaching and other professions.

Twenty-nine children's aspirations related to the hobbies, activities and
interests that they pursue outside of school, and these were predominantly
related to sports and the arts. School was also influential, being cited in relation
to 27 children's aspirations; 12 of these children aspired to become a teacher
and several others mentioned how their aspiration had developed through
interests and aptitudes developed at school (particularly in relation to science,
medicine and maths). Seven students said that their aspirations were influenced
by television, while 19 cited general interests which they did not have direct

TABLE 2.1 Sources of Year 9 interviewees' aspirations (Y8 in brackets)

Source of aspiration (most frequently mentioned occupational areas in brackets)	Number of Y9 (Y8) students*
Family member/s with same job: (medicine, teaching, other professional)	19 (30)
Family friend or neighbour with same job: (business and other professional)	15 (10)
Family push/steer (no direct contacts):	3 (2)
Interest developed through hobby/out-of-school activity: (sports, arts)	29 (28)
Television: (medical-related)	7 (15)
School: (teacher (n = 12), science, medicine, accounting/finance)	27 (21)
General interest (no specific direct experience): (business, actor, journalism, law)	19 (6)
Money (job perceived to be well paid): (business and professions)	3 (6)

Note: * Numbers add up to more than 83 because some children expressed more than one aspiration.

experience in (or could not trace a direct source). Only three seemed to be directly or primarily attracted by the perceived financial returns of particular careers (notable in business and the professions). Interestingly, and in contrast to the Year 8 interviews, eight Year 9 students claimed that their interest in a particular career had been sparked by information they had found on a careers website. These sites were usually suggested by the school (rather than something they encountered on their own), although on the whole students claimed that careers advice in their schools was minimal and generally uninformative. Nevertheless, it does appear that by Year 9 at least some schools are offering careers advice and guidance, although it would seem to be of variable quality.

Although our data-sets are small and the analyses necessarily tentative (and indicative rather than definitive), there are some discernible patterns across spheres of influence and types of aspiration and for differently socially located children and young people. It is also noteworthy, though perhaps not surprising, that the patterns are fairly consistent across our Year 8 and Year 9 interviews. We now discuss these, focusing in particular on family, out-of-school activities, school and television.

The interplay of family habitus and capital

As detailed in Table 2.1, 'family' was a frequently cited source of aspirations (and the most cited source in the Year 8 interviews), with 19 out of the 83 children who were re-interviewed at age 13/14 specially mentioning a family member who does the job that they aspire to as being an influence on their aspiration. A further 15 pupils cited family friends or neighbours as the inspiration for their aspiration. The prominence of family and family friends as a source of aspirations in our study is further reinforced by findings from the UPMAP study (Simon et al., 2012), which highlights the importance of key adults (usually family members or other significant adults) as influencers on the routes that young people take post-16.

The ambitions of the 34 students who aspired to the same occupations as family members or family friends covered a range of careers, but the majority were for professional, managerial and technical jobs, with the most frequently mentioned specific careers being medicine (doctor or surgeon) and teaching. For example, Heather's mother taught Health and Social Care at a local secondary school and encouraged her to work with disabled children ('my mum is like "You're really good with children" and stuff and especially people with disabilities and stuff like that'). Likewise, Rachel was interested in pursuing 'something using maths', such as accountancy, following in her father's footsteps. Other children with interests related to family careers included Roger, who was considering becoming a police officer like his father. Likewise, in Year 8 LemonOnion wanted to become a physical training instructor in the RAF ('cos my brother's a Royal Marine I thought I might go into the forces so I thought I'll be in the RAF, quite fun') and was still considering pursuing a career in the RAF a year later.

We found that students from socially advantaged backgrounds (e.g. with parents in senior, professional occupations) were more likely than their working-class counterparts to locate the source of their aspirations within their (privileged) social capital (networks of contacts). For example, in the Year 8 interview sample there were 17 students categorised as 'working class' (from unskilled manual or unemployed, impoverished households) and 17 students categorised as from professional/managerial families. Comparing these two groups, the 'working-class' students were much less likely to cite a family member's career as the inspiration for their aspirations (n = 3) than those from professional/managerial backgrounds, whose aspirations were much more likely to be shaped by a family member (n = 11). As Bourdieu argues, social capital can play a part in the re-production of privilege by providing valuable social links and contacts that can be exploited for advancement. Our evidence suggests that 'middle-class' children (those from professional and managerial backgrounds) are more likely to have access to social capital (in the form of family and friends who are doing the sorts of jobs they aspire to) to help them in the pursuit and realisation of their ambitions. In contrast, working-class children may also aspire highly (not least to achieve social mobility and 'exceed' the status of their parents' careers) but are far less likely to be able to access this form of social capital to aid the achievement of their ambitions. This differential is quite salient in the experiences of the students in our sample. For instance, Rachel spoke about how she could always work in her father's accountancy firm if she experienced difficulty finding work post-university. In contrast, the mother of Charlie was quite clear that she simply did not know any lawyers at all, much less have any in the family.

In the absence of direct social capital, some students specifically talked about their families providing the impetus for their aspirations for upward social mobility. For instance, Victor2 described how 'Dad knows he doesn't want me to have a job like his' and how his parents encourage and support Victor's science-related aspirations for an 'interesting', professional career. Likewise, Victoria2 explained how 'they both [parents] didn't go to college or university, and . . . they want me to do better than they did'. Similar sentiments were expressed by some of the (working-class) parents as well. For example, MacTavish's mother remarked that she hoped her son would have a 'good job . . . not like me . . . a job that's interesting, that's going to keep you interested . . . I'd just like him to be able to do something where you can be comfortable.'

We suggest that the uneven distribution of capital between differently socially located families plays a key role in structuring young people's aspirations and post-16 progression. We found an increasing use of family narratives among the Year 8 and Year 9 sample compared to the Year 6 sample, with Year 8 students more likely to evoke taken-for-granted notions of particular occupations as 'something that we do in our family'. For instance, Tom4 is from a professional, British Asian family. His father is a medical consultant and his mother is a businesswoman. His aspirations (to study science at Oxbridge and then pursue a career in either medicine or, possibly, business) are strongly grounded within intergenerational family narratives of success in these fields ('I think that would be following my family's footsteps'). Tom4 talked at length in both his Year 6 and Year 8 interviews about his grandfathers' and great-grandfathers' highly successful and wealthy careers in business and his father's successful career in medicine. Likewise, Amy2 described how:

> Yeah, well both my grandmas used to be teachers . . . Yeah, they talk about it quite a lot so we have discussed things about that . . . Yeah, they all know that I want to be a teacher. [Int: Yeah. What do they think of that?] They think it's a good idea. They think I'd be quite good at it.
>
> *(Amy2, White, middle-class girl)*

Similarly, Rachel commented about her father's accountancy practice: 'My dad said that his place that he works now, if anything does go wrong that's always a back-up for me as well so . . .' As Amy2 and Rachel indicate, for some students these aspirations are not just 'ideas', they are woven into the fabric of family life and personal identities – they become regular topics of conversation and form the basis of their sense of (personal and collective/familial) identity and aptitude.

We also noted increasing disparities between families in terms of the reported deployment of capital in relation to children's aspirations, with middle-class families appearing more likely to step up the 'hot housing' of children as they get older, through practices that Lareau (2003) calls 'concerted cultivation'. For example, Poppy (White, upper-middle-class girl who attends private school) first told us in her Year 6 interview that she aspired to an 'adventurous' job. At her Year 8 interview she had settled on the idea of becoming a safari vet, which derived partly from her father's new hobby and partly from the popular television series (*Safari Vet School*, ITV1, 2012), while including her desire for an adventurous career.

> My Dad has learnt to fly and it's like a small plane and there was a programme on TV, like a safari vet, so it[aspiration]'s still adventurous but still . . . so it's like a mixture of both.

As Poppy also explained, her family not only supported this idea, but were actively nurturing it through a programme of capital-building aimed at improving her 'CV' for future application to highly competitive veterinary science courses. For instance, Poppy described help in arranging work experience with a local veterinary practice and looking to exploit social capital:

> My Mum's cousin is something high up in the RSPCA . . . Well, my mum has tried . . . to talk to him, because he is something to do with the dog sanctuary in Africa and to see if I could go for two weeks when I'm older, because it will help for the university [application].

Tom4 (mentioned above) also talked about his family as being strategic and future-orientated, paying close attention to the news and developments in education and the job market ('we discuss what happens and we discuss how the kind of education system goes'), which informs ideas about Tom4's future plans. For instance, he recounted how his mum raised the value of studying mathematics at university after hearing a report on the news that 'the government doesn't exactly have many mathematicians today'. However, there was also a theme of safety/risk within the accounts of Tom4 and some of the other children from minority-ethnic backgrounds that was less obvious within the accounts of White middle-class children, hinting at the intersection of class privilege with racialised inequalities that has been noted within wider research on the minority-ethnic middle classes (see Archer, 2010, 2011, 2012). As Tom4 put it, 'my dad thinks yes, I should go into medicine, because he advises it because it's the safest route'.

In contrast, we found that young people from working-class families tended to report their families adopting a more 'hands off' approach (being supportive but without engaging in the active fostering of aspirations via the deployment of capital), encapsulated in the maxim that parents supported their ambitions 'as long as I'm happy', exemplifying an approach that Lareau (2003) terms the 'accomplishment of natural growth'. Such a perspective was reflected in comments made by a number of working-class parents when speaking about what choices and decisions their children might make that could impact upon their futures:

> So I don't believe in nurturing kids that way . . . they have to learn their own path . . . and I'm here just to support him, guide him, and if he needs any information or wants any help with them, I'm here.
>
> *(Tasha, Black/White mixed race, lower-middle-class mother)*

Similarly, although Danielle's mother would like to see her do A levels, she remarks that she would not want to 'pressurise' her into something she feels she could not do. Such statements contrast markedly with those of some middle and upper-middle-class parents, for whom the decision is not whether or not to pursue the A-level/university route, but what university to attend, which subjects to study to secure places at desirable/desired universities and whether or not to take a gap year prior to starting university and/or to attend summer programmes at elite universities abroad. In this way, we suggest that young people's aspirations to follow in the 'family footsteps' can be read as both a mechanism of social reproduction and (particularly in the case of the middle classes) as a strategy to protect against potential downward mobility (through a pragmatic use of immediate capital).

Previous research has found that children's aspirations tend to match parental expectations (Helwig, 1998b). Looking across the interview data from Years 6, 8 and 9, we were also able to detect some examples of children realigning their previous aspirations to fit family-class backgrounds. For instance, as discussed above, Poppy realigned her 'adventurous' Year 6 aspiration to a more socially conservative ambition of becoming a vet. Similarly, by Year 9 Chloe (White, middle-class background) had changed from wanting to be a professional dancer to aspiring to be an architectural/spatial designer (following in the footsteps of a woman she met at her father's workplace), keeping dance as a hobby. By the time of his Year 8 interview, Bob (mixed Asian-White, professional/managerial background) had given up his earlier ambition to become a firefighter and now aspired to a more professional career as an electronic engineer (like his uncle), an aspiration he maintained through his Year 9 interview. This change aligned him more closely in both social class and disciplinary terms with his parents' professional STEM (Science, Technology, Engineering, Maths) careers. A process of alignment was also evident among some working-class pupils. In her first interview, Laylany (White British, working-class girl) had aspired to become an architect but by her second interview she had developed food-related aspirations, aligning with other family members' jobs (her mother worked in food retail and, as Laylany put it, 'one of my stepbrothers works in a restaurant, he's a cook there'). She explained:

> My Mum always says to me 'You're a really good cook' and my grandma says to me 'We've got cooking in the family' cos my grandma cooks, my

mum cooks, my nan cooks, my great grandma used to cook . . . so I think it's just like in me in a way.

We interpret Laylany's quote as illustrating how working in food was more than just 'a job'; it was also a keen interest and a collective identity discourse within the family. As we discuss in Chapter 5, family habitus is normative but not deterministic, as exemplified in this same case by Laylany's return to her architecture aspiration by the time of her Year 9 interview.

The data contain several cases of young people who are 'bucking the trend' of family traditions and 'going against the grain'. This was exemplified by working-class children whose families provided the impetus for their aspirations (strongly pushing children towards particular jobs), but in the absence of social capital relating to these careers. It was also evident among a couple of middle-class pupils who explicitly resisted following in the 'family footsteps'. For instance, as Bill (White British, upper-middle-class boy) explained:

> Well my dad's sort of keen for me to follow in his footsteps sort of as a scientist. I mean he's already like got my brother into like a [international pharmaceutical company] tour . . . and he thinks that would be a good job. [Int: And what do you think about that?] Uh, it's not really something I would want to do.

In Year 6 Bill had aspired to join the army, and in Year 8 he was still resisting his father's push for him to pursue a career in science by aspiring to be a food writer. This resistance continued into Year 9, with his journalism aspiration. While resisting the strong push to science, it was also notable that Bill had actually aligned himself with a more 'middle-class' aspiration, which we would suggest indicates the strong imperative within middle-class family habitus to resist downward social mobility. Likewise, in Year 8 and Year 9 Raza (British Asian, upper-middle-class boy) was still trying to resist his parents' strong desire for him to go into medicine, in order to pursue his ambition to become a writer:

> Yeah, my mum says 'Oh, be a doctor' but then I go 'But I don't want to be a doctor' but that's what she wants me to do but then she wants me to be happy as well so it's sort of . . .

In contrast to many of the middle-class parents, the working-class parents often evoked a discourse of upward social mobility and 'doing better than I did'. But this was frequently couched in some uncertainty about whether this was attainable, due to the competitive nature of the job market. As Hedgehog's father remarked about his son's aspiration:

> I've told him that it's going to be tough, because you know the majority of kids will say, want to be a PE teacher. Whereas if he's saying be a science

> or a maths teacher you're not going to get so many kids want to do that,
> so but obviously the competition out there for PE teacher is going to
> be tougher.
>
> *(Larry, White British, working-class father)*

This comment resonated with Dave's mother's view:

> Yeah, but I would like him to go on to further education, because obviously
> at the moment the way the world is, you know hard to get jobs and stuff,
> so yeah, so and you know I'd prefer that he did.
>
> *(Jane2, White British, working-class mother)*

Similar sentiments were expressed by Football Master's mother, among others;
these parents were uncertain as to whether their children would be able to
achieve their high aspirations, due to the challenges life presented. While middle-
class parents certainly recognised the challenges their children would face due to
a competitive job market and, possibly, economic recession, they were more
confident in their ability to help their children compete successfully, as would
be expected given the greater capital they had to draw upon.

In Chapter 5, we articulate our theorisation of family habitus, a framework of
dispositions that play an important role in guiding action and shaping members'
perceptions of choices. Here, we argue that the influence of family on young
people's aspirations can be understood as exemplifying the interplay of habitus
and capital (resources), shaping young people's sense of what feels 'right' and
'appropriate' for 'people like me' (habitus) and providing resources (social
and cultural capital) that enable children to gain an understanding of what the
career might entail and often a direct social contact working in the field to
facilitate progression. While not the only factor shaping aspirations, the interplay
of family habitus and capital can be powerful and tends to produce patterns of
alignment between children's aspirations and parental class backgrounds, especially
among professional/managerial families. We explore this interweaving of family
habitus and capital further in Chapter 5.

Interest developed through hobbies

As detailed in Table 2.1, 29 (out of 83) children indicated that their aspiration
was inspired by a hobby, interest or activity that they undertook outside school.
These were predominantly in the arts (n = 8, including writing, art/design, music
and acting/drama) and sports (n = 4), but also included childcare (n = 4),
cooking/baking (n = 3), electronics, engineering/mechanics, computer games
(n = 2) and animals/pet care (n = 2). While sports and music were largely undertaken through organised clubs/orchestras, the other pursuits were mostly done
informally, by individual children on their own or with a parent (e.g. a couple

of boys talked about their hobby of fixing cars with their fathers, while a girl talked about rock pooling with her father).

The importance of such activities to the sustaining of aspirations is indicated by Azevedo's (2011) research, which suggests that initial interests must be sustained through lines of practice (distinctive, recurrent patterns of long-term engagement in an activity) if they are to develop and flourish. Likewise, Hidi and Renninger's (2006) four-phase model of interest development points to the importance of situational interest being sustained and supported externally by learning activities that provide meaningful and personally involving experiences. This research also indicates that interests are shaped by conditions of practice, and that these can impact on persistence in a practice. In other words, we might extrapolate that taking part in hobbies and extra-curricular activities on a long-term basis may shape aspirations, but that this influence will be mediated by the conditions and context of the activities.

Drawing on analysis of PISA data, the OECD (2012a) shows that students who experience more extra-curricular science activities attain more highly and have more positive attitudes to learning. However, only one of the children in our sample mentioned an 'academic' club in the context of their aspirations (and he attended a very-well-resourced, independent boys school), although one other did mention a school trip to a newspaper as sparking her interest in journalism. However, it might be hypothesised that where a child's activities have a close match to particular areas of the academic curriculum (e.g. writing/ English), there might be a relationship with increased attainment and/or attitudes to the subject.

As detailed above, interests developed through out-of-school activities and hobbies were particularly cited in relation to sports and the arts. We find it noteworthy, however, that so few students mentioned hobbies as contributing to an interest in STEM-related careers, particularly given the role that informal science learning is argued to play in stimulating interest in science (Bell et al., 2009b). In contrast, sports aspirations were almost entirely linked to this source – only one student with a sports-related aspiration (whose family member had been a professional boxer) cited any other influence on their ambitions. Students holding sports and arts-related aspirations (as well as games designer) predominantly described these as areas of personal interest and practice and held little, if any, social capital in these fields (e.g. only one student, who aspired to be a writer, also had a family member in this line of work). We suggest that for these young people their comparative lack of cultural and social capital (along with the competitive jobs market in such popular/desirable fields) may contribute to the difficulty that many experience in attaining their aspirations in these areas.

School influence

Nearly one third of the students interviewed in Year 9 (26 of 83) indicated that their aspirations had been influenced by their experiences of school. Twelve of these young people aspired to be teachers, while another 12 explained that their aspirations related to specific interests and aptitudes that they had developed through their lessons and learning at school. A further six students (not included as part of the 26 above) also related their aspirations to a careers convention or website recommended by their school.

The students who aspired to be teachers generally talked about how their aspiration derived from positive experiences of school, especially primary school, and their enjoyment of the primary school context. A few students (e.g. Amy2, Millie, Heather) also had relatives who worked as teachers, who were cited as additional sources of inspiration for their aspirations. A number of students (e.g. Millie, Danielle) also reported discussing teaching careers with teachers in primary (Millie) or secondary (Danielle) school. Of the 12 pupils who aspired to be teachers, there were two boys and ten girls. Four of the 12 pupils aspiring to be teachers were from working-class backgrounds, seven were from lower-middle-class (e.g. technical occupations) families, and only one (Amy2, cited earlier) was from a professional (upper-middle-class) background. This pattern is in alignment with previous research highlighting the way in which teaching has traditionally been considered a suitable and 'respectable' job for women (Maguire, 2005) and has provided a route for social mobility among women from working-class backgrounds since the 1960s (Hoskins, 2012). However, no specific patterns in terms of social class were detectable (not least given the small numbers) of the children whose aspirations had been fostered through specific areas/subjects.

Compared with the Year 8 interviews, slightly more Year 9 students report being inspired by school-related careers information (a careers convention or websites), as described earlier. While this might be taken as encouraging in some ways, it is also noteworthy in that these eight students are only a small fraction of those who have apparently been exposed to some sort of careers information via their schools by the time of their Year 9 interview. (Careers education or advice seems to have begun more formally in at least half of the schools attended by the students participating in the Year 9 interviews.) Moreover, this careers education seems to be of variable usefulness, as perceived by the students who mentioned it. For instance, one Year 9 student described her meeting with a careers adviser in this way:

> I found it a little useful, not as useful as I thought it would be because . . . but he told me like where to go to get the information [rather than providing specific advice].
>
> *(Emma, White British, upper-middle-class girl)*

In other schools, students were aware of careers advice (as one student put it, 'there is this Connexions person') but had not experienced it personally. This was, at least in some schools, due to very limited availability. For instance, Millie explained that there was a careers adviser, whom she hoped to arrange a meeting with, but 'who's only there on I think a Monday'. While Emma is upper middle class and likely has access to other sources of information (indeed, her aspiration follows her sister's plans to pursue psychology), as a working-class girl in a relatively rural area Millie's parents are likely to have fewer resources to draw upon in informing her decisions.

We suggest that the relatively negative (or at least limited) experience of careers advice by these 13/14-year-old children is concerning. Indeed, it might be taken as reflecting that careers education is currently 'too little, too late'. It is widely agreed that young people can benefit from receiving high-quality, appropriate advice and guidance to inform their aspirations (e.g. OECD, 2012b). Indeed, from a Bourdieusian perspective, we might suggest that high-quality careers education and related resources (e.g. high-quality work experience) might be particularly beneficial for those who do not otherwise enjoy privileged access to dominant forms of cultural and social capital, which enables middle-class families to 'play', and succeed in, the educational 'game' (Bourdieu and Wacquant, 1992).

Other sources of aspirations: television and money

Although popular discourses claim that both media (and television in particular) and the desire for money (often motivated by images of wealthy celebrities portrayed in the media) are key influencers of aspirations, our interview data suggest otherwise. More specifically, only seven young people cited television as an influence on their aspirations, and three suggested that money (specifically the perception of their chosen career as being well paid) influenced their ambitions. Television was cited primarily by those aspiring to medical/related careers (n = 4), such as doctor and forensic scientist, inspired by popular series such as the US show *CSI* and the UK series *Casualty*. There were no discernible patterns by class or gender in terms of likelihood of being influenced by television. However, all three of the young people citing money/good pay as a key motivation for their aspiration were from working-class backgrounds, suggesting that the desire for social mobility can be an important driver of aspirations.

It is also noteworthy that, despite popular concerns that the media is influencing many young people to aspire to be celebrities/pop stars/footballers,[4] our data paint a different picture. Although a number of children did aspire to such careers in Year 6, this proportion had decreased considerably by Year 9, as noted earlier. Moreover, by Year 9, not one of the children we interviewed held footballer or singer/actor/musician/dancer as their sole aspiration. Indeed, while several felt that they would enjoy such a career, they no longer considered it particularly realistic. Additionally, only one of the children we interviewed specifically articulated a desire for fame:

> I don't just want to be a scientist, I want to become a famous scientist.
>
> *(Kaka, British Asian, middle-class boy)*

While Kaka's comment is entertaining, it is also indicative of children's perceptions of fame. That is, while some of the children in our sample were not averse to the notion of fame or celebrity, it was often perceived to be a potential outcome of doing well in a career in which they already had an interest, such as music or sports. Relatedly, 36% of the students completing the survey agreed that they would be interested in – or enjoy – being a celebrity. In line with other research (Mendick et al., 2015), we argue that the motivations underpinning these responses are likely to be mixed – with some being interested in celebrity for the sake of celebrity and others aspiring to careers which could, potentially, lead to fame. The high level of agreement (though lower than for most other items, such as that indicating an interest in business) may have also been influenced by the way in which the question was asked.

It is unclear exactly how – or to what extent – television influences children's aspirations overall. For instance, McMahon and colleagues (2001) found that, while children in their study cited the media as a useful source of information, only a very few felt that it influenced them towards or away from a particular occupational aspiration. Our research would seem to be aligned with these findings and certainly does indicate that television is less influential on young people's aspirations than home, school and out-of-school activities.

Some young people do appear to recognise that television has provided them with representations of desirable potential future careers, which either inform or reinforce particular ambitions, but the majority of young people do not consciously recognise television as an influence on their aspirations.

Aspirations in science

Our study provided insight not only into young people's aspirations more broadly but also into their aspirations in science in particular. Although science – particularly participation in science post-16 – is not unique compared with patterns of participation in other subjects (cf. Smith, 2010a), our analyses suggest that aspirations in science are raced, and especially gendered and classed, perhaps even more so than aspirations more broadly. That is, our data suggest that issues related to structural factors (e.g. gender, social class) that shape aspirations play out quite strongly in science. At the same time, although structural factors have a role in shaping aspirations, they are not determinative. That is, as our survey data reflect, experiences within the family (see Chapter 5) and in school science (Chapter 3) seem to have a larger influence on aspirations than structural factors alone. However, in line with our conceptual framework as outlined in Chapter 1, we believe that family influences and school experiences are raced, gendered and classed, and we would argue that it is the complex interweaving of structural factors and experiences that leads to some children developing and maintaining aspirations in science, while others do not.

Who aspires to science careers?

In order to explore who does aspire to science careers, we created 'pen portraits' which highlighted the (structural) characteristics of students with strong aspirations in science. In order to form this picture, we focused on the 'aspirations-in-science' composite variable. Students' scores on this variable were used to divide them into two groups: those with strong science aspirations and those without. At Year 6, 727 of the 9,319 (7.8%) students completing the survey fell into the strong science aspirations group, while at Year 9, 392 of 4,600 (8.5%) were included. (As the Year 8 patterns were so similar to those of Year 9, for simplicity we are focusing on Years 6 and 9 here. Doing so also maximises the time frame spanned by the comparison.) At Year 6, students in the group with strong science aspirations were 62.5% male; 60.7% White, 18.2% South Asian, 9.4% Black and 9.5% Other ethnicity; and 56.5% with high or very high levels of cultural capital. At Year 9, students in this group were 52.4% male; 57.1% White, 21.9% South Asian, 8.4% Black and 11.7% Other; and 53.6% with high or very high cultural capital. In addition, 45.9% of these Year 9 students reported having a family member who used science in their work (as compared with 24.8% in the total Year 9 sample) and 48% reported being in the top set – or top grouping – of their school's science classes (as compared with 33% in the total sample). (Students are not put into sets for science in Year 6.)

Logistic multi-level models were also created to explore statistically which of these background variables were most closely related to children's science aspirations. These analyses revealed that the following variables were the strongest predictors of whether or not a child is likely to have strong science aspirations at Year 6: gender, ethnicity (Black, Other and Asian) and cultural capital (low, high and very high). At Year 9, we were able to incorporate further information (which had not been available for the Year 6 data) about science set and family background into the model. The logistic multi-level model for the Year 9 dataset revealed that the following most strongly predicted whether or not a child is likely to be part of the group with strong science aspirations: gender, ethnicity (Black, Other and Asian), cultural capital (low, very low and very high), family member using science in their work and science set (top). Table 2.2 displays the

TABLE 2.2 Characteristics of students with strong science aspirations – Year 9

	Coefficient	SE	Odds multiplier
Intercept (constant)	−2.85	0.13	N/A
Gender (female)	−0.341	0.12	0.71
Ethnicity – Asian	0.668	0.15	1.95
Ethnicity – Black	0.415	0.21	1.51
Ethnicity – Other	0.652	0.18	1.92
Cultural capital – very high	0.450	0.13	1.57
Cultural capital – low	−0.407	0.15	0.67
Cultural capital – very low	−1.484	0.51	0.23
Family member whose job uses science	0.768	0.12	2.16
Science set – top	0.681	0.12	1.98

coefficients and standard errors (SEs) for the logistic MLM for aspirations in science at Year 9.

Rather than effect size, this analysis produces an 'odds multiplier', which reflects how likely an outcome is for one category of independent variable as compared to the reference categories (male, White, medium cultural capital) and thus gives a perspective of the relative strength of the relationship between an independent variable and the outcome. At Year 9, girls and students with low or very low levels of cultural capital are less likely to fall into the strong aspirations in science group. South Asian students as well as those of Black or Other ethnicities are more likely than White students to have strong science aspirations. Students with very high levels of cultural capital are more likely than those with medium levels to have high science aspirations. Those who have a family member working in a science-related job are 2.16 times as likely to fall into this group as those who do not. Finally, students who are in the top set for science are nearly twice as likely to fall into this group as those who are in middle sets. Taken together, these analyses contribute to our picture of the child most likely to have strong science aspirations (in terms of background or structural variables) at Year 9: a boy with very high levels of cultural capital and a family member whose job uses science and who is attaining well in science (as indicated by set). He is also likely to be non-White. Apart from the additional information about family members and science set (which was not available for Year 6 students), this picture has changed very little compared with the Year 6 data.

Patterns of aspirations in science

As noted previously, boys, students with higher levels of cultural capital (who tend to be from families with higher socio-economic status) and Asian (and, to a lesser degree, Black) students were more likely to agree that they wanted to 'become a scientist'. However, as indicated by Table 2.3 below, our multi-level models of the aspirations-in-science composite variable across our survey suggest that other factors – family and experiences of school science in particular – are more closely related to science aspirations than are structural factors.

These models (which were very similar to the multi-level models using data from the Year 8 survey) are consistent with the qualitative data in suggesting that the sources of aspirations in science lie in family and school in particular. Within the qualitative data, there only seemed to be three exceptions to this pattern, and they are 'partial' exceptions. That is, two Black girls – Vanessa and Selena – had aspirations in forensic science, which were at least initially sparked by television programmes (e.g. *CSI*). However, Vanessa's father had a science degree, worked in the science department of a secondary school and provided a strong family 'push' for science. Although possessing considerably less science capital, Selena's family also encouraged her interests and she also reported positive

TABLE 2.3 Effects of structural and latent variables on aspirations in science (Year 6 and Year 9)

Effect	Year 9 coefficient (Y6)	Year 9 SE (Y6)	Year 9 effect size (Y6)
Intercept	−5.770 (13.944)	0.321 (0.072)	
Gender (female)	−0.438 (−0.651)	0.110 (0.074)	−0.09 (−0.13)
Ethnicity − Indian	N/A (0.602)	N/A (0.197)	N/A (0.12)
Ethnicity − Pakistani	N/A (0.663)	N/A (0.254)	N/A (0.13)
Ethnicity − Bangladeshi	N/A (0.833)	N/A (0.283)	N/A (0.16)
Ethnicity − 'Other' South Asian	N/A (1.253)	N/A (0.424)	N/A (0.24)
Ethnicity − Chinese	1.233 (1.271)	0.409 (0.424)	0.24 (0.25)
Ethnicity − Black Caribbean	N/A (−0.665)	N/A (0.284)	N/A (−0.13)
Ethnicity − Mixed, Black and White	N/A (−0.447)	N/A (0.203)	N/A (−0.09)
Ethnicity − Mixed, Asian and White	N/A (0.779)	N/A (0.340)	N/A (0.15)
Cultural capital − very low	0.647 (N/A)	0.258 (N/A)	0.13 (N/A)
Cultural capital − low	N/A (−0.317)	N/A (0.092)	N/A (−0.06)
Cultural capital − very high	N/A (0.298)	N/A (0.098)	N/A (0.06)
Family member using science in job	0.757 (N/A)	0.118 (N/A)	0.15 (N/A)
Science set − top	0.510 (N/A)	0.114 (N/A)	0.10 (N/A)
Parental attitudes to science	0.519 (0.668)	0.026 (0.021)	0.35 (0.44)
Attitudes to school science	0.320 (0.343)	0.015 (0.009)	0.48 (0.53)
Self-concept in science	0.161 (0.134)	0.013 (0.009)	0.24 (0.20)
Participation in science-related activities	0.159 (N/A)	0.013 (N/A)	0.21 (N/A)

Note: Year 6 coefficients, standard errors and effect sizes are shown in brackets. 'N/A' is used to indicate when a variable did not form part of a particular model (Year 6 or Year 9).

experiences of school science. The other (partial) exception was that of Neb, whose initial interest in science seemed to have been sparked by the *Horrible Science* books and visits to a museum with his grandmother. However, he had family members working in science and reported very rich science experiences at school.

Additionally − and as captured by the multi-level models − the concept of 'aspirations in science' is more nuanced than simply wanting to 'be a scientist', or not. Indeed our variable 'aspirations in science' is made up of five items, reflecting varying levels of participation in or affiliation with a career in science: (I would like to:) study more science in the future, have a job that uses science, work in science, become a scientist; I think I could be a good scientist one day. That is, 'I would like to become a scientist' is suggestive of a greater affiliation with science than 'I would like to have a job that uses science'. The latter would seem to be consistent with a general interest in science, whereas the former suggests a tight identification with science and requires seeing oneself as a scientist.

TABLE 2.4 Science aspiration items – agreement over time

Items	% agreeing/strongly agreeing		
	Y6	Y8	Y9
I would like to study more science in the future.	40.0%	42.9%	41.8%
I would like to have a job that uses science.	28.5%	32.4%	34.7%
(When I grow up) I would like to work in science.	23.4%	28.8%	31.0%
I would like to become a scientist.	16.6%	14.5%	15.0%
I think I could be a good scientist one day.	30.7%	26.8%	26.1%

That these items are perceived as reflecting different levels of engagement or identification with science is also borne out by the proportions of students agreeing with these items, a pattern that was consistent across all three administrations of the survey, as seen in Table 2.4 above.

The relatively small proportion of students with aspirations in science (particularly those wanting to 'become a scientist') is not reflective of a broader disengagement from the subject. Overall, students report a general liking and valuing of science, as indicated by the proportions agreeing that they learn interesting things in science lessons (73.8% at Y6, 73.2% at Y8, 65.7% at Y9) and that studying science is useful for getting a good job in the future (68.4% at Y6, 69.9% at Y8, 71.4% at Y9). The low levels of aspirations would seem to be more indicative of what we have termed the 'doing/being divide' (Archer et al., 2010a). That is, while students may enjoy doing science, much more is needed for this interest to translate into a desire for a career in science.

Taken together, these analyses highlight the key role of school experiences and, especially, of family on who does and does not have aspirations in science. Such a picture is also consistent with our qualitative analyses of science capital – i.e. the students most likely to maintain STEM aspirations over time tend to be those whose families possess medium to high levels of science capital, something we discuss further in Chapter 5.

Summary

In this chapter we have considered the aspirations expressed by the young people in our research. Although we have included a particular focus on science-related aspirations, we have also examined young people's aspirations more broadly, as the majority of students in our study did not have aspirations in science. Regardless of the area of their aspirations, it is clear that the young people (and their families) in our sample generally appear to aspire highly and, as such, might be regarded as part of an 'Ambitious Generation'. However, they also appear somewhat less confident in the likelihood of 'success' than previous cohorts, perhaps reflecting contemporary labour-market uncertainties and global recession. Our analysis identified the most consistently popular aspirations in our study to be for medicine, teaching and the arts. Although aspirations in sports are very popular among younger students, these decrease over time, while aspirations to careers in business become increasingly popular in Years 8 and 9. The main spheres of influence on aspirations were families (especially family social capital – family members or family friends who do this job), hobbies/activities engaged in out of school, and school factors. Aspirations to careers in science are notably less popular (a pattern that remains consistent across all of our data-sets), but the sources of these aspirations are similar to those for other areas – with family influences and school experiences playing a particularly key role, though there is a notable lack of hobbies/out-of-school experiences cited as an influence on STEM-related aspirations.

Our analysis indicated patterns of association between particular sources of influence and types of career aspiration. For example, aspirations for sports and the arts were overwhelmingly related to children's out-of-school activities. Middle-class children were more likely to cite family capital in relation to professional careers in the fields of medicine and teaching. Working-class students were much less likely to aspire to follow in a family member's footsteps or to develop their aspirations through an out-of-school hobby/activity. They were more likely to be influenced by schools (especially to aspire to be a teacher), television, other significant adults and money. We also found that careers education and resources featured very little within our sample of 10–13 year olds' accounts of the development of their aspirations. They were mentioned more frequently in the Year 9 interviews but still did not seem to have a major role in influencing aspirations.

We have argued that uneven interplays of family habitus and capital produce differential patterns of aspiration and differential chances that children will achieve their goals, a point to which we return in Chapter 5. We also suggest that schools (and careers services) are particularly important for disadvantaged children in that they can potentially provide a fairer distribution of cultural and social capital and opportunities for supporting, developing and informing children's interests. For Bourdieu, the education system plays a key role in social reproduction (e.g. Bourdieu and Passeron, 1990), helping to shape both the image people have of their own destinies (e.g. their perceived choices) and the resources (capital) available to them to achieve their goals. Our analyses indicate that there is still much work that needs to be done if schools are to play a greater role in challenging, rather than reproducing, inequalities in aspirations.

Notes

1 Note that the proportions expressed in Figure 2.1 represent the proportion of aspirations in each category, out of all aspirations expressed.
2 E.g. as expressed by politicians in the media (www.telegraph.co.uk/news/politics/9835365/David-Cameron-too-many-British-children-want-to-be-popstars-and-footballers.html (accessed 25/5/16)) and by some teachers in our study.

3 Note that not all of the items from the Year 8 survey could be included in the Year 9 survey.
4 E.g. the *X Factor* television programme is often popularly referred to as being the epitome of all that is wrong with young people's aspirations – www.telegraph.co.uk/education/ educationnews/10714089/Top-head-teacher-attacks-closed-mindset-of-The-X-Factor. html (accessed 25/5/16).

3

SCHOOLS, LESSONS AND SCIENCE IDENTITIES

As we argue throughout this book, aspirations are closely linked with identity and how individuals perceive themselves and are perceived by others. With regard to aspirations in science in particular, students' aspirations and educational choices are influenced by the extent to which they are able to develop and maintain a 'science identity'. That is, when students perceive themselves as scientific and 'good at science' and, importantly, are recognised as such by others, they are better equipped to maintain interests and aspirations in science (cf. Carlone and Johnson, 2007), leading to increased possibilities for future participation and engagement in science – whether in future study or in engagement with issues as a scientifically literate adult. In this chapter we explore the relationships between science identities and students' experiences of school science.

Previous research has highlighted that the development of a science identity is influenced not only by students' enjoyment of/interest in science and their attainment in the subject but also, critically, by how they are recognised (or not) by others as 'scientific'. In a study of women of colour working in science-based fields, Angela Johnson and colleagues (2011) found that recognition of these individuals as scientific was key to their ability to find a place for themselves in science, particularly in the face of other, unwanted, identities being ascribed to them on the basis of structural characteristics such as 'race'/ethnicity and gender (Johnson et al., 2011). Other work has identified similar issues and tensions at play in school settings. That is, the extent to which students are recognised as 'scientific' – and the spaces available in which to perform oneself scientifically – are critical influences on the development and maintenance of a science identity (e.g. Basu and Calabrese Barton, 2007; Carlone et al., 2011; Carlone et al., 2014). Put simply, children's experience of science in school, while not the only influence on science identity, plays a major role in whether or not they come to see science as 'for them'. (See also Chapter 2 for our analyses highlighting the close relationship between attitudes to school science and aspirations in science.) Moreover, adopting a 'science-learner identity' (seeing oneself as someone who is capable of learning science) has implications not only for future aspirations and participation, but also for attainment, which, in turn, facilitates future participation (e.g. Kane, 2012). The school science experience includes not only pedagogical elements and the activities students engage in (e.g. practical work) during lessons but also the influence of peers and, especially, the recognition and overall environment created by teachers. Here we explore each in turn.

The types of activities in which students engage in the science classroom not only influence whether students consider the subject to be interesting and enjoyable, but also how they perceive the discipline of science itself. Such perceptions are important as they can affect the extent to which students may be able to author a space for themselves in science. Research conducted over a number of years suggests that while students value science as important, they do not always find it interesting, which has clear implications for continuing participation (George, 2006; Jenkins and Nelson, 2005). Even more pertinent for issues of participation are students' perceptions of the relevance of science – it has been noted that science is frequently taught in a manner which obscures its relevance to students' lives, which, in turn, can lead to decreased interest (Lyons, 2006) and attainment (Hulleman and Harackiewicz, 2009), both of which are important enablers of continued student participation in school science. Interest and enjoyment can also be reduced by a pedagogical emphasis on memorisation and testing (Shanahan and Nieswandt, 2011), a practice which, moreover, promotes a view of science as a monolithic body of facts in which there may remain little still to be discovered. In contrast, there are pedagogical strategies and classroom activities which can support student interest, such as provision of clear instructions and explanations, fine-tuned to students' interests and understandings, varied use of ICT, practical work or experiments, appropriate levels of challenge and discussion of socio-scientific issues and relevance (Logan and Skamp, 2013; Toplis, 2012). These contrast with extensive repetition of material, test preparation, copying of notes from the board or textbooks or rushing through topics. At the same time, it is important to note that while practical work can increase interest, it is a complex issue, influenced critically by the way in which it is carried out (e.g. with an emphasis on following a recipe and getting the 'right answer' versus encouraging student exploration) (Toplis, 2012).

Students' experience of school science is not only influenced by pedagogy and classroom activities, but also by larger structures, particularly around assessment and progression. More specifically, students in most schools in England are not only put into levelled 'sets' for science, but also must go through attainment-based selection processes in order to progress in science. For instance, it is often only students in the top set who are allowed to enrol in Triple Science (the most advanced and prestigious option) at GCSE, and in many schools it is only students who do particularly well at GCSE who can progress to science at A level. For instance, 43% of those with an A★ (30% with grade A, 16% with grade B and 4% with grade C) in GCSE physics progress to AS physics, but nearly twice as many students with grade B at GCSE in English, history and geography go on to do AS in these subjects (DfE, 2012). Moreover, there are very limited, and generally undervalued, options for those who would like to continue with science post-16 but have not followed the prestigious Triple Science route. These structures, which exist in service of the science 'pipeline', serve to portray science as a discipline that is for the 'clever few'. Such an image, which can be reinforced by teacher discourses that value and promote 'smartness' in the science classroom (Carlone et al., 2014; Olitsky et al., 2010; Shanahan and Nieswandt, 2011), has clear implications for the development of science identities and post-compulsory participation in science (Archer et al., forthcoming).

Beyond choices they make about pedagogical strategies, teachers' actions play an even more critical role in the development (or not) of students' science identities in terms of the discourses they use and the environments they create. That is, the actions and discourses employed by teachers create contexts in which particular types of science identities and resources are valued (or not). In a poignant ethnographic study, Carlone and colleagues explored the development of three primary-school students' science identities over time. In fourth grade (ages 9–10) these students strongly identified with science and this identification was supported by the way in which their teacher's actions positioned them and their activities as scientific. That is, what it meant to be scientific in that classroom involved 'thinking critically, persisting, problem-solving, making unique observations, and creating scientific explanations and also being empathetic and nurturing with peers' (Carlone et al., 2014, p. 23), a construction of 'being scientific' which was quite broad and in which many students could perform themselves scientifically. By sixth grade (ages 11–12), however, these students no longer identified themselves as 'good science students', a shift which appeared to be linked very closely to the way in which their teacher constructed the 'good science student' space. Rather than the open construction they had encountered in fourth grade, their sixth grade teacher had narrowed the valued ways of being scientific or being 'good at science', thus seriously restricting who could be recognised as scientific (Carlone et al., 2014). Similarly, other studies have also identified the ways in which classroom norms and practices serve to recognise as scientific only those students who are able to occupy successfully the 'good student' position (e.g. who are well behaved, quiet, good at 'doing school' and so forth) (Carlone, 2003; Shanahan and Nieswandt, 2011; Varelas et al., 2011).

As Carlone and colleagues' (2014) work shows, it is possible for a range of science identities and resources to be valued and recognised in the classroom, with the result that more students – including those from non-dominant backgrounds – are able to take up science identities and perform themselves scientifically. For instance, various studies by Angela Calabrese Barton and colleagues have highlighted that when the funds of knowledge that students bring to the science classroom are recognised, valued and leveraged in support of the development of science understanding, and when students are able to use science to support valued goals of their own, their engagement and identification with science is increased, including for individuals from groups traditionally marginalised from science (Basu and Calabrese Barton, 2007; Calabrese Barton and Tan, 2009, 2010; Calabrese Barton et al., 2008; Furman and Calabrese Barton, 2006). Thus, by their actions and discourses, teachers recognise – in subtle and not-so-subtle ways – who is invited or allowed to occupy the space of a 'good science student'. When students' science identities are not recognised or valued in their classrooms, maintenance and further development become increasingly challenging or unlikely, and the chances of further progression or engagement in science are reduced.

In addition to the critical role played by teachers in creating a context in which the development of science identities is facilitated or hindered, another aspect of the school science field is that of other students. Students often have ideas about who is a 'good science student', impressions which are reinforced by teachers' attitudes and actions which send out strong messages about who is and who is not allowed/expected to have a science identity. Such images are likely to have an influence on their future choices and participation, with those who do not feel themselves to be 'good science students' being less likely to continue in science. Another, related, influence concerns how students perceive their peers who are 'really into' science or who are 'science people'. While this issue is addressed in detail in the following chapter, we note here that students' perceived 'match' between themselves and the prototype of a peer who chooses science is closely related to whether or not they are likely to choose to continue in science once it is no longer compulsory (Hannover and Kessels, 2004). That is, students whose self-image corresponds closely to images of a 'typical' peer who would choose science are more likely to want to continue with science themselves than those whose self-image is more distant from that of the typical science-keen peer (Taconis and Kessels, 2009).

Issues around the development of science identity are also central to the ASPIRES research, which we explore primarily through an investigation of science aspirations. That is, due to the intertwined nature of identity and aspirations, we utilise aspirations as a lens through which to explore the development of science identity. Later chapters in this volume discuss the way in which aspirations relate to structural characteristics of gender and social class, as well as how they are influenced by family contexts. In the current chapter, we explore the way in which experiences of school science may influence the likelihood of developing aspirations in science.

Attitudes to school science over time

Although some previous research has found a decline in student attitudes to school science as they move from primary to secondary school (Barmby et al., 2008; Bennett and Hogarth, 2009; Murphy and Beggs, 2005), the ASPIRES research unearthed a more nuanced picture. Drawing primarily on the survey data, it would appear that students continue to maintain relatively positive attitudes to school science over time, although there are changes in some aspects of these attitudes, which are described in more detail below.

Classroom factors

Across all three surveys, one component consistently emerging from the principal components analyses was an 'attitudes-to-school-science' component. Moreover, at each of the three time points (Year 6, Year 8 and Year 9), this component contained the following items: 'Science is one of my best subjects'; 'I look forward to my science lessons'; 'Science lessons are exciting'; 'We learn interesting things in science lessons'; 'If I study hard, I will do well in science'; 'Studying science is useful for getting a good job in the future'; and 'My (science) teacher expects me to do well in science'. In the Year 8 and Year 9 surveys, additional items related to school science were added, to reflect the changing experience of school science in secondary school (e.g. the presence of specialist teachers for different subjects). These items were: 'I like my science teacher'; 'My science teacher is enthusiastic about science'; 'My science teacher cares whether I understand science'. For the sake of comparison over time, a composite variable was created containing the seven items that were consistent across the three surveys.

Examination of the means of this composite variable for all three surveys reveals a remarkably consistent picture. The means for this variable (on a scale of 5–25) were 18.73 in Year 6, 18.76 in Year 8 and 18.29 in Year 9. Although there is a slight drop in the mean in Year 9, relative to the nearly identical means in Years 6 and 8, this difference was not statistically significant, suggesting that, for all practical purposes, attitudes to school science continued to be positive across all three surveys. Moreover, and as will be described in more detail below, attitudes did not translate into aspirations across all three time points. That is, the means for attitudes to school science were higher than those for aspirations in science at each of the three time points, with the means on the aspirations-in-science composite variable being 13.67 in Year 6, 14.28 in Year 8 and 14.30 in Year 9 (on a scale of 5–25) – consistent with the doing/being divide we discuss elsewhere (e.g. Chapter 2 in this volume; Archer et al., 2010a).

Despite the consistent means in the attitudes-to-school-science variable from Year 6 to Year 9, we drilled down into the particular items comprising this composite variable, in order to gain a sense of what it is that is remaining consistent and what might be changing over time.

The following table suggests considerable consistency among the three surveys in terms of most items reflecting attitudes to school science. However, it is noticeable that the items that directly correspond to science lessons themselves (e.g. 'I look forward to science lessons') show a decrease in agreement across all three time periods. This decrease is partly reflected in the lower mean in Year 9. Although it is non-significant, the item frequencies above suggest that the

TABLE 3.1 Student agreement with items in the attitudes-to-school-science composite variable

Items	% agreeing/strongly agreeing		
	Y6	Y8	Y9
Science is one of my best subjects.	40.1	43.5	41.4
I look forward to my science lessons.	51.7	47.8	42.7
Science lessons are exciting.	58.1	52.1	42.9
We learn interesting things in science lessons.	73.8	73.2	65.7
If I study hard, I will do well in science.	80.6	82.3	81.4
Studying science is useful for getting a good job in the future.	68.4	69.9	71.4
My teacher expects me to do well in science.	79.9	84.8	83.8

consistency among the means is more likely to be due to other positive attitudes (e.g. that hard work will be rewarded or high teacher expectations). It is also in alignment with the qualitative data, which suggest an increasing emphasis on test preparation and writing, in contrast with practical work, that may be leading to less enjoyment of the lessons themselves.

Qualitative data from interviews with students in both Year 8 and Year 9 confirm that attitudes to school science have not decreased generally since primary school. In particular, in Year 8 most (56 of 85) children interviewed said they enjoy science classes in secondary school more than they had in primary school, while 16 liked them equally well. As some of these Year 8 students remarked:

> It's changed like, because before in primary I didn't used to like science and now I like it more cos like they do experiments.
>
> *(Ali, Black African, working-class boy)*

> And like science, in primary school, we used to do like one experiment over a long time and now we do like one experiment every lesson and we have like science like nearly every day, so . . . and it's like a lot more advanced, like we don't put plants in a cupboard, we don't like do stuff like that, we like blow things up. [I: Yeah, yeah, so would you say that you like it more now or less?] Um . . . more cos like it's a lot more like advanced and that, there's more to do, like stuff, more danger.
>
> *(Charlie, White British, lower-middle-class girl)*

Similarly, of the 79 students interviewed in Year 9 who were asked this question, 50 claimed their interest in science had increased since Year 6, while 12 maintained that it had remained the same (generally staying high). A further seven reported that their interest had increased in some ways, while decreasing in others, and only ten students reported that they were less interested.

Students provided a variety of reasons for why they preferred science in Year 9, including having separate sciences (which often allowed them to understand the subjects in more depth), an increased level of complexity or detail, which made the lessons more interesting, 'good' teachers and increased relevance. However, of the students who preferred secondary school science, reference to practical work in some way was the most frequent way of explaining their preference, in both the Year 8 and Year 9 data-sets. For instance, in Year 9, 29 students claimed that experiments/practicals were the reason they found science more interesting than they had in Year 6. Some of these Year 9 students also highlighted that they enjoyed the greater independence or responsibility they had in conducting experiments, as well as the better equipment available.

> Well primary, it was boring and then Year 7, they started thinking 'Oh look, get interested in science, we'll use this, we'll do the Bunsen burner, we'll dissect . . .' whatever it was and then Year 8, it sort of faded a bit again, especially as our science [class] could not pull off an experiment, they'd always go wrong, and then this year it's been a lot more hands-on.
>
> *(Victoria, White British, middle-class girl)*

> [The teacher] has been really good because we do quite a lot of experiments with him and because he wants us to become more independent, ready for GCSEs, he's let us do . . . like find things out rather than giving us an experiment so we had to come up with them ourselves.
>
> *(Hailey, White British, upper-middle-class girl)*

> I think it's cos in secondary school you're trusted a lot more like with chemicals, like that could like put any old stuff and like fire and stuff, cos in primary, we were never allowed stuff like that. Like we had teachers like choose and stuff and you don't really learn anything and it was mostly writing so at secondary school, it's definitely improved.
>
> *(Heather, White British, middle-class girl)*

This pattern is consistent with previous research reporting limited availability of hands-on, practical work in primary school science (Murphy et al., 2012). As in the interview excerpts above, students often referred to the nature of the experiments they were able to do (more exciting or dangerous, involving more equipment), while in other cases they were simply pleased with the increased number of practicals or the overall science facilities in the school. A number of students specifically referred to chemicals and/or explosions in secondary school and seemed to find the more 'dangerous' nature of secondary school science to be exciting, echoing findings from other research on students' attitudes towards practical work in science (e.g. Delamont et al., 1988). At the same time, for the few students whose interest in science had decreased, their reasons were similar to those above, only in reverse. For instance, they reported dislike of particular subjects (e.g. biology, chemistry or physics), problematic teachers, increased complexity (which led to difficulty or confusion), fewer practicals, too much writing or bookwork and a lack of relevance as reasons for their decreased interest.

The reasons students provided for the increase – or decrease – in their interest in school science aligned with what they reported liking or disliking about school science more broadly. For example, they consistently enjoyed practicals/experiments, including the equipment (especially Bunsen burners) and increased responsibility they often had in conducting them. Not surprisingly, they tended to prefer subjects (often biology and chemistry) that they felt they understood or 'got' better. In contrast, many were put off by the increased writing and revision they encountered in Year 9 science, as well as the complexity of some topics (often, though not always, in physics).

> But we don't do many [practicals] because you'll have to revise. Cos it's Year 9, you have to like get ready for the real tests, so . . . sometimes I get confused in science, cos there's so many long words to remember.
>
> *(Celina, White British, working-class girl)*

Teachers were also mentioned as both a 'like' and a 'dislike' about school science in the interviews. Students who reported their teacher(s) as a positive factor in school science tended to offer as an explanation that their teacher explained things well, did not repeat material too much or go too quickly, and maintained order in the classroom (as well as encouraging practical work). In contrast, if teachers covered material too quickly, did few practicals or just read notes off PowerPoint slides, they were likely to be considered reasons for students disliking science.

> Our chemistry teacher he just tells us to copy it down . . . next slide, just copy it down.
>
> *(Kaka, British Asian, middle-class boy)*

Such sentiments are congruent with previous research identifying pedagogical strategies likely to increase or decrease students' interest in school science (Logan and Skamp, 2013) and serve to highlight the importance of teachers and science lessons themselves in maintaining student engagement with science. The importance of teachers is also emphasised in other research showing that the quality of teachers was a major factor in encouraging further pursuit of STEM (Aschbacher et al., 2010; Lyons et al., 2012; Sjaastad, 2012).

Attitudinal and other factors

Further quantitative analyses reflected that not only did the mean of the attitudes-to-science composite variable remain quite stable over time, but the pattern of related variables was also similar. That is, multi-level modelling analyses reflected

TABLE 3.2 Effects of structural and composite variables on attitudes to school science

	Y6 effect size	Y8 effect size	Y9 effect size
Gender	N/A	N/A	.05
Ethnicity – Black African	.15	N/A	N/A
Ethnicity – Indian	.11	N/A	N/A
Ethnicity – Pakistani	.07	N/A	N/A
Ethnicity – Bangladeshi	.10	N/A	N/A
Ethnicity – Other South Asian	N/A	.12	N/A
Ethnicity – Other Far East (Y6 only)	.17	N/A	N/A
Parental occupation – professional	−.10	N/A	N/A
Parental occupation – managerial	−.06	N/A	N/A
Parental occupation – unskilled	.07	.12	N/A
Parental occupation – student	.15	N/A	N/A
Parental occupation – unemployed	.09	N/A	N/A
Parental occupation – some other job	N/A	.08	N/A
Parental occupation – unknown	.06	N/A	N/A
Cultural capital – low	N/A	N/A	.09
Cultural capital – very high	N/A	N/A	−.10
Science set – bottom	N/A	N/A	.09
Science set – no sets for science	N/A	N/A	−.10
Aspirations in science	.34	.43	.31
Participation in science-related activities	N/A	N/A	.14
Parental attitudes to science	.23	.19	.41
Peer attitudes to science	.29	.33	.25
Self-concept in science (across)	.42	.50	.49
Positive views of scientists	.26	N/A	.20

Note: N/A means that this variable did not feature in the MLM for that year's data.

that similar variables were related to the attitudes-to-school-science variable at all three time points. As described in Chapter 1, multi-level models (MLMs) were created for the composite variables emerging from the principal components analyses. The multi-level model for the attitudes-to-school-science variable, then, demonstrates what variables are related to attitudes to school science. Such a model was created from each of the survey data-sets – Year 6, Year 8 and Year 9. Thus, an additional perspective on attitudes to school science is provided by a comparison among the MLMs at all three time periods. The table above displays the variables that were included in each model, along with their effect sizes. (Coefficients and standard errors are not included, for simplicity.)

The above data suggest that, at all three time points, structural variables (e.g. gender, ethnicity, parental occupation/social class, cultural capital) are not as consistently related to attitudes to school science (if at all), compared to the composite variables. At all three time periods, attitudes to school science are most closely related to aspirations in science and self-concept in science, followed by parental attitudes to science, peer attitudes to science and positive views of scientists. Thus, while what happens in the classroom is clearly important, other aspects of the environment are also related. Although directionality or causality cannot be determined from MLMs, it is possible to say that attitudes to school science are closely bound up with other attitudes and environments, and thus positive attitudes should not be a cause for complacency. That is, there are a variety of factors that could serve to increase – or depress – attitudes to school science. Moreover, the existence of a relationship between attitudes to school science and aspirations over time suggests that school science lessons must not be neglected when considering what is needed to nurture aspirations in science.

The relationship between attitudes to school science and aspirations in science, as well as between attitudes and self-concept in science, is also highlighted by analyses of the matched data-sets, which contain survey data from the same students collected at different time points. (We have Year 6 and Year 9 survey data from 1,036 students, and Year 8 and Year 9 data from 1,304 students.) Using the matched data from the Year 6 and Year 9 surveys, a multi-level model of students' attitudes to school science at Year 9 indicated that the variables most closely related to this outcome were their Year 9 self-concept in science (effect size = .52) and their aspirations in science at Year 9 (effect size = .35). The Year 6 attitudes-to-school-science variable was not strongly related enough to Year 9 attitudes to be included in the model. A similar pattern emerged in the MLM for Year 9 attitudes to school science which used the matched data-set with Year 8 and Year 9 data. Here again, the Year 9 self-concept-in-science variable (effect size = .50) and the Year 9 aspirations-in-science variable (effect size = .31) were most closely related to attitudes to school science, though Year 8 attitudes to school science were also included. However, the relationship was very weak, with an effect size of 0.01.

It might not be surprising that students' Year 8 attitudes to school science are only very weakly related to their Year 9 attitudes (compared to other variables) once other composite variables are taken into consideration. Likewise, it could be expected that Year 6 attitudes to school science are not strongly enough related to Year 9 attitudes to be included in the model of Year 9 attitudes to school science at all (as the experience of school science can certainly change from one year to the next due to different content, different teachers and so forth). Nevertheless, these models (along with the pattern of responses to items about science lessons) are a reminder of the importance of what happens in school science lessons – in any given year, attitudes to school science are most strongly impacted by what is happening in the classroom at that time, rather than by previous experiences.

The above findings also serve to highlight again the relationship between attitudes to school science and aspirations, reinforcing the implication that these attitudes must be attended to when considering how to foster and maintain aspirations in science. Additionally, the principal components analyses for the Year 8 and Year 9 surveys indicated that the 'attitudes-to-school-science' composite variable also included items about teachers (e.g. 'I like my science teacher',

'My science teacher is enthusiastic about science' and 'My science teacher cares whether I understand science'). These items were not included in the Year 6 survey because most primary schools do not have separate teachers for science. That these items grouped with other items indicative of attitudes to school science is not surprising, but it does serve as a reminder that teachers have an important influence on attitudes to school science. This pattern is also consistent with the interview data described above and, altogether, emphasises that teachers too are likely to have an important influence on aspirations in science.

Self-concept in science

As noted above, the other variable most consistently related to attitudes to school science (and more strongly than aspirations in science) is that of self-concept in science. That is, how students perceived themselves in terms of science (i.e. the extent to which a student sees him/herself as 'good' at science or not) was, not surprisingly, closely linked to their attitudes to school science. Moreover, while it is impossible to attribute causality based on statistical analyses of relationships, it is also noteworthy that both self-concept in science and attitudes to school science are linked to aspirations in science. (See the multi-level model of aspirations in science presented in Chapter 2.)

The self-concept-in-science component comprised seven individual items on all three surveys: 'I do well in science', 'I learn things quickly in science', 'I get good marks in science', 'I understand everything in my science lessons', 'I am just not good at science', 'I find science difficult', 'I feel helpless in science lessons'. As with attitudes to school science, the means of the self-concept composite variable remained quite stable across all three time points of the survey, only decreasing slightly in Year 9. The means on this variable (on a scale of 7–35) were 25.19 in Year 6, 25.06 in Year 8 and 24.38 in Year 9. This stability is also reflected in the percentage of students agreeing with the individual items, as seen in Table 3.3 below.

TABLE 3.3 Proportions of students agreeing with self-concept-in-science items

Items	% agreeing/strongly agreeing		
	Y6	Y8	Y9
I do well in science.	67.0	68.9	62.9
I learn things quickly in science lessons.	56.5	53.8	48.4
I get good marks in science.	64.8	71.3	64.5
I understand everything in my science lessons.	48.1	42.4	37.0
I am just not good at science.	19.2	17.1	17.7
I find science difficult.	20.7	19.1	22.7
I feel helpless in science lessons.	16.8	12.8	12.7

Note: The final three items were reverse-scored for analysis.

The pattern seen above does not indicate a dramatic drop in self-concept, although there are decreases on a few items (e.g. about learning things quickly and understanding everything). This pattern is generally consistent with perceptions of science as becoming increasingly difficult as students progress further with the subject.

Comments made by students in the Year 9 interviews about how they were doing in science are consistent with the survey data, suggesting that most students felt they were doing at least average, if not better, in science, though a few were struggling as well. For instance, many students seemed to feel they were doing 'all right' in science: 'I find it, like, medium' (Dave, White British, working-class boy); 'I'm average at science' (Celina, White British, working-class girl).

However, there were a few who identified very closely with science and were clearly excelling in the subject:

> I think physics is sort of my thing.
>
> *(Yogi, British Asian, upper-middle-class boy)*

> I think my teachers would kill me if I didn't take [Triple Science] . . . I'm kind of fine with more detail, it's . . . I can remember quite a lot of stuff and I like science so . . .
>
> *(Joanne, White British, middle-class girl)*

In contrast, some students seemed to feel that they really struggled with science, which would be consistent with a less positive self-concept in science:

> I don't think I'm good enough to do the Triple.
>
> *(Danielle, White British, working-class girl)*

> It's just like this is too much to learn for me . . . it's increasingly difficult and my brain's just like no you can't handle that.
>
> *(Millie, White British, working-class girl)*

This difficulty seemed often to be manifested in noting that the Triple Science option at GCSE would be 'too difficult' or 'too much':

> I think as much as I like Science, I think Triple is just too much and Double is better.
>
> *(Victoria2, White European, working-class girl)*

> Yeah, I don't know if I'm up to it, I mean I could do it . . . well, maybe I could but I don't know that yet because I haven't tried it so I'm not really too sure.
>
> *(Raza, British Asian, middle-class boy)*

Finally, a number of students indicated that they were 'better' in some areas of science (or found them easier) than others:

> Oh, oh no, I can't . . . Biology just goes straight past.
>
> *(Victoria, White British, middle-class girl)*

> I would say my best science is probably physics cos biology I sometimes don't understand and chemistry can be extremely confusing.
>
> *(Mitchy, White British, lower-middle-class girl)*

It is worth noting that when asked how they were doing in science, students often referred to whether or not they had been chosen for (or were planning to do) Triple Science at GCSE, with those likely to take it considering themselves to be quite talented at science, while those who were unlikely to be enrolled in it concluded that their strengths were probably not in science. Indeed, one student remarked that she planned to do Triple Science as a 'reflection of my skills' (Bethany1, White British, middle-class girl), while another said Triple Science was 'quite likely because I'm good at science' (Indiana, White British, working-class boy). But another student, who wanted to take Triple Science but was not chosen, noted:

> I was quite gutted that I didn't get Triple Science, but obviously I'm not as good in lessons . . . I was planning on doing Triple Science and then obviously going on and doing a science career, but I didn't get Triple Science, didn't get picked for it.
>
> *(Georgia, White British, lower-middle-class girl)*

Such alignment of Triple Science with notions of who could be considered to be 'good' at science – or with students' self-concept in science – highlights the strength of the discourses of 'cleverness' surrounding Triple Science, as well as the power of the school in determining who was 'allowed' to take Triple/take up a science identity, a theme we continue to explore in ongoing work (Archer et al., forthcoming).

While the above interview excerpts reflect that students expressed or constructed their self-concept in science in a range of ways, we also utilised multilevel modelling analyses of the survey data to explore what other variables were related to self-concept in science, as seen in Table 3.4.

As might be expected from the MLMs for attitudes to school science, aspirations in science and attitudes to school science are the variables most closely related to self-concept in science and structural variables are not as closely related. However, in contrast to the attitudes-to-school-science variable, gender is related to self-concept in science at all three time points. (See Chapter 6 for more about the gendered nature of aspirations in science.) Moreover, although it remains quite small, the effect size of gender does increase over time, suggesting

TABLE 3.4 Effects of structural and composite variables on self-concept in science

	Y6 effect size	Y8 effect size	Y9 effect size
Gender	−.06	−.13	−.23
Ethnicity − White Irish	N/A	N/A	.35
Ethnicity − Black African	−.15	N/A	N/A
Ethnicity − Pakistani	−.16	N/A	−.16
Ethnicity − Other South Asian	−.25	−.14	.24
Ethnicity − Chinese	−.19	N/A	N/A
Ethnicity − Other Far East (Y6 only)	−.28	N/A	N/A
Ethnicity − Black and White	.13	N/A	N/A
Ethnicity − Asian and Black	−.30	N/A	N/A
Unclassifiable ethnicity	−.32	N/A	N/A
Parental occupation − professional	.13	N/A	N/A
Parental occupation − managerial	.10	N/A	N/A
Parental occupation − skilled	N/A	−.05	N/A
Parental occupation − semi-skilled	N/A	−.11	N/A
Parental occupation − unskilled	−.12	−.15	N/A
Parental occupation − student	−.32	N/A	N/A
Parental occupation − unemployed	−.19	N/A	−.17
Parental occupation − some other job	−.12	−.10	N/A
Parental occupation − unknown	−.21	−.18	N/A
Cultural capital − very low	−.21	N/A	N/A
Cultural capital − low	−.10	N/A	−.08
Cultural capital − medium	N/A	.12	N/A
Cultural capital − high	N/A	.14	N/A
Cultural capital − very high	.15	.21	.07
Science set − top	N/A	N/A	.18
Science set − bottom	N/A	N/A	−.27
Science set − no sets for science	N/A	N/A	.13
School type − state	N/A	N/A	.17
Aspirations in science	.67	.27	.25
Attitudes to school science	.24	.71	.73

Note: N/A means that this variable did not feature in the MLM for that year's data.

that the relationship between gender and self-concept in science does become stronger over time. This change is also consistent with the increasing size of the gap between the means of boys and girls on this composite variable, as seen in Table 3.5.

In addition to gender, Table 3.4 also reflects that one of the structural variables for ethnicity (Other South Asian) and one for cultural capital (very high) also appear in all three models. (Recall that no structural variable featured in all three models for attitudes to school science.) Thus, although from a survey perspective structural variables appear to have fairly minimal relationships with attitudes to school science per se, they may have some kind of interrelationship with students' experience of school science via their self-concept in science. That is, a student's

TABLE 3.5 Means of self-concept in science, by gender

	Boys	Girls
Year 6	25.61	24.76
Year 8	25.79	24.79
Year 9	25.65	23.38

identity as 'good at science' (which would be aligned with our self-concept-in-science variable) would seem to be related in some ways to structural variables, especially gender (although potentially ethnicity and cultural capital as well).

Summary

Taken together, findings from the survey, as well as the interview data, suggest that, in general, students' experience of school science remains positive well into secondary school. That is, the steep decline in attitudes to school science which conventional wisdom asserts happens as soon as students enter secondary school was simply not borne out by our data. That said, our data – particularly from the interviews, but also from some of the survey items (i.e. about science lessons themselves) – reflect the kinds of factors that support the maintenance of positive attitudes to science, as well as those that are beginning to contribute to a decline. In particular, practical work/experiments have the potential to nurture and maintain interest, while excessive revision and focus on bookwork and note-taking can suppress it. Additionally, the data point to the key role that teachers play in supporting positive attitudes or fostering negative attitudes to school science. Indeed, this was evident in interview data from some individual students, who described the way in which their interest in science varied from year to year, depending on their teachers.

Despite the students' generally positive attitudes to school science (as well as their self-concepts in science) over time, their aspirations in science remained comparatively low. That is, the doing/being divide, or the discrepancy between students' attitudes and their aspirations in science, remained doggedly persistent across all three data collection time points. Nevertheless, the link between their attitudes to school science, self-concepts in science and aspirations in science remained as well. Thus, it would seem that helping students see science as 'for them' (and consequently reflected in their aspirations) is not simply a matter of increasing interest in school science, nor even a matter of improving self-concept in science, although both are areas that should not be neglected as we seek to foster students' identification with and aspirations in science. At the same time, our findings align with other work in highlighting the central role that classroom experiences of science play in shaping the extent to which students identify – or not – with science (e.g. Basu and Calabrese Barton, 2007; Calabrese Barton and Tan, 2009; Carlone et al., 2014; Olitsky et al., 2010).

4

THE 'BRAINY' SCIENTIST

As we have argued elsewhere (cf. Chapter 1 of this volume), aspirations are inextricably bound up in issues of identity and are profoundly shaped by the extent to which individuals can imagine themselves pursuing a particular route. Whether students consider certain jobs as both 'possible' and 'achievable' is influenced by the images they hold of those career paths and the individuals who pursue them. This chapter argues that the portrayal of scientists as very clever or 'brainy', and of science careers as requiring exceptional intelligence, acts as a barrier to many students seeing science as 'for them'. We argue that this situation is exacerbated by young people's perceptions of science qualifications as leading to a narrow range of jobs. Moreover, we discuss how this association of science with 'braininess' is reinforced by the current organisation of 14–19 science education in England and is inherently racialised, gendered and classed, which may act as a further barrier to young people from underprivileged social groups seeing post-16 science as 'for them'.

Where do these influential images of scientists and those who work in science come from? Students may encounter images of science and scientists from a wide range of sources, including home, school, out-of-school contexts and the media (Scherz and Oren, 2006; Steinke et al., 2007; Whitelegg et al., 2008). Popular media portrayals of scientists still often present them in stereotypical ways – as crazy-haired, old White boffin males, wearing lab coats and probably glasses (Barman, 1999; Schummer and Spector, 2008; Whitelegg et al., 2008), epitomised by the character of 'Doc' Brown in the 1980s film *Back to the Future*. These associations are, unfortunately, still prevalent today. For instance, upon typing 'scientist' into a Google images search in July 2015, seven of the top ten images were consistent with this stereotype. Moreover, one of the categories that Google offers to help users refine their search is 'mad' (another is 'lab'). There has been some awareness in the media of the need to broaden representations of scientists (both to challenge old stereotypes and to engage wider audiences), but only to fairly limited effect. For example, Professor Brian Cox and Dara O'Briain both present popular science or mathematics-related television programmes: Brian is a former member of a rock band and Dara is a comedian, but both are White, middle-class men (and Professor Cox is unambiguously 'brainy'). Despite decades of campaigning by gender and STEM organisations, there still seems to be a dearth of women who embody or represent scientific expertise within science television programmes, at least in the UK – although lead women scientist characters do appear prominently in some fictional US television crime series, such as *CSI* and *Body of Proof*. The popularity of the US comedy series *The Big Bang Theory* has been associated with the rise of 'geek chic' (discussed later), although this programme still depicts the four lead scientist characters as highly intelligent (White or South Asian) men. Indeed, one of the lead characters, Sheldon, is distinctive on the basis of his superior intelligence and social awkwardness.

Despite these small shifts in popular media portrayals of scientists, internationally considerable concern remains among policy-makers and academic researchers that the popular, narrow, stereotypical image of scientists (and engineers) is detrimental because it is putting young people off pursuing STEM (e.g. Congressional Commission on the Advancement of Women and Minorities in Science, Engineering and Technology Development, 2000; Truss, 2014). Consequently, there have been numerous initiatives and interventions that have aimed to change young people's views of scientists. For instance, most professional STEM societies and organisations now consciously attempt to present a more diverse 'face' of science in their promotional images and public materials (e.g. see the Institute of Physics' 'Girls in Physics' videos[1]).

Considerable resource has also been put into schemes which attempt to broaden young people's views of scientists by bringing young people into direct contact with 'real' practising scientists (often from a variety of backgrounds). In the UK, for instance, substantive public funding has been provided for STEMNET, which organises the STEM Ambassadors programme. STEM Ambassadors are individuals working in science, or using science in their work, who volunteer their time in school classrooms with the intent of engaging children and young people in science and engineering; see Gartland (2015) for a useful critical discussion of STEM Ambassadors. Another initiative, 'I'm a Scientist, Get Me Out of Here!'[2] invites students to meet and ask questions of scientists online. This *X Factor*-style competition encourages participating students to vote on their favourite scientist. While presenting a broader image of those who work in science is *not* the primary goal of either of these initiatives, they do present an opportunity for students to engage with a wide range of individuals, and STEMNET in particular attempts to recruit Ambassadors not only from a wide range of professions but also from diverse backgrounds. As the STEM Ambassadors website notes, currently 60% of STEM Ambassadors are under 35 years of age, 40% are women and approximately 13% of Ambassadors describe themselves as from BAME (Black and Minority Ethnic) backgrounds (www.stemnet.org.uk/ambassadors/).

Another attempt to address narrow views of scientists among children concerned the new Lego 'Research Institute' mini-figures, which are all women scientists (featuring an astronomer, a palaeontologist and a chemist).[3] These were the prize-winning idea of a female geochemist (Dr Ellen Kooijman), who wanted to respond to long-standing calls for Lego (and other toy providers) to create less gender-stereotypical children's toys. However, these efforts to broaden images of scientists do not always go smoothly, as evidenced by the controversy around a video produced at the beginning of the EU's 'Science: It's a Girl Thing' initiative. This, now infamous, video was an attempt to encourage more girls into science. It adopted a highly heterosexualised catwalk/pop video style, in which three attractive young women, clad in short skirts, high heels and make-up, dance sexily and pose together, 'distracting' a young male scientist from his 'work' (looking at a microscope). The shots are intercut with sexualised images of make-up (e.g. a thrusting lipstick!) and lab equipment (e.g. bottles, beakers), with the final shot featuring a pair of lab safety glasses with an image of a lipstick imprinted on. The video was quickly removed from the EU website (http://science-girl-thing.eu/en), though not before going viral and attracting a barrage of outrage and criticism, not least from feminists and women scientists who complained that it trivialised, sexualised and misrepresented women in general and women scientists in particular.

Concerns around young people's narrow images of scientists and the possible impacts of these on their engagement with science are reflected in academic research, as well as policy circles. Research suggests, for instance, that it is not unusual for students to subscribe to a view of scientists as White, male, intelligent, having limited social skills, and working long hours alone in a lab (e.g. Chambers, 1983; Finson, 2002; Huber and Burton, 1995; Koren and Bar, 2009; Newton and Newton, 1998). Other research suggests that although the stereotype of scientists as White and male does begin to appear from quite a young age (Losh et al., 2008), many children actually hold complex and even internally contradictory views of scientists and their work (Driver et al., 1996; Mead and Metraux, 1957; Palmer, 1997; Solomon et al., 1994; Song and Kim, 1999). That is, students do not precisely buy into the stereotypes presented in the media (e.g. of 'mad scientists') but tend to hold more complex images with both positive (e.g. altruistic, intelligent, dedicated) and negative (e.g. socially inept, physically unattractive or unkempt) aspects. These sorts of complex images seem to have changed little since Mead and Metraux's 1957 study, despite numerous intervention attempts. Moreover, and as we discuss in more detail later in this chapter, we suggest that even the more positive aspects of students' perceptions (e.g. seeing scientists as exceedingly intelligent, altruistic and dedicated) still reflect a positioning of those who pursue science as exceptional, 'not normal' and hence 'other'. Similarly, more recent research has found that although students' views of scientists are not uniformly negative, many students do seem to have narrow perceptions of what scientists are like and limited awareness of what their work might involve (Cleaves, 2005; Scherz and Oren, 2006). Such perceptions can be resistant to change, with shifts generally requiring longer-term, more intensive interventions, often involving extended personal interactions with scientists (Avraamidou, 2013; Buck et al., 2002, 2008; Cakmakci et al., 2011; Finson, 2002; Flick, 1990; Painter et al., 2006; Scherz and Oren, 2006; Smith and Erb, 1986). Finally, although a number of these studies have been critiqued for assessing student perceptions using the Draw-a-Scientist method – because the task encourages participants to produce stereotypical portrayals of scientists (cf. Losh, 2010; Matthews, 1996) – studies using a wider range of methods, such as interviews and/or other mixed methods, have pointed to similar conclusions about the narrow images students hold of scientists and jobs in and from science.

Exploring images of scientists

Our study found that most parents and young people had relatively narrow views about where science qualifications lead, with the majority only being able to name scientist, science teacher or doctor as jobs that science qualifications lead to. Indeed, of the 81 students asked in the Year 9 interviews, 66 (81%) could name no more than four careers in or from science. Thus, it seems that most students had difficulty considering post-16 science qualifications as personally useful or relevant unless they aspired to one of these few careers. As discussed in Chapter 5, the exceptions to this were students with high science capital, who saw science qualifications as transferable and useful for informed citizenship. In other words, most students and their parents associated school science, but particularly post-16 science, with the 'pipeline' – that is, as a means of training the next generation of scientists. As we discuss next, young people also tend to hold quite narrow views of scientists as 'brainy' and science as a 'hard' subject, which you need to be 'clever' to continue with – a discourse which, we argue, can be socially challenging (requiring additional 'identity work' and resources to balance it with social popularity) and, more significantly, precludes the majority of young people from considering a career in science as being 'for me'.

So how do young people make sense of the concept of 'scientist' (and the identity of a 'science-keen' person) in their everyday lives and interactions – and how do these develop over time? The ASPIRES interview data provide some insight into these questions. In the interviews, we elicited students' opinions of their peers who were 'really into science' (or highly engaged with science) in order to explore the extent to which they considered these peers as similar to or different from themselves. It seemed that how students regard their science-keen peers over time could provide useful insights into the emerging trajectory of their relationship with science and the extent to which they might ultimately come to perceive science as 'other'. Our interest in gaining a richer understanding of the context in which children come to identify – or not – with science led us to explore not only how children perceive their peers who are highly engaged with science but also the way in which their parents perceived adults who are likewise highly engaged with science, namely, scientists.

In response to our research concerns, our analyses focused in particular on students' responses to questions about their science-keen peers such as what characteristics they shared or what kind of 'image' they had in the school, as well as whether or not they could be popular. Due to the semi-structured nature of the interviews, as well as time constraints, not all students were asked identical sets of questions. However, we were able to gain some impression of the image (or images) students felt their science-keen peers had at their schools. We also focused on parents' impressions of the images of scientists, or those who are pursuing science careers.

Although we read all of the Year 6 and Year 9 student interviews to develop initial impressions of how children perceived their peers who were highly engaged with science, we focused particularly on their responses to questions about peers who were 'really into' science. We also compared the way children described their science-keen peers in Year 9 (the images they felt these students held in their school) with their descriptions from Year 6. The longitudinal nature of our interview data allowed us to explore the ways in which their images and perceptions may have changed – or not – since primary school. However, as we were focusing on change since primary school (and thus what pupils' attitudes had become), most of our transcript excerpts come from the Year 9 data-set. We were also able to explore the way parents perceived those who pursue science careers, though only in the interviews conducted when their children were in Year 6. (The Year 9 parent interviews focused on different topics.)

The analyses presented in this chapter are organised as follows. We begin by discussing students' and parents' prevalent association between scientists/science-keen peers and 'braininess' and 'cleverness', which is reinforced by (and a product of) the 'hard' image of science. We then move on to discuss the (less prevalent) association of scientists/science-keen peers with geeky/nerdy identity. We outline three main problems with such associations of science/scientist with 'braininess'/'cleverness' and geekiness, namely: (i) that these are inconsistent with social popularity and thus require more identity work to 'balance'; (ii) that these associations render science and scientist as 'other' and 'not for me'; and (iii) that cleverness is a gendered, classed and racialised discourse which excludes the majority of students. Finally, we discuss students' and parents' non-stereotypical associations, i.e. views of scientists/the science-keen as 'normal' people, and reflect on ways that these might provide helpful future avenues for broadening images of science.

'Brainy' science people

The data from the ASPIRES surveys emphasise that the perception of scientists as 'brainy' is widespread. Indeed, 81% of students responding at Year 6, 80% at Year 8 and 79% at Year 9 agree that scientists and those who work in science

TABLE 4.1 Student agreement with survey items about scientists

Items	Proportion agreeing or strongly agreeing		
	Y6	Y8	Y9
(Scientists and people who work in science)			
can make a difference in the world	76.7	78.7	79.4
make a lot of money	66.2	63.4	59.3
have exciting jobs	58.6	55.4	51.1
are brainy	81.1	79.8	79.1
are respected by people in this country	60.3	62.0	57.4
do valuable work★★	N/A	N/A	78.1
have to be creative in their work★★	N/A	N/A	60.2
are odd★	23.5	19.2	14.4
don't have many other interests★	31.5	22.9	17.6
spend most of their time working by themselves★	42.0	31.2	25.3
are geeks★,★★	N/A	N/A	21.0

Notes: ★ These items form the 'negative-images-of-scientists' component.

★★ These items are from the Year 9 survey only (and so cannot be compared over time).

are 'brainy'. However, the data caution against interpreting this as a necessarily negative perception. Principal components analyses of survey items clearly group the 'brainy' item with more positive items about scientists such as 'Scientists can make a difference in the world', 'Scientists have exciting jobs' and 'Scientists make a lot of money'. Moreover, the 'brainy' item and these other items did not group together with items reflective of negative perceptions of scientists, such as scientists 'are odd', 'don't have many other interests' and 'are geeks'. In other words, young people see scientists as 'brainy', but most do not tend to associate this with socially undesirable characteristics. For instance, as shown in Table 4.1 above, only 14.4% of Year 9 students agree that scientists are 'odd' – and this percentage declines markedly from Year 6 to Year 9.

In some ways, these views appear to echo representations of popular 'brainy' scientists in the media (e.g. Brian Cox, Sheldon) whom we discussed earlier. Moreover, research suggests that STEM professionals themselves may be fiercely proud of such associations, not least because 'braininess' can be linked with high status within certain contexts. For instance, Mendick and Epstein (2010) found that male mathematics undergraduates were highly protective of their 'special' (exceptional) intellectual abilities.

'Brainy'/'clever' science-keen peers

These views of scientists as 'brainy' were also evident within students' constructions of their science-keen peers. Indeed, 'cleverness' was the characteristic that students most strongly associated with peers whom they described as being 'really into' science. In Year 9, 30 (out of 85) students articulated a strong and clear association between science and cleverness when describing these individuals:

> There are a lot of really really clever people . . . And then when you're friends with all the people that are really good at science, 'Oh God I wish I was that good and stuff' – then you kind of doubt yourself, you think 'I'm not going to be a scientist, cos I'm never that clever'.
>
> *(Luna, White British, lower-middle-class girl)*

> People keen on science . . . um they're sort of . . . they're not average people, they're more . . . they're more clever, they're cleverer than most people but yeah . . . but they're good at science and then there's the few people that can muck around whilst being really clever at the same time.
>
> *(Victor2, White British, lower-middle-class boy)*

> If the teacher like just suddenly asked them the question, they'll just know it like straightaway. Like even if we haven't learnt it, they'll just know it.
>
> *(Rachel, British Asian, middle-class girl)*

In addition, a further 26 students described their science-keen peers in ways that reflected *some* relationship between science and cleverness, although not necessarily as strongly as the perceptions held by others. Of the 30 Year 9 students depicting their science-keen peers as clever, 25 asserted that someone did not necessarily have to be clever to be 'really into' science. Nevertheless, the link between science and cleverness was apparent in the interviews of 56 (of 85) students. This association, although not shared by all students we interviewed, is aligned with perceptions held in Year 6, in which the 'clever scientist' discourse was invoked by 43 of 92 students interviewed. While these perceptions would seem to have been largely maintained (with only 12 Year 9 students appearing to move away from their Year 6 images of those who are highly engaged with science as clever), they are simultaneously becoming more nuanced. For instance, some students argued that while it was not necessary to be clever in order to be really into science, cleverness was required to do well in science:

> I think you have to be clever to be good at it. But I don't think you have to be clever to like it.
>
> *(Louise, White British, lower-middle-class girl)*

> Like to be into science obviously you don't need to be clever, but to be good at science . . . you kind of do need to be clever really.
>
> *(Cristiano, Black African, working-class boy)*

Similarly, science is perceived as one of various academic subjects that clever individuals may strive to do well in:

They're more of people who are more into school, more people who actually want to do science, want to learn. And they just are smart.

(LemonOnion, White British, lower-middle-class girl)

Such perceptions are also congruent with notions of science as a difficult, strongly academic subject, as well as with an image of scientists as highly intelligent. Put differently, while cleverness may not be a prerequisite for a Year 9 (or Year 6) student to be strongly interested in science, it is a requirement to continue to pursue it as an advanced subject or career. That this is the case is reinforced by other students, who asserted that 'Triple Science'[4] was very difficult, or only for intelligent students:

That [Triple Science] is so hard.

(Victoria2, White European, working-class girl)

You don't really like have to be classed as clever to do science but I think most people that are probably going to take Triple Science are going to be more clever.

(Rebecca, White British, middle-class girl)

This image also aligns with views expressed by parents, with 27 (of 78) describing scientists or those who are highly engaged with science as clever or intelligent. Thus, it would seem that while being clever is not necessarily required for being 'really into' science at Year 6 or Year 9, it becomes increasingly necessary in order to do well in science and, importantly, to progress in science, either in later schooling or, especially, into a career. This perception is likely to be exacerbated – or at least supported – by perceptions of science as a difficult subject (and career).

Science as 'difficult'

The construction of scientists as 'brainy', and science-keen peers as 'clever', was underpinned by the discourse of science as a 'difficult' subject. This difficulty derives from science's status as a prototypical academic subject.

Cos science is a difficult subject and you have to be pretty smart to understand it.

(David, White British, lower-middle-class boy, Y9)

That is, many students referred to science as a difficult subject, and this perception could underpin – or at least inform – impressions that students have of those who are 'really into' science. Put simply, if science is a difficult subject, students have to be clever to do well in it and to progress (e.g. to A level).

> They might just think oh I don't want to do an A level in science. That
> sounds to be really hard.
>
> *(Poppy, White British, upper-middle-class girl, Y9)*

The widespread image of science as a prototypical academic subject may
mean that it more easily lends itself to negative connotations (i.e. being geeky
– see below) and, especially, to associations with cleverness. Thus, while students
seem to agree that it is possible to be 'really into' science without being clever
at a younger age (late primary, early secondary), this relationship would seem to
be tested as individuals progress through the education system, not least as they
come to see that high attainment is required to continue along the science
pipeline and to pursue it into adulthood and as a career.

The 'geeky/nerdy' scientist

The term 'geek' is popularly applied to signify an unfashionable, socially inept and
often highly academic person. As Epstein and colleagues (2010) note, the popular
media often portray the geek as a White or South Asian (often middle-class) boy
or man who is closely associated with the STEM fields (as encapsulated by the
figure of Bill Gates or Sheldon from *The Big Bang Theory* television series). Our
previous research (DeWitt et al., 2013b) discusses how notions of the 'geeky
scientist' appeared quite regularly in interviews with parents, with 38 of 78 parents
referring to the image of the 'geeky scientist' in some way – although the veracity
or authenticity of these stereotypes were also often challenged by parents. The
association of scientists with geekiness was less prevalent among students. For
instance, only 21% of Year 9 students agreed that 'scientists are geeks', and very
few (2/92) Year 6 students agreed that their science-keen peers were geeky. A
similar pattern emerged from the Year 9 interview data, with only ten (out of 85)
students agreeing that science-keen peers have a geeky image at their schools.
Moreover, five of these students indicated that although such students were considered to be geeky, this categorisation had more to do with how these particular
individuals looked or behaved than with their affinity for science per se.

A number of students also asserted that although their peers who were 'really
into' science did not necessarily have a geeky image, an association between
science affinity and 'geekiness' was possible. Of the 85 students interviewed,
32 discussed this potential association, which seemed to be strongly mediated
by other characteristics and behaviours. That is, most of these 32 students
could think of someone who was into science and was also a 'geek', but nearly
all asserted that the geeky image was not due to their peer's liking for science.
For instance, in some cases being a geek was explained as due to the classmate
being a 'teacher's pet' or working really hard (or being 'swotty', Francis et al.,
2012) at school:

> I definitely think it [the association between science and geeky] is something
> that happens and I think there is a girl in my class that is like very, very

smart and hasn't got many friends cos she is very, like you know, like very hard working and like into school.

(Mitchy, White British, middle-class girl)

Such constructions echo the findings of Francis and colleagues (2012), who researched the identities and practices of high-achieving school students. They found that high-achieving students (those described variously as boffins, geeks, nerds, swots, brainiacs, etc.) are usually socially ostracised. Students in our study also referred to those science-keen peers who were seen as geeky as being linked with an unfashionable appearance:

Like their uniform is perfect, their ties are like really little knots, their skirts are like below their knees or they've got really like pointy shoes and like that's . . . yeah . . . they're always perfect and stuff.

(Gemma, Black British, lower-middle-class girl)

Other students described peers who were considered geeky due to focusing too much, almost exclusively, on science:

It's just the way they act and stuff, like even when . . . I don't know, if someone is really, really well-spoken and always talks about sciencey stuff, it just makes them sound nerdy.

(Josh, White British, middle-class boy)

However, in these instances of science affinity being potentially associated with being considered a geek, this affiliation was clearly not due to liking science, but rather to other behaviours or characteristics and, importantly, was not necessarily limited to science. That is, such behaviours, exhibited in relation to any academic subject, could lead a student to be considered geeky:

If they like maths, science or English, like some people like . . . and they're really good at it, people just call them a nerd or a geek.

(Hedgehog, White British, working-class boy, Y9)

Put differently, science, as a prototypical academic subject (core to the curriculum and with a reputation of being difficult or complex) may lend itself more to associations with geekiness than some other subjects, and this tendency extends to any academic subject.

Despite this potential association, 41 students overtly disagreed that their science-keen peers had a geeky image. At the same time, many students do continue to be aware of this stereotype, even while challenging it:

Stereotypically normally . . . you'd normally say like someone that's really good at science to be like a nerd or something, but obviously I don't see them like that.

(Millie, White British, working-class girl)

Although it is clear that our Year 9 sample on the whole did not believe that liking science was sufficient in itself for someone to be considered a geek, 15 of the students who acknowledged possible associations between science and geekiness in their Year 9 interviews had not done so in their Year 6 interviews. It is possible that, at least for some, this affiliation had simply not come up in their previous interviews, but such a trend does suggest the possibility of an increasing awareness that, at least in some schools, being 'really into' science can leave a student vulnerable to being labelled a geek.

Finally, traditionally the geek has been a social pariah, the butt of classroom jokes (albeit one who is also recognised as often getting the 'last laugh' by becoming rich/successful in the job market, as epitomised by successful 'geek' entrepreneurs such as Mark Zuckerberg and Bill Gates). But in recent years, in particular, the figure of the 'geek' has increased in kudos, with the rise of so-called 'geek chic':

> within popular culture there are many examples where 'geek' has kudos, notably in the 'geek chic' phenomenon that crystallised around the character of Seth Cohen in US TV series *The OC* (Mendick, 2005), and also where the heroic discourse of the geek plays out (from Spiderman Peter Parker to the male leads in Judd Apatow's movies, and the recent, hugely successful US series *Glee*).
>
> *(Mendick and Francis, 2012, p. 18)*

Although students tended not to refer to the notion of 'geek chic', a few middle-class parents did discuss the idea, saying that the media image of scientists was shifting towards 'geek chic' or 'cool geek', giving *The Big Bang Theory* and even the popularity of actors such as Benedict Cumberbatch and David Tennant as examples. That is, these parents felt that it can be 'cool to be geeky' and that this shift, as well as overall shifts in the image of scientists, meant that fewer students were likely to be put off science by its geeky image.

> There's geek chic and there's *The Big Bang Theory* isn't it, which has shown actually they're not geeky like that.
>
> *(Colleen, White British, middle-class mother)*

As Mendick and Francis (2012) discuss, for some 'geeks' their social positioning can generate capital. In other words, whilst popularly recognised as a disparaging term, some students are able to derive social and educational value from their 'geek' identities. As a T-shirt recently spotted on the streets of London noted, 'Geek is the new sexy' – although (as reflected by the relatively small number and distinctive profile of those parents discussing 'geek chic' in our sample) we might also speculate that this perception may only carry currency within particular social circles. In this respect, the association of scientist and science-keen identities with 'geekiness' is not necessarily (or inherently) wholly negative.

At the same time, the association between science/scientists and cleverness is not unproblematic. As we shall now argue, (i) it can be potentially problematic in terms of social status and popularity, and (ii) it signals a certain requirement for the pursuit of science, particularly as a career, which most individuals may feel they do not possess. That is, perceptions of science as being for the 'brainy' or 'clever' can serve to mark it as something that is for 'others' or 'not for me'.

The problem with 'brainy'/'clever'/'geeky' associations with science: (1) (un)popularity

Francis (2009) argues that highly academic 'brainy' students ('boffins') are positioned as 'abject' (Kristeva, 1982) within peer classroom relations and interactions. That is, they are subject to 'exclusion/ostracism . . . ridiculing . . . victimisation and bullying' (Mendick and Francis, 2012, p. 16). And as discussed above, the 'geek' is closely associated with notions of social ridicule and marginalisation/exclusion. Hence, the widespread association of scientist/ science-keen identity with braininess/cleverness also carries the inherent threat of being potentially socially unpopular.

Encouragingly, of the 66 students who were asked in Year 9 whether science-keen peers could also be popular, an overwhelming majority (58) agreed that it was certainly possible for a science-keen peer to be popular at their school, as many students (73 of 86) had also asserted in Year 6. In justifying this assertion, many argued, quite simply, that they knew individuals who were popular and simultaneously were very enthusiastic about science and/or in the top set at school.

> She's really, really into science . . . and she's smart at it and she's popular.
>
> *(Kelsey, Black African, working-class girl)*

> It doesn't matter what you do. You can still be popular, but be good at a subject as well.
>
> *(Colin, British Asian, lower-middle-class boy)*

Despite broad agreement that liking science made a person neither popular nor unpopular, a subset of students explained that being popular while also being 'really into' science would require extra work. For instance, some felt that, to maintain popularity in their school, science-keen peers would need to hide their liking for science:

> There is one popular girl in our science but when it comes to science, she acts a bit class clown so she . . . she does do well but she acts a bit like um . . . a bit funny and sort of very . . . to maintain that popular rank, yeah.
>
> *(Mienie, British Asian, middle-class girl)*

> Like this popular person don't go around telling people 'I'm into science'
> – that's probably something. He won't mind telling people, but it's
> something that he won't just bring up.
>
> *(Tom2, Black African, working-class boy)*

This echoes findings from wider research which suggests that, in order to
maintain popularity, boys (in particular) need to 'hide' their work and academic
effort from peers (e.g. Frosh et al., 2002). In other cases, students in our sample
suggested that someone could be popular and also into science as long as they
possessed other characteristics valued for popularity, such as being sporty:

> Someone like me, because I play football and so you can't really have a
> geeky image when you play football, so that kind of knocks it out, basically.
>
> *(Gerrard, White European, working-class boy)*

As Francis and colleagues (2012) found, it is only those high-attaining students
who are also attractive, fashionable and sporty, with strong social skills, who are
also able to simultaneously balance their attainment with being popular. This
exemplifies a general wider phenomenon, namely that high academic attainment
needs to be off-set by other identity work, e.g. attractiveness, being fashionable/
sporty, socially skilled – a phenomenon that may be exacerbated in the case of
science due to it being an archetypal 'clever', 'hard' subject.

The problem with 'brainy'/'clever'/'geeky' associations with science: (2) post-16 science is only for the exceptional few

As discussed above, braininess and cleverness are not necessarily considered by
students as negative characteristics per se – as, indeed, suggested by the survey
findings – but they can certainly be constructed as 'other'. That is, if students do
not regard themselves as clever but believe that cleverness is necessary to do well
and progress in science, they are less likely to take up a science identity and
continue to participate in science in the future (i.e. by studying science post-16
or pursuing a science-related career). Moreover, this association between science
and cleverness would seem to become more robust over time in that jobs in
science are regarded as for the 'clever'. As Rebecca (White British, middle-class
girl, Year 9) put it: 'You have to be quite intelligent to get quite a sciencey job',
a view that closely corresponded with that expressed by parents as well.

The increasing 'othering' of science is likely exacerbated by the strong links
between science and cleverness found in the Year 9 interviews. While this
association was apparent in the Year 6 interviews as well, it seems to have
strengthened, on the whole, by Year 9. It would seem that, by Year 9, images
of science-keen peers (particularly as clever), as well as perceptions of school
science as a difficult subject (which requires cleverness in order to do well), are
likely to underpin views of science as 'other'. This othering decreases the

possibility of identifying with science and, consequently, reduces the likelihood of students choosing to pursue it post-16.

The othering of science – particularly the affiliation of science with cleverness – is seriously compounded by the English school system itself. As we discuss in greater depth in Archer et al. (forthcoming), students must attain well in science in order to be allowed to pursue Triple Science (the most advanced option at GCSE). Moreover, access to post-16 science is also tightly controlled. The vast majority of entrants to A-level physics record the highest level of attainment at GCSE. Indeed, DfE (2012) figures show that only approximately 16% of students who gained a grade B in science at GCSE went on to study A-level physics (and 15% of those gaining a B in maths went on to study A-level maths). By contrast, twice as many students with a grade B in English, history and geography go on to AS (see also Bell et al., 2009a). Such a system clearly reinforces the message that science is only for the clever, a message which is underlined even further by policy discourses around the importance of the science pipeline. Overall, then, while it may not be necessary to be clever to be 'really into' science in school, students clearly subscribe to the view that the further someone goes in the system, the more clever they have to be. Such a perception can certainly impact on aspirations, as individuals are likely to aspire to careers that they see as 'for me'. Science's reputation as a career 'for the exceptionally clever' is likely to act against many individuals seeing it as 'for me'.

The problem with 'brainy'/'clever'/'geeky' associations with science: (3) cleverness as gendered, racialised and classed

The third problem with the association between science and braininess/cleverness is that the latter are dominantly configured in distinctly classed, racialised and gendered ways, which make it more difficult for non-dominant students to inhabit the identity of the 'good/ideal student' with any permanence or authenticity. We draw here particularly on the arguments and model set out by Archer and Francis (2007, pp. 66–67) and Archer (2008), which draw on empirical data to discuss how dominant educational discourse constructs the ideal student as White, male and middle class, against which Others are positioned as either pathologised (notably girls and British Chinese or Indian students) or demonised (particularly boys and White or Black working-class students). For instance, this work shows how dominant educational discursive configurations position White, middle-class masculinity as performing educationally in the 'right way' (e.g. as naturally talented, assertive, inquiring, independent, active). In contrast, educational attainment is 'explained away' among those who do not fit the ideal student identity, such as that among high-attaining girls and/or the British Chinese, who are pathologised as learning in the 'wrong way'. For instance, these students' achievement is attributed to 'plodding diligence', hard work and/or parental pressure, and these students are often described as being too 'passive', not questioning enough, and so on. In turn, demonised students are positioned as lacking intelligence, being unduly aggressive, disruptive, challenging, led by their peers, and so on.

In other words, we suggest that clever/brainy identity is not equally open to all students. Moreover, due to the close association between science and braininess/cleverness, it will be more difficult for Other students to perform – and be recognised by others as authentically performing – science identity.

Challenging the stereotypes: perceptions of scientists/science-keen peers as 'normal'

As discussed above, many students and parents in our sample indicated that there was something different about those who are strongly affiliated with science – and this was primarily identified in terms of their braininess/cleverness. However, some parents and students described scientists and/or science-keen students as essentially 'normal' – or as not differing in any discernible way from non-scientists, other than in their liking of science.

In Year 6, 52 students expressed opinions aligned with a view of science-keen peers as 'normal' and/or that being 'into science' is simply a reflection of a person's interest. More specifically, 37 Year 6 children described their science-keen peers in ways that suggested they do not consider being 'really into' science as indicative of a type of person, but rather as merely a reflection of their classmates' interest or activity.

> They're like, I don't know, they just like science. They just like doing it.
> *(Michael, White European, working-class boy)*

Moreover, a small subset of the 52 students more explicitly asserted that there was *not* a particular type of 'science person' or that those who were 'really into' science were *not* different or exceptional:

> I'm not sure how you can describe them cos they're normal people, they just like science a bit more than you.
> *(Mary, British Asian, working-class girl)*

Eighteen parents also insisted explicitly that there was not a 'type of person' who is likely to become a scientist:

> I don't think there's a type of person to do anything.
> *(Patsy, White British, working-class mother)*

In addition, of the 85 students interviewed in Year 9, 24 made statements in alignment with this image of science-keen students as normal:

> They're interested in science.
> *(Samantha, British Asian/White, upper-middle-class girl)*

I don't think you'd be able to like set them apart from everyone else.

(Hailey, White British, upper-middle-class girl)

Such perceptions of those who are 'really into' science as normal or not different from other students could also play a role in broadening images of science. That is, if a person does not have to be exceptionally clever to be keen on science, there are increased possibilities that other students – who may regard themselves as 'normal' or 'regular' – may also find a place for themselves in science. Of course, dismantling science's privileged status requires structural changes, such as improved post-16 access and broader options, as well as parity of status for technical and academic routes. Moreover, portraying scientists as 'normal' or 'just like you and me' is problematic in itself, given the ongoing disparities along gender, ethnic and class lines, particularly in the physical sciences and engineering (and at higher levels). Nevertheless, representing/portraying science as something that 'normal' people enjoy and do would seem to be a productive approach that might help contribute to 'opening up' the image of science.

Summary

In this chapter, we have explored the ways in which students – and their parents – perceive science and those who pursue it. We have also discussed the ways in which students view their science-keen peers. All of these perceptions point to a deeply entrenched alignment between science and cleverness – a relationship that acts as a major barrier to many young people coming to believe science is 'for them'.

This alignment is reinforced by widespread popular perceptions of science being a difficult subject, one in which exceptional intelligence is needed in order to do well. This view of science is strengthened by the structure of the school system, in which students must demonstrate achievement at a certain level in order to progress. In the final chapter of this volume we consider potential ways that the link between science and cleverness could perhaps be mitigated, suggesting that 'opening up' the image of science, and where science qualifications lead, might be helpful, particularly in light of our findings that most parents and students were only familiar with a very narrow range of possible jobs that science qualifications could lead to.

In sum, we have argued that the strong association between science and cleverness not only makes it difficult for those students who do not consider themselves to be exceptionally clever to perceive science as being 'for me', but also reinforces the doing/being divide. That is, while science may be something many young people enjoy doing, the link with cleverness is not aligned with most young people's sense of self or image of who they could visualise themselves becoming.

Notes

1 http://www.iop.org/resources/videos/people-and-events/gip/page_58728.html (accessed 25/5/16).
2 http://imascientist.org.uk/ (accessed 25/5/16).
3 http://www.theguardian.com/lifeandstyle/2014/jun/04/lego-launch-female-scientists-series (accessed 25/5/16).
4 Introduced as part of the 2006 curriculum reforms, 'Triple Science' is a popular, widespread terminology that refers to students studying for three GCSEs in biology, chemistry and physics. Entry to the Triple Science route is usually restricted according to prior attainment and is popularly considered to be the most challenging science GCSE option.

5

THE ROLE OF FAMILIES, SOCIAL CLASS AND SCIENCE CAPITAL IN YOUNG PEOPLE'S ASPIRATIONS

How do families shape children's science aspirations?

To date, the majority of interventions aimed at improving STEM participation have tended to be aimed at students/young people. Yet research tells us that families play a central role in shaping children's sense of themselves and their horizons of possibility. From a Bourdieusian perspective, families are key socialising agents, structuring the forms of capital that children possess and providing the primary context within which the habitus is developed. In the field of science education, studies have found that families exert an important influence on young people's science engagement, identities and/or attainment (e.g. Aschbacher et al., 2010; Ferry et al., 2000; Gilmartin et al., 2006; Stake, 2006). Yet, education policy and practice tend to pay scant attention to families – beyond pathologising accounts in some policy texts in which particular types of family are 'blamed' for low attainment or participation. For instance, working-class and some minority ethnic families have been described as suffering from a 'poverty of aspiration' or have been identified as having the 'wrong' knowledge, attitudes or values, particularly in relation to education (e.g. DfES, 2003, 2005). In this chapter, we consider the ways in which families may shape young people's science aspirations.

First, it is worth briefly reflecting on what we mean by the concept of 'family'. Scott and colleagues (2004) argue that it is preferable to use the terminology of 'families', rather than 'family', in order to acknowledge 'the plurality of family forms and . . . the dynamic processes of family formation and dissolution across time' (Scott et al., 2004, p. xvii). They point to how 'the family' is not a separate or universal structure, but families are diverse, ever-changing and inseparable from wider social spheres (e.g. of work, sexuality, gender, globalisation, and so on). Indeed, Beck and Beck-Gernsheim (2004) reflect that it is indeed difficult to 'objectively' define what a family is, since the concept of family is so diverse and has ever shifting boundaries. Recent times have seen significant and far-reaching changes in the forms that families take – such changes are notable across the world, from Europe (e.g. Kiernan, 2004) to the US (e.g. Elliot and Umberson, 2004) and beyond. Indeed, Edgar (2004) argues that family members' lives are interlinked to such an extent that we cannot focus on individuals without also looking at families. He suggests that a challenge for social research is thus to look at how families open up, or constrain, opportunities for individuals.

Research suggests that families can be highly influential on science attitudes and participation. For instance, Gilmartin and colleagues (2006) surveyed 1,126 tenth grade students in southern California and commented on 'the powerful role of family context' (p. 196), notably in terms of ethnicity and gender, on students' career aspirations, both generally and specifically in relation to their views of science and engineering. However, the ways in which families influence children's aspirations are complex and not fully understood (Atherton et al., 2009). It has also been noted that there may be different patterns of participation and engagement with science across different ethnic groups (e.g. Huang et al., 2000), and that the processes through which families influence children may vary between ethnic groups, with studies suggesting that Latino and South and East Asian families may promote STEM more explicitly as compared to White and/ or African American families (e.g. Gilmartin et al., 2006; Springate et al., 2008). As Aschbacher and colleagues (2010, p. 13) report within the US context, Asian American parents 'stand out' as providing their children with particularly 'strong expectations and support' for STEM careers.

Research indicates that families may also play a role in reproducing gendered (e.g. Dick and Rallis, 1991; Eccles, 1993; Frome and Eccles, 1998; Manis, 1989; Tenenbaum and Leaper, 2003) and classed (Aschbacher et al., 2010; Royal Society, 2008a) patterns in STEM participation. For instance, Tenenbaum and Leaper (2003) found that more parents tended to perceive science as being 'difficult' for their daughters than did for their sons. Researchers have also found that, on science museum visits, parents tend to offer their sons more complex and scientific explanations than their daughters (Crowley, 1999; Crowley et al., 2001).

In this chapter we explore how and why families matter to the development (or not) of children's science aspirations, asking why is science a more 'thinkable' aspiration in some families than in others? We begin by introducing the concept of 'family habitus' and how families' everyday practices, resources (both generic and science-related), values and sense of identity ('who we are') influence the extent to which children come to see science as a (im)possible and/or (un)desirable future career path.

Family habitus

In Chapter 1, we introduced Bourdieu's concept of habitus. As we discussed, habitus has predominantly been used in an individualistic sense, but in Archer et al. (2012b) we extended the concept to families in order to capture families' collective dispositions and ways of being, the family 'micro-climate', as Aschbacher et al. (2010) term it. We felt that this extension of habitus, from the individual to the family level, was not incommensurate with Bourdieu's conceptualisation of habitus, as he sees habitus as encompassing both individual and collective formations, such as gendered habitus (Bourdieu, 2001) and classed habitus (Bourdieu, 1984; Bourdieu and Passeron, 1990; see also the development of this idea by Charlesworth, 2000). Indeed, Bourdieu conceptualised habitus as a 'multi-layered concept, with more general notions of habitus at the level of society and more complex, differentiated notions at the level of the individual' (Reay, 2004, p. 434). Following Bourdieu, academics have theoretically and empirically developed further forms of collective habitus, such as institutional habitus (e.g. Reay et al., 2001; Reay et al., 2005) and collective rural habitus (e.g. Atkins, 2000, cited in Reay, 2004). Indeed, Diane Reay argues that 'collective understanding of habitus is necessary, according to Bourdieu, in order to recognize that individuals contain within themselves their past and present position in the social structure' (Reay, 2004, p. 434).

The term 'family habitus' is not our own invention – it can be found in a handful of previous studies that have explored student access to higher education using a Bourdieusian framework (e.g. Robb et al., 2007; Thomas, 2002; Tomanovic, 2004). However, as we discuss in Archer et al. (2012b, p. 5), 'it [family habitus] remains under-theorised and where it has been cited, its specificity and distinctiveness tend not to have been remarked upon . . . what family habitus actually "is", is rarely defined'. Hence we felt that it would be useful to theoretically elaborate on what the parameters and nature of family habitus might be. Moreover, we wanted to explore whether family habitus might be a useful conceptual tool for understanding how and why some children come to see science aspirations as 'natural' and 'for me', while others experience science careers as 'unthinkable'.

As we detail in Archer et al. (2012b), we conceptualise *family habitus* as referring to the ways in which families think, conceive of themselves and operate. This extends beyond shared attitudes, for example what families think about science, the extent to which they like, or dislike, science, and so on. We see family habitus as also encompassing families' values, collective dispositions, sense of identity and everyday practices. Extending this to science, we propose that family habitus captures the extent to which families construct a collective framework of dispositions towards, and a conscious and unconscious relationship with, science. This 'mindset' is further shaped by (and interacts with) a family's economic, social and cultural capital across and within different fields.

We could, of course, have chosen a different (perhaps more accessible!) term than 'family habitus', such as 'family identity' or 'family context'. However, we feel that the value of the concept of habitus lies in its capacity to:

> encompass a broad spectrum of family resources, practices, values, cultural discourses and 'identifications' ('who we are'). It provides a lens for

attempting to situate and contextualise individual child and parent identities (and orientations to science) within the family environment – for examining the extent to which the everyday family 'landscape' shapes, constrains or facilitates aspirations and engagement in science through the combination of attitudes, values, practices and ways of being that they engage in.

(Archer et al., 2012b, p. 6)

That is, we see the value of the concept of family habitus as lying in its potential for exploring the ways in which families socialise children to develop particular 'ways of being' in the world.

We now move on to consider how family habitus (and its interaction with science capital) plays a role in shaping children's science aspirations, particularly in terms of producing classed patterns in science aspirations. We begin by outlining evidence from the surveys that we conducted with students in Years 6, 8 and 9. We then explore the issues in greater depth, via analysis of the longitudinal interview data from children and parents.

Young people's engagement with science at home and parental attitudes to science: what the surveys tell us

In the surveys, we asked students to tell us about their (perceptions of their) parents' attitudes to science. On the whole, students reported that their parents have positive attitudes to science and value science as a school subject. Students' ratings of their parents' attitudes to science also appeared to be an influential variable with regard to student science aspirations. Statistical analyses using multi-level modelling revealed that parental attitudes to science, experiences of school science and student self-concept in science were the variables that had the strongest relationship with students' aspirations in science (see Chapter 2 and DeWitt et al., 2014).

The surveys revealed a mixed picture of student and family engagement with science. Overall, it seems that in general, as they grow older, young people engage less with science in their spare time, as detailed in Table 5.1.

As Table 5.1 sets out, by age 14, 40% of young people say that they 'never' do any science-related activities outside of school, and just 9% are regularly engaged in science-related activities at least once a week. Almost half of Y9 students say they 'never' read a book or magazine about science (less than 10% do so regularly) and about a third never look at science-related websites. Television appears to be the most prevalent medium through which young people engage with science in their spare time, with a fifth of Y9 students saying they watch science-related television programmes at least once a week and only 16% saying they never watch such programmes. In addition, over a quarter of Y9 students reported that they 'never' visit a museum or zoo.

Such patterns are not entirely unexpected and may reflect both young people's growing independence and autonomy (e.g. taking part in fewer whole-family

TABLE 5.1 Percentage of students regularly or never engaging in science-related activities in their spare time

	Regular involvement (at least once a week)			'Never'		
	Y6	Y8	Y9	Y6	Y8	Y9
Do science activities out of school	18.8%	13.2%	9.1%	23.4%	33.5%	40.4%
Read book or magazine about science	17.9%	8.5%	8.5%	31.1%	47.2%	47.6%
Go on science websites	15.2%	9.1%	11.7%	33.4%	34.8%	32.5%
Watch science-related television programmes	35.2%	24.8%	21.7%	18.7%	19.6%	16.2%

activities) and/or an increase in competing demands on their free time (e.g. schoolwork/homework, social life, etc.). As one of our interviewees, Georgia, put it:

> I used to be doing it [science activities] nearly 24/7 and now I'm not doing it as much. I don't know, because I had lots of time to do it, whereas now I've got lots of homework and then most of the time I'm out with my friends, so I don't get as much time.

Within these top-level figures there are, however, some further patterns of interest. For instance, the Y9 survey found that boys, minority ethnic students and those with higher levels of cultural capital are significantly more likely to engage in regular science-related activities in their spare time. A medium negative effect size was also found for the relationship between engaging in regular science-related activities and having low cultural capital (−.33). There is also a positive relationship (with an effect size of .40) between attitudes towards school science and engagement in science activities out of school. Looking across the three surveys, it appears that, overall, there is a decrease in student engagement with out-of-school science activities with age, particularly across the primary/secondary divide, but some social groups (particularly the more socially advantaged) are more likely to maintain their engagement compared to others.

This decrease in students' extra-curricular engagement with science stands in contrast to young people's perceptions of their parents' levels of interest in, and valuing of, science. Across all three surveys, we found that students generally reported high levels of parental interest in, and support for, science. Moreover, the level of parental support for science remained fairly constant over time. For instance, 58.6% of Y6 students and 56% of Y9 students agreed that their parents think science is interesting. Moreover, 72% of Y6 students and almost three quarters of Y9 students agreed that their parents think it is important for them to learn science. Multi-level modelling analyses (see DeWitt et al., 2014) also revealed that parental attitudes to science are closely related to students' aspirations in science – that is, students reporting the most positive parental attitudes to science were most likely to aspire to a future science career.

How do families make science 'thinkable' or 'unthinkable'? Evidence from longitudinal interviews with parents and children

We now turn to the qualitative data to examine in more detail how family orientations to science, and social class, play a part in producing patterns of student science aspiration. We classified 16 students in the qualitative sample as coming from high-science-capital families. Of these, nine expressed science or STEM-related career aspirations in their final Year 9 interview. Twenty students were classified as having medium levels of science capital, of whom 12 expressed science or STEM career aspirations in their final Year 9 interview. This compared with 47 students who were classified as having low science capital, of whom just 15 held science or STEM-related career aspirations in the final Year 9 interview (see Figures 5.1 and 5.2). In other words, there appeared to be a reasonably strong relationship between levels of science capital (high/medium versus low) and children's science-related aspirations, and, as shown by Figures 5.1 and 5.2, this relationship appeared to increase over time. There is then a discernible relationship between science capital and broad categories of children's aspirations. Overall, it appears that children from families with medium and high levels of science capital are more likely to aspire to science and/or STEM-related careers than those from families with low science capital.

We were struck by the relatively high level of consistency in student aspirations from Y6 to Y9, which was noted across all three broad categories of aspiration (science, STEM-related and non-STEM). Indeed, mapping student

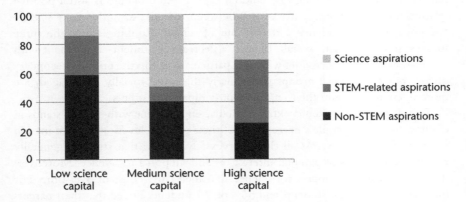

FIGURE 5.1 Percentage of Year 6 students (qualitative sample) with science/ STEM-related or non-STEM aspirations by level of science capital

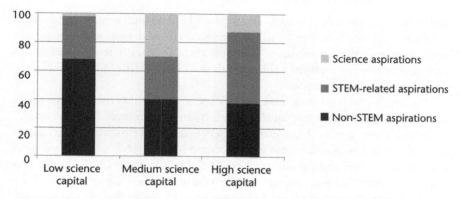

FIGURE 5.2   Percentage of Year 9 students (qualitative sample) with science/
STEM-related or non-STEM aspirations by level of science capital

aspirations over time showed that approximately three quarters of all students keep their aspirations within the same broad category (science/STEM-related/ non-STEM) from Year 6 to Year 9. While the precise aspiration often varied between time points (e.g. actress in Year 6, artist in Year 9), the broad type of aspiration tended not to change much.

As the figures also show, among our interviewees, students with high and medium levels of science capital are more likely to express science/STEM aspirations than not. Those with low levels of science capital are more likely to hold non-STEM aspirations, and it was notable that not a single student in this group expressed *consistent* science aspirations from Y6 to Y9 (that is, the students with low science capital who held science aspirations in Year 9 are different students from those who expressed science aspirations in Year 6).

We now move on to explore how the interaction of family habitus and science capital plays a part in producing these patterns of aspiration. In particular, we discuss how the extent to which science is 'woven' into (or is absent from) un/conscious family life seems to be important. We begin by discussing how children's science aspirations, interest and identification are strongly facilitated within families with high and medium levels of science capital. We then move on to discuss the implications of situations where young people and their families possess very little capital, and the effect this has on patterns of science aspiration.

'Science families': how families make science thinkable and realistic

Among the sample of parents and young people whom we longitudinally tracked via interviews from age 10 to 14, there were 16 families who were highly engaged with science and whom we classified as having 'high' science capital. These families had at least one parent who held degree-level science qualifications and either a current, or previous, career in a STEM-related area. These families exhibited high levels of interest in science and their children engaged frequently with science in their spare time. We term these families 'science families', to represent how science played a role in both the family sense of identity and their everyday values and practices.

The families with high science capital, 'science families', were overwhelmingly middle class and from White and/or South Asian backgrounds. They possessed, or could easily access, high-quality science-related resources and engaged in everyday family practices that supported and helped 'grow' children's potential science interest and aspirations. Not all children in these families aspired to science careers (indeed, several actively resisted science aspirations at some point between the ages of 10 and 14 and/or aspired to other non-STEM careers), although all did plan to study at least one science at A level. Moreover, a small subset of these children held science-related aspirations (in line with family expectations) but did not display any strong intrinsic interest in science. We suggest that it is a combination of family habitus and science capital that provides a particularly 'fertile ground' that renders post-16 science more thinkable/desirable for children in these families.

As the following interview extracts illustrate, the interaction of family habitus and capital resulted in: (i) making science highly 'visible' and familiar within everyday life, with regular and ongoing access to resources and support for children to develop a practical 'feel' for, and sense of mastery of, science; (ii) cultivating a perception of science as desirable, both for future careers and for informed citizenship; and (iii) a narrative of family identity in which science is constructed as 'part of who we are'.

Making science highly 'visible' and developing a 'feel' for/mastery of science

We found that children with higher levels of science capital, particularly those with a parent working in a science-related career, tended to have stronger aspirations in science than their peers. This was also borne out in the survey, in which, for instance, 47% of Y8 students with a family member who worked in a science-related job (versus 29% of the whole cohort) said that they would like to work in a science-related job. We suggest that among the reasons for this are that these families have particularly high levels of scientific knowledge to draw on, identify strongly with science (and convey this passion to their children) and are able to mobilise their capital to heavily promote and support science activities and resources both educationally and as leisure activities for their children.

These families tended to provide science resources and activities within a family habitus that is strongly 'pro-science' and which approaches child-rearing through the practice of concerted cultivation (Lareau, 2003), as discussed previously. For instance, Bob is a middle-class boy of mixed Asian/White ethnicity. His father has worked in IT and his mother is a chemist. Bob has a passion for electronics and does lots of electronics-related activities in his spare time. He also enjoys welding, woodwork and is a member of a coding club. As his mother Debbie explains, there is a strong interest in and identification with science in the family and she actively seeks out opportunities to engage her children in science-related enrichment activities:

> I don't just work in science, I am actually interested in it as well . . . So my interests probably come out in two ways. So I do things with the children that are science related. So for example I'm a member of the Royal Society of Chemistry . . . they had like some lectures where they were trying to aim them at families rather than on an academic level, so we took both kids in to London . . . along to one of these talks, so they could get a different sense of what's out there. And it wasn't an academic talk particularly . . . but the point was they were going into a sort of scientific institution and they were meeting other people that were, you know, not in their circle of friends and whatever. So you know I will do things like that and I'll take them to a science museum and that sort of thing . . . Oh yeah [and] we have *New Scientist* and Bob'll sit there over dinner reading that and telling me all about it and everything, yeah, he's fascinated by some of the things in that.

Like other 'science families', Bob's family had ample science-related social capital that he could draw on, and which seemed to have shaped his aspiration to become an electronic engineer. As Debbie explained:

> I know there were a few relatives that he was talking to when we had a big gathering at Christmas. So his uncle works on the electronics side of satellite design and whatever, so he talks to him about a few things. I think they're probably like quite similar personality types and interests. But he also went to talk to another relative . . . because this guy also studied electrical engineering or electronics . . . And so he was asking him about his career and what he did and . . . you know you could see him getting quite interested and excited in what this guy was telling him – that was quite nice. And then a few weeks ago I sat down to dinner and he [Bob] tore this article or this advert rather out of the paper, it was a job for an electrical engineer or something, he was going 'That's what I want to do, that's where I see myself' . . . Yeah I guess if he'd wanted to go into something like performing arts we'd be struggling. [laughs] But there's plenty of scientists and engineers in the family, so it's not that unusual for him to do.

The family were also able to mobilise their STEM-specific cultural capital to support Bob's option choices and attainment at school. For instance, Debbie described the actions they took in relation to a decision about whether Bob should take ICT as a GCSE subject choice during the Year 9 options process:

> The only one I had any concern over was the ICT . . . whether the school could teach it adequately . . . because it was relatively new to them. Because they couldn't like point to a lot of results to convince me that, you know, a lot of students went in for it and got good grades. My one concern was it could turn out to be one of those subjects that they offer, and people don't try very hard . . . or they put some of the less able children in and they're very disruptive . . . So we [parents] looked at the syllabus from the exam board itself and we decided that actually if the teaching turns out to be less optimal than we'd like we could probably teach him it ourselves or he could probably almost self teach it . . . So if it all fell apart at school . . . I knew we'd be able to rescue the situation.

Perhaps unsurprisingly, Bob expressed very consistent STEM aspirations across his interviews and firmly expected to study science to degree level and beyond.

Like Bob's family, other high-science-capital parents also talked about their specific, intentional fostering of science within the family habitus. For instance, Jack is the father of Kaka, a British Asian boy from the south-east of England. In his interviews, Jack clearly articulated his explicit agenda to actively foster and increase his son's science interest and aspiration through the provision of science-related toys and activities. Jack talks in some detail about his 'love' of physics and chemistry and how he hopes that buying Kaka science and electronics sets and providing enthusiasm for science in the home will contribute to Kaka choosing to pursue a science-related career in the future ('I mean definitely we'll give him a bit more of a push I think to actually get into the stuff . . . so hopefully yeah, we'll actually push him into that'). This strategy seemed to be working, with Kaka agreeing: 'I really, really love like science but I want to get better at science, so that's why I want to become a scientist.' Across all his interviews, Kaka identifies his aspirations as including science or scientist (alongside mathematician and footballer in his Year 6 interview and mechanic in his Year 8 interview). At his Year 9 interview, Kaka aspires to be a surgeon or scientist, plans to study science at A level and identifies the three sciences as his 'favourite' subjects at school.

We suggest that middle-class families' economic, social and cultural capital provides their children with opportunities to develop (new/wider forms of) scientific knowledge (for instance about a wide range of potential science careers, and understanding 'how science works'). It can also help develop children's familiarity and ease with science, for instance through participation in a greater volume and variety of science-related activities in their everyday lives. As discussed in the previous section, analysis of the survey data indicates that, overall, students with high or very high cultural capital were more likely to participate in science-related activities out of school (and students with low or very low cultural capital were less likely to participate in science-related activities outside of school). Aschbacher et al. (2010) also discuss how students who achieve highly in science tend to come from more affluent families which possess strong scientific social capital and a range of economic, social and cultural resources to help support their children's achievement. Likewise, we suggest that the active (concerted cultivation) parenting approaches of families with high science capital help to create opportunities for children to develop a practical mastery of and 'feel' for science in their everyday lives, which contributes to their favourable views of, and liking for, science – and makes post-16 science a more attractive, achievable and conceivable potential option for them.

Cultivating a view of science as important for future careers and informed citizenship

The second main way in which science families supported and fostered science aspirations and/or the intention to continue with science post-16 was through the cultivation of an understanding/appreciation among young people that science would be useful for their future lives, in terms of jobs and/or active citizenship.

For instance, Raza (British Asian, middle-class boy) aspires to be a writer but is considering taking physics at A level (along with English) due to his intrinsic interest in the subject ('Physics, yeah, I'm probably going to look into that . . . because I'm interested in it, yeah'). His father is an accountant and his mother works in a science-related job. Raza resists his mum's ongoing pushing for him to become a doctor, but he does seem to have developed an interest in physics and an appreciation of the value of science generally. Similarly, Amy2 (White British, middle-class girl) talks in her Y9 interview about the strong science interests within her family (both her parents have science degrees and her older brother is studying for a zoology degree). She describes how the family watch science programmes together, and she does some experiments at home. Amy2 has a long-term aspiration of becoming a teacher (expressed consistently from age 10 to 14) but also describes being 'very into' science and strongly values science. She plans to take chemistry alongside humanities subjects at A level.

As mother Debbie (a chemist) exemplifies, science parents often explicitly convey the value of science qualifications to their children:

> I'm certainly aware that Science doesn't just lead to science careers, that it can lead to lots of others. That was one of the reasons I think we supported our daughter in choosing a scientific career knowing that even if it didn't pan out and you know at the end of it she didn't want to do science jobs, that she could go into lots of other things.

Children from science families were often able to articulate a view of science as valuable for informed citizenship, 'knowing how the world works'. As Davina and Tom4 put it:

> I think it's just quite useful [to study science] just to be like you know . . . you understand the basics of the world around you. If you're completely isolated from it completely, then I think it's just a bit kind of weird, cos I think you wouldn't understand how anything works, why anything happens.
>
> *(Davina, White British/European, upper-middle-class girl, Y8)*

> I think it would be really useful to study science, because science is a really wide range and it gives you a choice of nearly everything.
>
> *(Tom4, British Asian, middle-class boy, Y8)*

Davina and a few others were also aware of the social status and standing of science, an understanding which Davina described as coming from her father (Dawkins):

> I think Science is quite good cos I think . . . something I've heard from my dad is that like . . . when companies look at all of your like qualifications and stuff, if they see science, they automatically think 'Oh they're actually quite clever' so like you know they wish to employ them. I think that's the only reason why, like, if you're not really sure what you want to go into and you know you're not going to be like something specific like a lawyer, then you might as well just do science, cos it's respected.
>
> *(Davina, Y9)*

Davina held among the most consistent science aspirations of all the girls we interviewed, maintaining a desire to be a scientist (Y6), 'something to do with science' (Y8), and to get a 'science-related job' (Y9). Since the age of ten she had always planned to continue with science at Oxbridge, following in the footsteps of her father, who had studied Genetics there. She talked about having already read the Oxford prospectus before her Year 9 interview. Davina was in the top set for science and was taking Triple Science at GCSE and was confident in her ability to attain her aspirations.

Young people's views about the future utility and value of science qualifications seemed to be inculcated from a relatively young age. Indeed, most of the young people classified as having medium or high levels of science capital had expressed an assurance from the age of 10/11 that they would take at least one science at A level. In this sense, the children from science families echo the middle-class young people in Reay et al.'s (2005) study of higher education choice who are described as 'always knowing' that they will go to university (in stark contrast to their working-class peers who are 'never sure'). That is, we suggest that, for many/most children with high/medium science capital, the powerful interaction of family habitus and intensive pro-science parenting practices results in them 'always knowing' that they will continue with science post-16. There is no single moment of choice or decision; it is something that is taken for granted, a 'given', within such families.

Science as family identity ('who we are')

One of the defining features of 'science families' was a strong alignment between family habitus, family (science) capital and the child's personal interests and identifications, producing a family discourse in which science is not just something 'we like' but is an aspect of family identity, 'who we are'. This family science identity was realised in a variety of ways, including through emotional bonds and family practices.

For example, Hannah is a middle-class, White British girl who attends Austen School. Her father (Maddison) is an IT professional who holds an engineering degree. Her mother is a dietician with a Master's level STEM qualification and an IT background. Maddison describes both himself and his wife as 'quite sciencey'. As in the case of other science families, Maddison portrays their everyday family life as embedding science-related interests and forms of capital ('there's always lots of *Scientific American* magazines and dietician magazines and . . . Natural History Museum magazines around'). Hannah's parents' interest in science is exemplified by, as Maddison explains, the 'magazines we get, the programmes we watch . . . the bits of newspaper we go to . . . And what we talk about it in the house – you know we do talk about it'. The family regularly discuss and debate media coverage of science-related issues. Maddison also describes how, as parents, they regulate their children's television viewing, pushing the Discovery Channel in particular. This commitment to science has also shaped their educational decision-making. Maddison explains that they chose Austen School on the basis that it is 'strong at science' with excellent facilities and teachers.

The strong embedding of science within the family 'habitus' appears to be fostering durable dispositions within Hannah too, who is developing a strong 'science identity' and aspires to be a chemist (Y6), work in a lab (Y8) or apply science (but particularly chemistry) potentially within the police/detective sphere (Y9). Her father says that she 'hero worships' her older brother, who is studying for a higher degree in nuclear physics. When asked to identify the person whom she most looks up to, or would like to be like in the future, Hannah replies 'Einstein'. She also describes herself as friends with 'the sciencey crowd' at school (something that her father concurred with). At home she describes watching 'all' the science programmes on children's television and the Discovery Channel.

For a number of families, an interest in science and STEM-related careers permeated both the nuclear and the extended family, often tracing back over generations. Notably, many of these parents themselves held science degrees and/ or were working within science-related fields.

> As the product of history, habitus produces individual and collective practices . . . It ensures the active presence of past experiences which, deposited in each organism in the form of schemata of thought and action, tend, more surely than all the formal rules and all explicit norms, to guarantee the conformity of practices and their constancy across time.
>
> *(Bourdieu, 1990, p. 91)*

Consequently, science is rendered not 'just another subject'; instead it suffuses all aspects of family life, such as daily topics of conversation, leisure time and family activities and joint interests, both consciously and subconsciously. As one mother put it:

> The other day in the car we were laughing about chemical symbols and things, so I guess it does come into the discussion quite subliminally really.
>
> *(Elizabeth, White British, middle-class mother, Y9 interview)*

The result – alignment between family science capital/habitus and student science engagement

As a result of these processes, families with high science capital were much more likely to produce children with science, or STEM-related, aspirations. The power of the interaction between science capital and family habitus was also such that even when children in these families did not hold science aspirations, they were more likely to plan to study science post-16. As Figures 5.1 and 5.2 also indicate, family science capital appears to produce alignment over time – something which is exemplified by the case of Poppy.

Poppy is a White, middle-class girl at Austen School. In her Year 6 interview she said that she enjoys science and would be happy to do 'something linked with science' in the future, but her real passion was for an 'adventurous' career and she describes herself as interested but 'not really into science'. Poppy engages in some science-related activities outside of school (e.g. doing science kits, watching television programmes, going on family visits to museums) but the science-related aspect of her aspirations seems to be driven by her parents, who regularly encourage Poppy to consider becoming a scientist (especially in the field of medicine or veterinary science) and emphasise her aptitude for this. As mum Lulu explained in the Y6 interview, 'I just think that her brain works that way really . . . I think she is interested and I keep telling her she's got a scientific brain. So that might make her think that way.' Lulu has a personal interest in science ('I think biology really is my thing . . . I'm fascinated by space as well') and indicated that her steering of Poppy is shaped by her regret that she herself was 'steered away' from science in her youth by her school. Lulu's persistence and motivation appeared to be paying off, as in both her Year 8 and Year 9 interviews Poppy expressed a firm ambition to become a vet. Whereas she had suggested in her Year 6 interview that she was unsure if she would continue with science in the future, in her latter two interviews Poppy was certain that she would continue with science and named her favourite subjects as biology and chemistry.

We suggest that Poppy is influenced by her family habitus, which is produced through an interplay of past and present and through which parents are actively seeking to cultivate certain dispositions towards science. This habitus is not deterministic; that is, she exerts agency at various points through her interviews. However, we suggest that it is possible to see how she becomes increasingly 'pro-science' over time, shifting her aspirations and post-16 study plans in line with her parents' interests and practices.

Making science 'unthinkable': interactions of family habitus and a lack of science-related capital

So far we have discussed how some middle-class families can mobilise resources and cultural discourses and practices to make science more 'thinkable' and potentially a more sustainable and achievable aspiration for their children. We now move on to consider how an absence of (both generic and science-specific) capital and a family habitus aligned with the 'accomplishment of natural growth' (Lareau, 2003) can disadvantage children from less privileged backgrounds by (1) hindering the realisation, development and continuation of science aspirations or (2) rendering science aspirations 'unthinkable'.

'Lost' science aspirations: the interaction of family habitus, capital and social inequalities

Our analyses suggest that even when working-class children hold a personal science-related interest/aspiration, the resources and family 'cultural infrastructure' (family habitus) available to them may be too thin to enable the child to build/ capitalise on and persist with their nascent interest. Hence, in such contexts, the child's science aspirations are likely to remain 'raw' and are more likely to wither away or be dropped over time, given the lack of opportunities and capital for them to become more 'cemented' in ways that will be resilient and persistent over time and which can generate social advantage.

For instance, Jake is a Black British, working-class boy who lives in London. In Y6 he aspired to become a doctor, scientist, lawyer or footballer. In Year 8 he was interested in being a lawyer or computer technician. By Y9 he aspired to become an accountant or lawyer. Jake had always done well at science, a view that had been reinforced by his teachers. Indeed, as Bunmi, his mother, reflected in the Y9 interview:

> He used to like science so much . . . even the teacher told me that he's very good in science . . . He's very good in science, I don't know why he wants to be an accountant.
>
> *(Bunmi, Black British, working-class mother)*

However, in his Y9 interview, Jake reflected on how being a scientist would be 'very hard'. His mother also wondered whether Jake had dropped his science aspirations because 'I don't know, maybe he believes science is too difficult'.

Bunmi's parenting style fits with Lareau's notion of the accomplishment of natural growth, in that educational decisions are devolved to Jake. For instance, during the Year 9 interview, Bunmi had to ask Jake which subjects he had chosen for his options – and Jake explained to her then that he had chosen additional (Double) science. This 'child as expert' approach is also illustrated by Bunmi's comment that: 'When he said he wanted to be an accountant I was like "Well I'm not going to discourage you – it's your choice".'

Bunmi admitted that she had little interest in science herself ('I don't like it') and the family appeared to be disadvantaged by a lack of science capital and, consequently, provided little support for or fostering of Jake's science interest. For instance, in the Year 6 interview, Bunmi explained that while she is generally supportive of Jake's science interests, she finds it hard to offer further support or reinforcement. She described how Jake calls out to her when he's watching science television programmes, asking her to look at what is going on, but she feels she lacks the time and interest to join him. Consequently, Jake's self-reported out-of-school engagement with science at age 10 (e.g. his self-directed 'experiments') came across as somewhat sporadic and haphazard, and by age 14 he had stopped doing science activities at home.

Bunmi also talked at some length in the Y9 interview about having little idea where science qualifications might lead ('you know he [Jake] loves science – [but] what can I do? . . . if you do science, what can you be later in the day?'). Jake appeared to be at a similar loss to know where science might lead ('Well like jobs that use study of science are actually important jobs, but like there's not really many there that I know of anyway', Jake, Y9 interview). Bunmi explained that she knows science can lead to a job as a scientist but does not actually have much of an idea what being a scientist involves, saying 'I don't know the jobs they do anyway when they're a scientist'.

As Bunmi explained about her son Jake's aspiration to become an accountant, 'I don't want to discourage him . . . because I wanted to be an accountant as well'. But Bunmi also feels disadvantaged by a lack of cultural capital, as she doesn't know what subjects Jake would need to study in order to become an accountant, nor whether he would need to go to university. The family do not know anyone who is an accountant and Bunmi describes being at a loss to understand the UK system and feels dependent upon the school for advice and help:

> Well in this country I don't really know what are they doing . . . I know in my country if you want to be an accountant or banker you have to be very good in maths and English . . . I don't know about this country you know . . . So if he say he want to be an accountant, I think they should . . . tell him in school the kind of subjects, what he's got to be good, what you have to be good in.

In sum, it is perhaps unsurprising that young people like Jake, despite liking science, end up opting for 'safer', 'known', more pragmatic aspirations. Jake and Bunmi's case also exemplifies the difficulty that some working-class parents experience (particularly those from migrant backgrounds and those not fluent in English), unable to enjoy the resources of time and sufficient cultural knowledge/ educational understanding to share and develop their child's science interest. They may lack the dominant forms of cultural capital to enable them to support their children to make choices that might sustain/promote, rather than close down, avenues that could enable them to continue with science post-16.

We argue that the loss of science aspirations among these children was often a gradual process of erosion, rather than a single moment of choice or a conscious decision to 'drop' science. For instance, Brittney (White British, lower-middle-class girl) aspired in Y6 to 'something involving chemistry' or 'something involving beauty'. In Y8 she was unsure but was still interested in pursuing 'something involving science, maybe chemistry'. By her Year 9 interview, however, she was fairly decided on becoming a primary school teacher. Her interest in science remained ('I sort of quite like science . . . I've always been quite interested in science, so it's not really changed that much') but her favourite subject was now food technology (followed by drama, dance, sport, history and languages). She still does well in science at school but explains the dropping of her previous science aspirations in the following way:

> I just don't really think that I'd enjoy it as much as being a teacher because you get a broader variety of things being a teacher than just doing you know one thing.

None of her friends are really into science and, unlike with science, Brittney has social capital relating to teaching ('Someone in my family is a teacher at a college'). She also indicates that, despite her interest in science, she does not engage with science in her spare time, largely because she has no idea what opportunities there might be ('there isn't really much to do about science outside of school, so I don't really do anything').

There appears to be some resonance here with the young people that Aschbacher et al. (2010) describe as 'lost potentials' (students who initially described themselves as highly interested in science but who later dropped it). Aschbacher and colleagues suggest that these young people are characterised by a waning family 'pushing' of science: 'by high school, less than half reported that family members were still encouraging such activities' (2010, p. 10). We suggest that such combinations of family habitus and capital (within an albeit benign/ neutral family view of science) may provide a rather 'poor soil' in which science aspirations may find it difficult to take root and flourish. This point is underlined by Hidi and Renninger (2006), whose four-phase interest model suggests that an initial interest has to be sustained through lines of practice (Azevedo, 2011) if it is to develop and flourish. If there are no lines of potential practice and/or only restricted opportunities available to develop lines of practice, then it risks diminishing/'withering'.

'Science as unthinkable'

For most young people in our sample, however, science had never really featured within their aspirations. This is not to say they did not like science – as the survey data also show, the majority of young people in our study report finding science interesting. However, their enjoyment of 'doing' science (in and out of school) tends not to translate into an interest in 'being' a scientist (Archer et al., 2010a). Here, we discuss how, for many children, the configuration of family habitus and the unequal distribution of science capital within society combine to render science more of an 'unknown' and 'unthinkable' option.

Most young people's families were certainly not 'anti' science. Rather they expressed views that might be characterised as benign or neutral. But it was notable that, outside the 'science families', most young people's early instinctive enthusiasm for science was enacted without the formalised support and embedding within the family enjoyed by 'science family' children. In other words, while many children may describe themselves as being 'into' science, the majority enact these interests alone; they are not shared or threaded through most families. For instance, at Year 6 MacTavish (White British, working-class boy) describes himself as 'into science', enjoying various science books at home and watching some children's television science programmes. He attains well in science at school and he does engage with science in his free time – although his home experimenting is of the exploding Coke/Mentos[1] variety (see Archer et al., 2010a) and science is not woven into his family habitus. Indeed, like numerous other children, MacTavish said he had 'no idea . . . not a clue' what his family think of science.

We suggest that where there is an absence of strong family science capital and identification with science, this can produce a formidable barrier to potential future science participation, even among well-resourced middle-class families. Moreover, we suggest that the limits of possibility are even more constrained for working-class families, where the interplay of family habitus and the unequal distribution of both generic and science-specific capital in society means that, for a sizeable proportion of working-class families and children, science is simply an 'unthinkable' aspiration.

The first of these points is illustrated by the cases of Tom3 and Gus, both White upper-middle-class boys who attend an independent boys' school. Both boys achieve highly (across different subject areas), both enjoy science, have a small amount of science capital within their families and think that their teachers are excellent. At age 10, Tom3 aspires to become a sportsman or to work in business and become a millionaire. Aged 12, he wants to become a cricketer or cricket commentator. At age 14 he is undecided. His favourite subjects are languages and science is a fairly 'unthinkable' aspiration. As Tom3 puts it, 'I just can't really picture myself being a scientist'.

For both boys, their aspirations appear to align with a family habitus that identifies strongly with 'the arts' (which are constructed as dichotomous to 'science'). As Tom3's mother Terri explains, 'We know more arts people than science people'. Likewise, Gus expresses a consistent ambition across all three interviews to become an author, writer or journalist, which he links to an established family narrative ('Well my granddad was an author and my great granddad was as well'). Unsurprisingly, Gus's favourite subject is English. His science self-efficacy appears to decrease over time, such that by his Year 9 interview he claims, 'I'm not very good at sciences'.

We suggest that the absence of any science-related family discourse (and the construction of science as distinct from and even oppositional to 'the arts') can contribute to children coming to regard science as 'interesting, but not for me'. However, as we shall now discuss, the consequences and potential mutability of this perception may 'weigh' differently for those (predominantly working-class) children who lack Tom3 and Gus's privilege and their likely continued accrual of science-related social and cultural capital over time.

In our interview sample, the majority of children who did not express science aspirations came from less privileged social backgrounds. These children tended to enjoy 'doing' science but did not see a career in science as desirable or likely. That is, they were 'interested, *but* . . .'.[2] They all enjoyed science and, while at primary school, reported doing science activities in their spare time. Yet their out-of-school engagement with science typically dwindled considerably once they reached secondary school. These young people tended to have some notional science-related capital at home, with most families having a parent or extended family member who 'enjoys' science and finds it interesting. However, they were much less likely to have parents with formalised science capital (e.g. post-compulsory qualifications or science-related jobs). Hence this parental interest tended to have less 'exchange value' (i.e. less capacity to capitalise on resources and translate them across social fields to generate advantage), as compared to the 'science families' discussed earlier. Moreover, this interest was not embedded either materially or discursively within (and hence was not actively woven into) the family habitus.

For instance, Hedgehog is a White working-class boy. He consistently aspires to be a teacher across the three interviews, ideally a PE teacher, reflecting his sports interests. He also finds science interesting, for instance describing how he loves researching space and NASA in his spare time ('I'm a bit of a space fan . . . I've got books and DVDs and everything'). Like others, at age 10/11 he occasionally did science experiments at home, watched various children's television science programmes and sometimes looked up science-related topics on the internet. But he also explains that science is only a moderate interest ('I'm not really, really into science, but yeah, I do like it'). By the age of 14, Hedgehog no longer engages in as many science-related activities out of school. As he explains in his Y9 interview, 'I had like science kits when I was little and that and just experimented because it was fun, yeah. [Int: Yeah, yeah, so what kind of . . . why don't you do that anymore?] Well I just think I've grown out of it a bit now, yeah.' Hedgehog does not seem to have any particular science capital within his family and there is no evidence of any strong scientific habitus at home ('I've never really heard [parents] them say anything about science'). Like most of his peers, he cannot imagine following a science career ('I don't know. I'm into science, but I don't think I'd ever become a science teacher, well you know science, scientist'). We suggest that, for students like Hedgehog, with lower levels of science capital, science largely remains enjoyable at school but becomes less 'thinkable' out of school because engaging in science is not normalised within the family habitus.

Analysis of the survey data indicates that low (and very low) levels of cultural capital are negatively associated with student science aspirations. In other words, students from more socially disadvantaged backgrounds are less likely to express science aspirations. In the interviews, working-class children also tended to have lower levels of science-related capital and were much less likely to aspire to careers in science, or STEM-related areas. We suggest that, for these students, science might be described as marginal or *peripheral* to their everyday lives.

That is, where science is not part of the daily 'fabric' (habitus) of family life, children are less likely to engage in science in their spare time as they get older and/or to consider science as something that might be a feature of their daily, or future working, lives. As Jane2, the mother of Dave (White working-class boy), explained: 'I suppose in everyday life you don't get that much really to do with it [science] now.' Likewise Robyn (mother of Charlie, a White lower-middle-class girl) agreed that her daughter does not really have much interest in science, which Robyn feels reflects her own lack of any real interest in science ('I don't think that any of us are really that . . . [sciencey]').

Although many of the families we interviewed said that they do go to museums (especially when their children are younger) and watch some science-related television programmes, they do so 'generically' and/or sporadically. They do not weave these activities into an active science interest or promotion of science – it remains just one element, among many, of their leisure and entertainment consumption. Working-class parents and children were also more likely to describe parental practices exemplified by the 'accomplishment of natural growth' (Lareau, 2003), in which children's pastimes and aspirations were described as their personal choices and interests (rather than being steered or 'pushed') and were not embedded within an intensive, future-orientated family project of 'development'. Thus, rather than 'hot housing' their children, these parents were more likely to say, 'I just want her [daughter] to be happy really and to achieve as much as she can' (Shelly, White, working-class mother).

A few families also suggested that a lack of money and/or time also prevented them from engaging more with science. For instance, families on lower incomes, or those comprising lone parents or parents who work long hours, found the 'costs' of going to museums and science events prohibitive.

One of the outcomes of this widespread lack of science capital was a lack of awareness (among both children and parents) of the potential usefulness of science qualifications. As Tasha (Alan's mother) put it: 'The problem is the lack of knowledge, the lack of awareness, where you know certain subjects like this can take them [children].' Research conducted by Michael Reiss and colleagues, as part of the UPMAP project (e.g. Mujtaba and Reiss, 2012), found that a sense of the transferability of STEM qualifications can be strongly linked to students' post-16 plans. Their survey of 7,000 Year 10 and Year 12 students found that 'perceived material gain' (e.g. agreement with statements such as 'I think physics will help me in the job I want to do in the future') is one of the most important factors predicting whether or not students will choose to study the subject post-16. Indeed, most young people in our project could only name a very small number of future careers that science qualifications might lead to (notably 'scientist', 'science teacher' and 'doctor'), which we would interpret as one of the indicators of lower levels of science capital.

Summary

In this chapter, we have suggested that the relationship between family habitus and science capital can be very powerful and can play a key role in making science known, thinkable, desirable and achievable for some children, and that these children are disproportionately likely to be from the middle classes. However, not all middle-class families will have high science capital – and we found that where parents have higher level science qualifications and/or jobs, their children were significantly more likely to aspire to continue with science post-16. We argued that where families have the resources and inclination to create a 'pro-science' micro-climate, which embeds science within family life and identity, children are much more likely to aspire to continue with science post-16. As Aschbacher et al. (2010, p. 15) argue on the basis of their own study:

> Students who participated in and found solid support for science in multiple communities were more likely to consolidate their science identities and persist in their STEM aspirations . . . than students with less breadth and depth of support. They were buoyed by perceived strong and aligned support for their science identities at home, at school, and in extracurricular activities.

In sum, we suggest that when families adopt a practice of concerted cultivation and possess not only middle-class social, cultural and economic resources (privilege) but also science-specific forms of capital ('science capital'), their children are much more likely to aspire to continue with science in the future. Moreover, we suggest that these families are also particularly well positioned to support and help their children to maintain and achieve these aspirations over time.

Notes

1 A fun experiment that is popular among children, in which mint sweets (e.g. Mentos) are put into a bottle of fizzy Cola drink, resulting in a spectacular eruption.
2 As we have written elsewhere (DeWitt et al., 2010), this lack of interest in becoming a scientist emerged strongly in our separate qualitative pilot sample of London primary-school children, who expressed an interest in science but who stated that they did not want to become scientists in the future (and is borne out by the main survey data).

6

GENDER, GIRLS AND SCIENCE ASPIRATIONS

The persistent under-representation of girls/women in the physical sciences and engineering post-16 remains an intractable problem that continues to perplex policy-makers and educationalists alike. Indeed, decades of investment and interventions aimed at encouraging more girls and women to continue with science seem to have had little impact on gendered patterns of STEM participation (Phipps, 2008). While, in overall terms, boys' rates of participation in the different sciences tend not to be regarded as particularly problematic, closer inspection suggests that there are noticeable patterns in terms of *which* boys tend to participate – namely, mostly White and South Asian middle-class boys (see Archer et al., 2014a). In this chapter we examine our data through the lens of gender to focus on these questions: why do so many girls come to see science as 'not for me'? What role does femininity play in this? And how do those girls who maintain science aspirations manage to do so?[1]

We begin by reviewing data from our surveys in relation to gendered patterns of aspiration, showing how even from a young age – and despite equally liking science – boys and girls seem to hold different views about the possibility of science as a future career. We then discuss in detail findings from the longitudinal interviews, exploring first how science careers are rendered 'unthinkable' for many girls due to the construction of science careers as 'masculine', which sits in opposition to performances of popular femininity. Here we argue that science aspirations are rendered unthinkable for girls because they sit in tension with traditional performances of femininity as 'caring', 'creative', 'glamorous/ attractive' and because science demands masculine performances of 'cleverness'. As a result, girls receive less encouragement from significant adults (and peers) to develop science aspirations and to continue with science and they can feel excluded within some science spaces. We then consider in detail the girls in our sample who did maintain science and STEM-related aspirations from age 10 to 14, exploring what performances of femininity they engage in and how they manage to reconcile (or not) their gender and science identities.

Gendered aspirations age 10–14

Across all three surveys, we found gender stereotypical patterns of aspiration. For instance, girls were more likely than boys to agree that they would like a career in the performing arts, whereas boys were much more likely than girls to be interested in a career in engineering. A few aspirations appeared more gender neutral – i.e. there were some careers that boys and girls were equally likely to aspire to – with business emerging as not only one of the most popular aspirations among 12–14 year olds, but also the most 'open' aspiration, with relatively equal proportions of boys and girls from a range of ethnic and class backgrounds aspiring to a career in business. Of course, care must be taken with these figures, not least given that the category of 'business' is open to wide interpretation (for instance, ranging from an aspiration to own your own small business to an ambition to be the CEO of a major multinational). However, the point that we wish to convey here is that, in a multitude of ways, 'business' is eminently 'thinkable' for a diverse range of students – it seems to be associated with meritocracy and is flexible enough that most young people can imagine a space within it for themselves. In this respect, we feel that the construction of 'business' provides an instructive counterpoint to the ways in which young people construct science careers, which, as we discuss below, tend to be seen as elitist, masculine and middle class.

Overall, most of the students we surveyed aspired to continue with full-time education after the age of 16, although these aspirations did also vary significantly by gender, with girls being more likely to plan to continue in full-time education than boys. Another significant difference also emerged, with nearly twice as many boys as girls aspiring to get a full-time job or pursue an apprenticeship.

In terms of young people's *science aspirations*, across all three surveys boys were significantly more likely than girls to agree that they would like to 'be a scientist' in the future. For example, in the Year 8 and 9 surveys, about 18% of boys and 12% of girls aspired to a career in science. Boys also scored significantly higher than girls for the 'science-aspirations' composite variable. In the multi-level modelling analyses of science aspirations, the effect of gender was small, but it did appear in the models at all three time points (Y6 = −0.13; Y8 = −0.017, Y9 = −0.09). (Note that the negative effect size means that being female was negatively related to aspirations in science.)

However, these somewhat subtle gender trends around science aspirations were dwarfed by the huge gender differences that emerged for engineering aspirations. Boys were significantly more likely than girls to aspire to a career in engineering, and MLM analysis showed that, for the engineering-aspirations composite variable, gender has a very large negative effect size (−.88). Indeed, gender is by far the most influential factor on students' engineering-related

TABLE 6.1 Categorisation of interviewee aspirations at Y6 and Y9, by gender (all aspirations)

	Science aspirations		STEM-related		Non-STEM	
	% girls	% boys	% girls	% boys	% girls	% boys
Y6 (n = 92, 55 girls, 37 boys)	31	27	24	32	45	41
Y9 (n = 82, 47 girls, 35 boys)	11	9	17	34	68	49

aspirations. Looking across the three surveys, these trends appear to remain consistent.

Due to a different methodology and sample composition, a slightly different pattern of gendered aspirations emerged within the interview sample. As detailed in Table 6.1, looking across from Y6 to Y9, the popularity of science aspirations decreased dramatically among both boys and girls (from 31% of girls and 27% of boys in Y6 to just 11% of girls and 9% of boys in Y9). The popularity of STEM-related aspirations (e.g. in medicine, engineering) also decreased among girls by age 14 (from 24% of Y6 girls to just 17% of Y9 girls), but maintained popularity among boys (32% of Y6 boys, 34% of Y9 boys). Over this age period, non-STEM aspirations increased among both boys and girls, but particularly for girls (from 45% of girls in Y6 to 68% of girls in Y9). These figures present a slightly different picture of science aspirations compared to the survey in that the girls we interviewed were equally, if not slightly more, likely to aspire to a science career compared to the boys. However, we would caution that the interview sample was self-selecting and included from the outset a greater proportion of students and their families with an interest in science – a trend that was amplified in the case of girls through the inclusion of science-specialist girls' schools in the sample (in order to be able to explore in depth how some girls manage to aspire to science). Moreover, due to the different data collection methods, in the interviews students were able to (and mostly did) express more than one aspiration at a time (whereas the surveys made greater use of closed response questions). Indeed, slightly different aspirational patterns are produced within the interview sample according to whether we code only a student's primary aspiration (as in Table 6.2) or we code interviewee aspirations as 'science-related' if *any* of the stated aspirations include a science job (e.g. 'scientist'), as in Table 6.1. Yet, even with these provisos, we suggest that the interviewees' aspirations point to a common wider picture, like the survey, in which over time we see girls drifting away from science aspirations and a notable increase in the proportion of girls not expressing *any* science or STEM-related aspirations by age 14, while boys, in general, seem to maintain a stronger interest in STEM-related aspirations.

We now explore some of the reasons and factors that might underlie these gendered patterns of STEM aspiration among boys and girls and why, despite liking science, girls are on the whole more likely than boys to 'aspire otherwise', perceiving science or a STEM-related career in science as being 'not for me'.

Girls and science aspirations: not 'normal' for girls?

The complexity of gender issues in relation to science participation is highlighted by an Ofsted (2011) report. The English education regulatory body found that although many girls state that gender makes no difference to their aspirations and future choices, their *actual* choices (of subjects and careers) remain highly gender-traditional, falling into established gender stereotypical patterns. In other words, many students may have little awareness or understanding of the ways in which their seemingly 'personal' and individual life choices and decisions may be structured and influenced by wider identities and inequalities, such as gender.

As detailed in the previous section, for the majority of girls in our qualitative and quantitative samples, science aspirations were not experienced as a 'natural' choice. We now try to unpick the various ways in which gender (notably the construction of science careers as 'masculine' versus girls' performances of popular hetero-femininity) plays out, such that choosing otherwise (i.e. non-STEM aspirations) is a more 'natural' (taken-for-granted) choice for many girls.

The prevalent association of science with masculinity was not just limited to students. The majority of parents whom we interviewed also associated science careers with masculinity and held a perception of science as being an area that more men than women study and work in – as two mothers explained:

> It's [science] always seen as men, isn't it? But geeky men – sorry!
>
> *(Shelly, White British, working-class mother)*

> I think more males go into science careers, but the girls seem to enjoy it more at school.
>
> *(Amelie, White British, middle-class mother)*

Indeed, science careers were associated with masculinity by over 50% of interviewed parents (see Archer et al., 2012b, 2013), although views differed considerably among parents as to the reasons for this imbalance, being divided between those who suggested that this association was due to 'natural' (biological and/or neurological) gender differences (i.e. girls and boys are predisposed to like and/or be good at different subjects) and those who saw it as due to social differences (e.g. science has become male dominated for sociological reasons). Often participants found it hard to articulate why femininity sits at odds with science aspirations – to quote one mother, it was often felt that a science career would just somehow not 'suit' a particular girl/daughter. We now unpick some of the ways in which dominant constructions of science careers sit in tension with dominant constructions of femininity. To do this, we draw on the interview data collected from girls who did not aspire to science or STEM-related careers.

In Year 6, there were 25/55 girls (45%) who did *not* aspire to science or STEM-related careers.[2] By Year 9, there were 32/47 girls (68%) who did not aspire to science or STEM-related careers. The overwhelming majority of girls (and boys) expressed multiple aspirations at each interview, which we categorised in an earlier paper as falling into a number of main job categories: caring professions; creative/artistic; professional; 'glamorous'/girly; and active/sporty aspirations (see Archer et al., 2013).

We now extend this analysis, classifying these non-STEM aspirant girls by their primary (strongest/main) expressed aspiration, in order to compare overall patterns in these aspirations between Y6 and Y9. As detailed in Table 6.2, we can see that aspirations to 'nurturing' careers (predominantly 'teacher') remain popular among girls at both time points, although overall levels of interest in these jobs decline with time (from 55% of non-STEM aspirant girls in Y6 to 25% in Y9).

As Table 6.2 shows, there is a notable increase over time in girls' aspirations to 'other professions' (particularly lawyer, psychologist and journalist), from just 5% of non-STEM aspirant girls in Y6 to 34% of these girls in Y9. There also appears to be a growth of interest in creative industries, from 5% of Y6 girls to 13% of Y9 girls, and a marked decline in aspirations for 'girly/glamorous' jobs (e.g. in hair and beauty, show business), from 27% of Y6 non-STEM aspirant girls to just 6% of Y9 girls.

We identified four key themes, or dimensions, within the girls' constructions of their aspirations, which reflected particular performances of femininity. These

TABLE 6.2 Classification of primary aspirations expressed by girls who did not hold science-related aspirations (Y6–Y9)

Coding of job type	No. of Y6 girls (n = 22) expressing aspiration*	Y9 (n = 32, incl. 2 'don't know')
Nurturing jobs (e.g. teacher, childcare)	12 (55% of non–STEM aspiration girls)	8 (25%)
'Glamorous' and 'girly' jobs (e.g. show business, actress, model, hair and beauty)	6 (27%)	2 (6%)
Active/sporty (e.g. athlete, swimming instructor, personal trainer)	2	1 (5%)
Businesswoman (e.g. own business, work in City/finance)	2	2
Other professional (e.g. psychologist, architect, lawyer, accountant, journalist, advertising)	1	11 (34%)
Creative (fashion designer, interior designer)	1	4
Other (police)	–	2

Note: *Because most girls expressed more than one aspiration, these add up to more than 25.

were: a desire for (i) caring/nurturing, (ii) creative, and (iii) glamorous/girly careers which align with dominant performances of popular femininity, and (iv) a construction of themselves as 'not the cleverest'. As we discuss next, girls sought to actualise and perform these dimensions of femininity through their aspirations – and resisted science aspirations due to their lack of fit with these key dimensions of popular femininity.

Caring/nurturing femininity

As illustrated by Table 6.2, across the 10–14 age period a sizeable proportion of non-STEM aspirant girls aspired to caring/nurturing professions, such as teaching. However, some of the 'other professional' careers, such as lawyer and psychologist, could also fall under this banner, as a number of the girls framed their motivations for these careers in terms of wanting to 'help others'. Analysis of our survey data also shows that Y9 girls are significantly more likely than boys to agree that what is important to them in their future career is to 'help other people', $t(4298) = -5.848$, $p < .001$.

As Francis (2000b) discusses, vocational career motivations are among the most common reasons that girls give for their aspirations – and are consistently found among girls, irrespective of their ethnic and/or social-class backgrounds (see also Archer and Francis, 2007). As Francis (2005, 2010) argues, a discourse of 'care' (of others and of the self) is integral to 'traditional' (dominant) constructions of 'good' femininity and is not found among boys to the same extent.

Girls explained their motivations for wanting caring jobs, such as teacher or childminder, through a desire to nurture others (e.g. 'I just want to help children learn for the future, like the teachers are doing for us now', Celina, White British, working class, Y6). Like many of the other girls, Celina explained that her aspirations derived from her own family experiences and her admiration of a significant female's nurturing femininity (often that of a mother or favourite teacher):

> Because she [mum] has a way with children, like when my sister is crying and I can't stop her, like she can stop her and she can calm her down and that when she's really angry, yeah and she gets me to calm down when I'm really angry and I just wish I could be like her.
>
> *(Celina, Y6)*

Families played a key role in socialising girls and embedding the primacy of caring within constructions of popular femininity. For instance, girls described receiving considerable support and recognition of their nurturing capabilities from their parents, which bolstered their sense of being competent and well suited for this particular area. Parents also concurred; for instance, Celina's mother (Leah2) described her daughter as 'good with children' and emphasised that she felt Celina would make a good teacher. As Charlie, who aspired to be a teacher, explained:

> When I go round my nan's and my cousins', mum and dad come in and all that and they go 'oh you're so good with babies . . . they say you're really good with babies and you should be like someone who looks after children . . . like a childminder or a babysitter or something.
>
> *(Charlie, White British, lower-middle-class girl, Y6 interview)*

We might infer that these girls did not perceive science as offering an obvious arena within which to perform 'caring' femininity (cf. girls discussed later in this chapter who aspired to STEM-related careers, predominantly in medicine, which they constructed as 'caring' professions). Indeed, a couple of the non-STEM aspirant girls explained their reasons for not aspiring to science-related careers as due to a perception of science as *not* nurturing. For instance, Flower (White European, working class, Metropolitan School), who aspired to become a teacher, explained in her Y6 interview that she would not want to become a scientist 'because I love animals and I don't want to harm them'. This view seemed to derive from her sister's account of dissection at secondary school ('because my sister said when she was in school she used to do science in secondary school, they used to have to cut frogs and mouses [*sic*] and she loves animals and she doesn't want to harm them').

'Creative' femininity

Science has long been associated with rationality and, within public discourse, is popularly positioned in opposition to 'the arts' (which are aligned with creativity), as encapsulated by C.P. Snow's (1959) famous reference to the 'two cultures' of the arts and sciences. This discourse continues, despite vociferous critique, not least from within the scientific and engineering communities, some of whom argue that their subjects involve, or even require, creativity (e.g. Burns, 2014).[3]

The popular notion of an arts/science divide was evident in the interviews with parents and students, expressed for instance through the notion that children who are creative/artistic are unlikely to also aspire to science careers. This was brought up predominantly (although by no means exclusively) by girls and/or by parents in relation to their daughters. For instance, Mary (White British middle-class mother) explained that her daughter's aspiration to be a teacher reflected her 'creative' nature, and Sally-Ann (White British working-class mother) described her daughter (and friends) as being into the 'arty side of things', rather than science. Indeed, we would argue that the arts/science divide is constructed in explicitly gendered terms, illustrated through comments by girls like Lucy (White British working-class girl), who stated that 'girls are more into literacy and boys more into science'. We suggest that this dominant societal discourse (in which femininity is aligned with the arts and masculinity with science) reflects the historical construction of science through masculinity (e.g. Harding, 1986) and is so embedded within our culture that, for many girls, choosing 'creative', arts-based subjects is just 'natural'. Indeed, girls who aspired to careers such as journalist or author framed these aspirations as fulfilling a wish for a 'creative' career and/or a job that would match their creative interests and aptitudes.

While strongly aligned with femininity, creativity is not solely constructed as 'feminine' but is also, arguably, an increasingly popular interest among contemporary youth. Research has found that young people in advanced Western societies generally express less positive attitudes to science than their counterparts in the less economically developed world (Schreiner and Sjøberg, 2004). One factor contributing to this pattern may be that the arts and creative industries appear to offer a closer fit with the current 'age of desire' (Kenway and Bullen, 2001, p. 7) that is prevalent in capitalist developed economies, where consumerism has become a key aspect of identity (Bauman, 2000). In such societies, consumer-media culture plays a key role in young people's lives, the ways they see themselves and even their dis/engagement with education (Archer et al., 2007, 2010b), and some tenets of this were already evident in these girls' descriptions of their aspirations and interests – not only for creative careers, but also for jobs in fashion and celebrity culture, as discussed next.

'Glamorous' femininity

Although, as detailed in Table 6.2, the popularity of 'glamorous'/'girly' careers declined in prominence among girls' main aspirations from Y6 to Y9, we suggest that another key reason why science aspirations were resisted by girls relates to their perception that these are not 'glamorous' careers. That is, some girls may reject science careers because they do not seem to offer them ways to perform heterosexually attractive versions of 'girly' femininity. Particularly at age 10/11, the girls' aspirations seem to reflect high levels of interest in the body and appearance, reflecting dominant discourses of hetero-femininity (Renold, 2005). As we discuss elsewhere (Archer et al., 2013), there is also an intersection of gendered and classed discourses (e.g. Skeggs 1997, 2004), such that working-class girls are more likely than their middle-class counterparts to aspire to glamorous careers.

For instance, Celina2 (White, working class/lower middle class, Y6 interview) explained how 'when I'm older I want to be an actress and, um, I've got loads of role models that are actresses'. Celina2 was adamant that she did not want to continue with science or pursue a science-related career when she grows up. Instead, her aspirations were firmly entrenched within 'feminine' occupations from age 10 ('I really want to do beauty, as well as acting') through to age 14 (primary school teacher). Pop stars such as Lady Gaga were also mentioned as being the inspiration for girls' aspirations to become celebrity fashion designers. For instance, Lucy (White British, working class) maintained an aspiration to be a fashion designer across all three of her interviews.

The girls' 'glamorous' aspirations were often based in their family life and experiences and reflected their feminine social capital and the practical competencies they gained through their everyday performances of femininity. For instance, in her Y9 interview, Connie (White British working-class girl) described how her aspirations to do hair/beauty or modelling were based on these being things that she is already 'good at' (as a result of her everyday practices of femininity) and for which she possesses the 'right' embodied resources to enable success (e.g. she has been told that she has 'nice eyes' and is familiar with hair and beauty jobs as a result of her social capital, specifically through female family networks):

> My nan's friend used to be a hairdresser and she used to come and cut our hair and stuff and my mum has always said that I have nice eyes so I should go in to do something to do with eyes like eye modelling.
>
> *(Connie, Y9)*

Some mothers articulated how 'masculine' science aspirations did not fit easily with their daughters' performances of 'girling'. For instance, one mother, Ella, felt that girls are often put off science because 'it's not very girly . . . it's not a very sexy job, it's not glamorous'. As Sandra (mother of Danielle, White British, working-class girl) put it, 'girls are more interested in fashion usually and things with peers. You know and it seems to be a bit geeky to be into science', although Sandra also lamented that 'she's got this impression that only people who don't have a life do science, which is terrible', and blamed television for promulgating these stereotypes of scientists as geeky men:

> I have to blame TV . . . Oh she watches these things, you know on TV if somebody is good at something like science don't they always say they're a boffin and they just sit at the computer or they do something and they don't have a life. They're like geeks. They put them with big heads and glasses. It's just stereotyping.
>
> *(Sandra, White British, working-class mother)*

While interests in fashion, appearance and celebrity culture can be found among girls from all different social-class backgrounds, research suggests that they may be particularly important for working-class girls. Since the 1980s, feminist academics have drawn attention to how working-class girls may resist education through hyper-heterosexual femininities that are organised around themes of heterosexuality, appearance and romance (e.g. Griffin, 1985; Hey, 1997; McRobbie, 1978; Skeggs, 1997). Indeed, analysis of the survey data suggests that girls are less likely than boys to agree that their peers find science 'cool'. Numerous girls in our study discussed how practices such as shopping, wearing make-up and being fashionable were all important aspects of their lives, but they were particularly significant among working-class girls. We suggest that, for many girls (from across the class spectrum but particularly working-class girls), science did not seem to offer the opportunity to express (and value) performances of ('girly') popular hetero-femininity.

'Not the cleverest' femininity

Although, in the UK, girls are outperforming boys in the national GCSE examinations at age 16 (DfE, 2014), it has long been recognised that girls' success 'on paper' is not matched by their levels of self-confidence in their abilities, particularly in relation to STEM subjects. For instance, Mujtaba and Reiss (2012) found that while girls performed as well as, if not better than, boys on a physics test, they reported significantly lower levels of confidence in their abilities. These trends were also noted in our study; for instance, across all three surveys, boys expressed a significantly higher self-concept in science than girls.

Across the survey and interview data, children strongly associated science with 'cleverness'. For instance, around 80% of students in each survey agreed or strongly agreed that 'scientists are brainy', and an association between science and 'cleverness' was evident across both parent and child interviewees. The association between science and cleverness/braininess was voiced by both those who personally aspired to science-related careers and those who resisted science aspirations, reflecting a historic discourse of the sciences as 'hard', difficult and high-status subjects. Yet, as Mendick (2005) writes, 'clever' identities can be difficult for girls to occupy comfortably. At a general level, this tension reflects a long-standing discursive construction in which masculinity is aligned with 'the mind' and femininity with 'the body' (Paechter, 2000). This is further ampli-fied in the case of subjects such as science and maths, which are aligned with masculinity, such that those who are marked out as 'science people' (those who find science interesting and do well in it) are widely regarded not just as being 'clever' but as being *exceptionally* clever students. For example, when asked by the interviewer 'Who is into science?', Louise (Y6) replied: 'Well the clever ones are . . . it's just strange how all the clever ones are into science.' Likewise, in her Y6 interview, Victoria2 gave her reasons for not wanting to become a scientist as 'cos most scientists are brainy and I don't want to be brainy'. Flower (White European, working–class girl) was adamant that she personally would not want to follow a science career 'because I'm not that smart'. Likewise, Celina (White, working–class girl, Y6 interview) described those who are 'really into science' as 'brainiacs'. Consequently, the association of the sciences (and mathematics) with cleverness and masculinity means that a sustainable science identity may be 'more challenging for girls than it is for boys' (Carlone and Johnson, 2007; Ong, 2005). Hence, we argue, science aspirations are less 'thinkable' for many girls because they require taking up (and being recognised by others as performing) not just a 'brainy' but also a 'cleverest' subject position, which is predicated upon a performance of masculinity.

The power of these discourses is such that even girls who really like science can rule themselves out of it if they do not feel that they match/can perform 'brainy' student identity. For instance, several of the girls who expressed non-STEM aspirations also confessed that, although they loved science, they did not feel 'clever enough' to aspire to continue with it. This is exemplified by the case of Danielle, a White working-class girl. Danielle describes herself as a 'middle' student, a view that her mother Sandra concurs with ('Um, I think she's more of a middle of the range child. There's nothing really that she excels in') but, among her various interests, Danielle does enjoy science and says it is one of her favourite lessons ('I'm not being a kiss-up[4] but my favourite lesson is actually science'). Her mother is strongly supportive of Danielle's science interests and her father works as a (non-graduate) engineer. Yet, science aspirations are unthinkable for Danielle, who feels 'I'm not clever enough to be good at science'. This theme of 'not being clever enough to continue with science' continued through all Danielle's interviews.

We suggest that it is harder for girls to own and perform 'cleverness', irrespective of their actual attainment, because dominant gendered discourses construct the 'naturally brainy' and the 'natural science student' as male. Some of our previous work (e.g. Archer, 2008; Archer and Francis, 2007) has argued that dominant educational discourses construct the 'ideal pupil' in gendered, racialised and classed ways, such that (White, middle-class) boys' attainment is attributed to 'natural intelligence', whereas girls' (and Other students') attainment is explained away as due to 'hard work'. Carlone's (2003) research further underlines this point – she found that teachers in an advanced physics class perceived boys as more 'naturally' able in physics than girls, despite girls tending to achieve higher marks. Echoing wider gender and education research (e.g. Francis, 2000a), girls' achievement was attributed to their plodding diligence and 'hard work', whereas boys' lower achievements were explained as due to a lack of application (rather than a lack of aptitude). Moreover, as Carlone and colleagues' (2008) research indicates, the ways in which teachers reproduce (or challenge) these dominant gender constructions can make a significant difference to the extent to which girls and Other students feel that they can identify with science and be a good science student (irrespective of their actual attainment in the subject).

Moreover, the alignment of science identity with rationality, 'the mind' and 'clever/cleverest' (masculine) student identities means that popular hetero-femininity, which is relationally associated with 'the body', sits in direct tension with performances of science identity. Some girls, like Davina, suggested accordingly that performances of cleverness are respected and valued among boys but are ostracised or resisted among girls:

> I think like boys just kind of respect intelligence a bit more, whereas I think girls kind of . . . I think they're kind of a bit more 'Oh they're intelligent, oh that's really annoying, oh go away' kind of thing. . . . I mean it's obviously the same with boys, obviously they all want to be the cleverest, but if someone is cleverer than them, rather than sort of shunning

them, they'll maybe try and be friends with them, so then they can kind
of . . . because they interact with them, they'll then become like more
clever themselves in a way.

(Davina, White British/European, upper-middle-class girl, Y9)

Moreover, across the interviews, a number of girls described how they felt that
some popular girls work to 'hide' their intelligence and to appear 'stupid' in order
to maintain their popularity. Consequently, we suggest that science identity –
which requires performances of 'cleverness' – may be antithetical to some girls'
performances of popular femininity (as 'not academic').

The result – science is not for 'normal' girls and girls receive less encouragement to continue with science

As feminist theorists such as Francis (2000a) and Paechter (2000) argue, femininity
and masculinity are inherently relational concepts. Accordingly, we suggest that
constructions of popular femininity as caring, creative, glamorous/girly and 'not
clever' sit in direct tension with science aspirations (which are aligned with
masculinity, i.e. rationality, 'the mind' and 'cleverest' identity), which renders
science aspirations largely unattractive and unthinkable for many girls. Instead,
non-STEM aspirant girls constructed their preferred career aspirations in ways
that value and facilitate performances of popular hetero-femininity (as caring,
creative, 'glamorous' and 'not the cleverest'). By default, science aspirations
occupy an imagined space that is incompatible with these girls' usual, desired
performances of self. In other words, for these girls, science offers little space
for them to be 'normal', 'girly', caring and creative – science aspirations simply
do not 'fit' with their sense of identity. Moreover, the dominant alignment of
science with masculinity and middle-classness would imply that science aspirations
are even less likely to be experienced as a conceivable and achievable option by
working-class girls – who may need to engage in considerable identity work if
they are to come to see science aspirations as 'for me'.

So far we have concentrated on the ways in which girls' self-identifications
and performances of gender are implicated in the perception that science
aspirations are 'not for me'. Yet these gendered patterns in aspirations were not
solely due to girls ruling themselves out of science. We suggest that the popular
discursive alignment of science with masculinity had an equally strong impact on
the extent to which others (e.g. family members, teachers and peers) interacted
with and influenced boys' and girls' aspirations. For instance, although we found
no clear patterns[5] by gender in the surveys in terms of the young people's
reporting of their parents' attitudes to science or in the extent to which they felt
their parents were involved in their education, we did find a marked gender
difference in terms of parental ambitions for their children. For instance, on the
Y9 survey boys were more likely than girls to agree with items such as: 'My
parents want me to make a lot of money when I grow up'; 'My parents want

me to get a good job when I grow up'; 'It is important to them that I get good marks in school'; and 'They expect me to go to university'. In other words, it appears that, compared to girls, boys seem to feel that their parents hold higher expectations of them.

The UPMAP study found that encouragement from a significant other to continue with maths or physics was one of the most important predictors of whether a student does continue with the subject, or not. For instance, Mujtaba and Reiss (2012) found a significant difference between the amount of support that boys and girls report receiving from their physics teachers in terms of encouraging them to continue with physics post-16. Likewise, they found that boys report higher levels of parental motivation to continue with physics.

In the interviews that we conducted with parents and students, we also noted a feeling among some parents that science might be a more 'suitable' aspiration for boys than girls. Our surveys also found that boys are significantly more likely than girls to report participating in out-of-school science activities. Moreover, the interview data provided some examples in which a few girls recounted their negative experiences of particular out-of-school science spaces, which they felt were 'male dominated'. For instance, Georgia (White British, lower-middle-class girl) was interested in science but did not want to attend her school's extra-curricular science club. She explained, 'I know it [STEM club] goes on, but it's mainly just boys and I don't want to be on my own with just a load of boys.' She was quite disparaging of the boys who attended the club:

Interviewer: Oh right, so why do you think it's mostly boys who do that?
Georgia: I don't know. Most of them are like, I know it's really stereotypical, but like the geeky boys. [laughs]
Interviewer: Oh really?
Georgia: Yeah, they're all geeks. No offence to them or anything.

Instead, by Year 9 Georgia was running the eco-club at her former primary school, a more girl-friendly, less 'masculine' and less 'geeky' science space. Another example is provided by Sandra, who describes how her daughter Danielle had stopped attending an after-school science club because 'it was all boys'. This had led Danielle to see science as 'a boy thing', despite being passionately interested in the subject:

I said why can't you do science? She [Danielle] said well, 'oh no it's a boy thing'. And I said 'it's not'. They had [science club name] at school. It's an after school club on Monday and she said 'I'm not going because it's all boys'. . . . I said 'well you should at least go along and see if you enjoy it. It's all these experiments' and she said 'oh, it's fun, we did all this' . . . She went twice and then she stopped going because it was all boys and she had no girls to talk to.

(Sandra, White British, working-class mother)

In other words, in a variety of ways and through a diverse range of contexts, spaces and media, girls seemed to experience a consistent message that science – but particularly non/post-compulsory science – is 'for boys'.

Girls who aspire to science/STEM – precarious balancing acts

In earlier papers, we classified the girls (Archer et al., 2012a) and boys (Archer et al., 2014a) who expressed science and STEM-related aspirations by their performances of gender (femininity and masculinity). We noted that, of the 17 girls aged 10/11 who expressed science/STEM-related aspirations, performances of 'bluestocking' (highly academic, 'not girly') femininity (11 girls) outnumbered those of 'feminine scientist' (popular hetero-femininity) identity (six girls).

By Year 9, we identified five girls as expressing science aspirations and a further seven as holding STEM-related aspirations. Most of these girls had expressed science or STEM-related aspirations in Year 6, but one had previously held non-STEM aspirations. Several 'bluestocking' girls who had expressed science/STEM-related aspirations in Y6 either aspired to non-STEM careers or had dropped out of the study by Y9. Of the 12 girls who expressed science/STEM-related aspirations in Y9, we found just two girls to be performing 'feminine scientist' identity (one girl with science aspirations and one with STEM-related aspirations). Three previous 'feminine scientists' had changed their ambitions to non-STEM aspirations, and one girl (who had kept her STEM-related aspirations) had become less 'girly' with time, such that by Year 9 she was classified as performing 'bluestocking' femininity.

In comparison, by Y9 we categorised 14 boys as holding science and STEM-related aspirations: six boys with science aspirations and eight with STEM-related aspirations. But whereas by Y9 the girls were overwhelmingly performing 'bluestocking' identity, the boys were almost exactly evenly split between those performing 'young professor' (highly academic, 'uncool' masculinity) and those performing 'cool footballer scientist' (performances of science identity and popular masculinity) identities. See Archer et al. (2014a) for a full discussion of the boys' data and the role of masculinity in relation to science aspirations.

We suggest that these patterns fit with the hypothesis that we posited in our 2012 paper (Archer et al., 2012a), namely that the number of feminine scientists decreases over time due to the particularly difficult balancing acts that these girls are engaged in, trying to reconcile the 'masculinity' of science with performances of popular femininity. We now explore the ways in which science aspirations are either opened up or closed down through particular performances of femininity, starting with the 'feminine scientists'.

'Feminine scientists': an endangered species?

While various girls across the wider sample engaged in performances of popular femininity, these performances were much less noticeable among girls who aspired to science/STEM-related careers. We identified performances of 'feminine scientist' identity as involving enactments of popular hetero-femininity, such as being fashionable, sociable, popular and engaging with popular culture. As per the earlier discussions, these performances also tended to value core feminine tropes such as 'care' and 'creativity'. Yet the girls who we classified as performing 'feminine scientist' identity also balanced these performances of popular femininity with science aspirations – which required performances of 'cleverness' and 'rationality'.

We begin by reflecting on the Y6 'feminine scientists' who, by Y9, had dropped their science aspirations and the extent to which femininity might play a role in these changes. We then consider the case of Luna, a 'feminine scientist' who changed her ambitions from science (in Y6) to STEM-related aspirations in Y9, bringing her aspirations into an easier alignment with her performances of popular femininity. Finally, we discuss the case of Davina, the only girl who expressed consistent science aspirations from Y6 to Y9 who also performed 'feminine scientist' identity, exploring how she managed this balancing act – albeit noting tensions and disruptions within these performances which we suggest may be precarious in the longer term.

'Lost girls' – feminine scientists who lose their science aspirations

As noted above, between Y6 and Y9 there was a notable decline in the number of 'feminine scientists' in our sample. Three of these girls (Carol, Emma and Katherine) changed their aspirations over time into non-STEM aspirations. While the girls identified many reasons for these changes, there also seemed to be a common thread in which science just did not seem to provide the girls with a means/space for performing popular femininity. For instance, while Carol (White European, middle-class girl) described in her Y9 interview how she still really enjoyed science and found it interesting (and still engaged in a variety of informal science learning activities in her leisure time), she explained that she now aspired to more 'creative' jobs, such as magazine editor or bilingual secretary. These careers fitted better with her everyday performances of femininity, which involved 'designing' (especially at home with her mum) and acting, dancing and singing with friends. The new aspiration was also prompted by her existing social capital, with a friend of a friend's mother providing an exemplar of a desirable, 'exciting' and glamorous career (in journalism):

> I know my friend's sister, her friend's mum works in one of them, she writes articles about celebrities . . . And like what they're wearing and everything and she said that it's really exciting.

Carol also seemed to be increasingly aware of (and acknowledged that her own views had been influenced by) the popular stereotype of science as 'geeky':

> It's easy to be popular if you like English more than Science. [Interviewer: Right, right. And why is that then?] Because . . . when you like Science, it's the way people sometimes talk. So people in my class who like Science they're quite hard to talk to and they're called geeks because of that.

This notion of 'geeky' science identity was exacerbated by the 'brainy' image of science (as discussed in Chapter 4), which made it hard for Carol to continue to imagine herself (a 'normal' girl) as a viable scientist:

> I don't think I would be a very good scientist . . . Like if you don't know what's happening . . . it would be a bit complicated and hard for me to understand.

Shifting aspirations: from feminine scientist to 'caring/creative' STEM-related femininity

In contrast to Carol, Emma and Katherine, Luna did not completely lose her science-related aspirations. However, she did modify her ambitions considerably between age 10 and 14 in ways which, we would argue, sought to bring them more closely into line with her performances of femininity. Luna is an attractive, sociable, fashionable, White, middle-class girl. She attains well at school (and is in the top sets), although she does not consider herself 'clever'. In Y6 she was very keen on science and aspired to be an astronomer/astronaut – an ambition that had been sparked by an earlier school visit during which she had met a woman scientist. The visit had been highly significant and inspirational for Luna, and she had maintained her aspiration over a couple of years, supported by her family (see Archer et al., 2012b). However, as she moved into secondary school, Luna lost her science aspirations and, while she always maintained an interest in science, she developed more 'creative' and 'caring' aspirations ('In primary school I used to like science a lot but now I'm more like art, music', Y9). In particular, Luna's Y9 aspirations were all focusing on 'helping others', in line with a nurturing/caring performance of femininity:

> I'm quite interested in midwifery . . . counselling . . . paediatric nurse or something like that . . . working with children . . . I'm quite interested in like helping people – I'm a caring person.

In line with her artistic family habitus, Luna increasingly identified herself as both a creative and a caring person, and felt that this also reflected what she is 'good at'. Although she recognised that 'there could be quite a scientific part to all the jobs I just mentioned', she no longer saw science as a defining aspect of her identity and felt that she would ideally like a career that could combine both art and caring, such as art therapy.

Alongside seeking aspirations that could better align with the creative and caring aspects of her femininity, Luna's shift away from science also seemed to be underpinned by the association of science with 'cleverness' – a positioning that she seemed to experience as being too risky and untenable for her personally to attempt to inhabit. Despite being in the top set, Luna's Y8 and Y9 interviews were peppered with references to no longer feeling 'clever enough' at science. For instance, she compared herself unfavourably to her friends ('a lot of my friends are very clever, they come from really wealthy backgrounds . . . most of my friends are really intelligent'), and she explains that she felt that there are so many 'really clever' girls at secondary school that maybe she shouldn't continue with science. She suggested that the change in her science aspirations was prompted by her experiences of secondary school science ('At end of primary I was really, really into science . . . I think science kind of changed when I got to secondary school . . . it got harder . . .'). Thus, although Luna still enjoyed science both in and out of school (e.g. she named various topics that she found interesting at school and described engaging in various out-of-school science-related activities, such as watching particular television science series), science was no longer a central part of her identity and the STEM-related aspirations that she did maintain were made possible only to the extent that they enabled performances of caring and creative femininity.

Last girl standing: the lone feminine scientist?

Davina was the only girl in our sample who maintained her science aspirations from Y6 to Y9 and also performed what could be classified as a form of popular hetero-femininity in Years 8 and 9 (she had previously been classified as performing 'bluestocking' femininity in primary school at Y6). Davina is an upper-middle-class girl who attends an independent girls' school. As discussed elsewhere, she has substantial family science capital (Archer et al., 2012a/b). She is chatty, confident and comes across (and self-recognises) as being quite 'mature' for her age ('I think I'm quite mature like within my year'). At her Y8 and Y9 interviews she was classified as performing popular hetero-femininity through her fashionable appearance (e.g. her clothes, hair and eye make-up), her references to her boyfriend and sociability (e.g. going to parties) and her resistance to, and distancing of herself from, the 'geeky' science femininity of other 'hard-working' science girls at her school. For instance, she describes herself as more 'chilled' and sociable than her science peers:

> I think I'd say I am actually a bit of an exception . . . I mean I see all the people that are sort of in the top set . . . most of them are people that kind of do work really hard and like really do focus on their school work a lot. Whereas in my case I'm kind of a bit more just chilled. Like as in . . . yeah

> I'm interested in science and I do want to do well, but I'm not like . . . as in my life isn't completely focused around schoolwork like I do have like other activities that I take almost just as seriously . . . The people who tend to be like good and interested in science do tend to be like . . . on average tend to be like quite sort of geeky and like hard-working and like whatever. But I wouldn't say that's true for everyone.
>
> *(Davina, Y9)*

Davina recognises, and repeatedly makes mention of, how her balancing of popular femininity and her science interest and aspirations ('I want to take it all the way') makes her different ('strange', 'weird', 'not the norm') from other girls:

> I think I'm quite strange, like I mean I'm interested in science and I do want to do science like . . . and I want to take it all the way . . . but then I think I'm still like quite social, I do like going out to like parties and stuff, and I do like . . . for example a lot of the people that do science, like a lot of them like don't have boyfriends. And I'm like well I'm kind of weird, cos I have one but then . . . and I'm like friends with people who have in the past or currently do have . . . but then they have completely different interests, and they like completely different subjects. So I think I am sort of not the norm really.

She suggests that there is a social pressure on 'normal' girls (those performing popular femininity) to give up science, but argues that her focus on the 'future' and her independence of mind enable her to resist this pressure and maintain her 'difference':

> I think maybe the reason why [other girls] they gave it [science] up is probably just because they felt that they wanted to fit in with their friends. But I think your friends aren't going to be there for the rest of your life necessarily . . . So I think, to be honest, it's more important to focus on your career, it's just really going to determine your lifestyle for the rest of your life, than be like 'Oh okay I'm going to give up what I love, like the subject that I'm good and like give up the job that I'm good at, just so I can be with my friends'. And obviously if they are real friends they'll respect the fact that you like science and they'll just be like 'Okay fine, she likes science, she's different, you know that's her'.

In this respect, Davina engages in a delicate and precarious balancing act – simultaneously she is trying to be recognised as a 'normal' girl (through her performances of popular femininity) but is also trying to perform an authentic science identity – which, as she recognises, marks her out as not just 'different' but also 'strange'. We suggest that a further paradox arises within Davina's identity performances, namely that although she performs some aspects of popular hetero-femininity (e.g. through her appearance, heterosexuality and sociability), Davina's productions of self as a science person also involve various performances of *masculinity*. For instance, her construction of herself as 'chilled' in her performance of science identity evokes dominant societal notions of ('masculine') effortless brilliance/natural intelligence rather than ('feminine') hard work/plodding diligence (Francis, 2000b). She also recognises that she is different, strange and exceptional, not only different from other science girls but also different from girls in general – by dint of both her love of science and also her intellect – and, crucially, her own *confidence* in her intellect ('I also think I know a lot more') and her rational 'science mind':

Interviewer: And in what ways would you say you're similar and what ways are you different to the other girls?

Davina: Uh . . . well I think I'd probably say that I'm definitely more interested in science, certainly than people that I hang around with anyway. Definitely a lot more. I think I also sort of know a lot more . . . I think it's just maybe cos I think that's just . . . I think science as a subject kind of makes you think in a certain way, like quite different from a lot of other subjects, and I think that's just naturally the way I think anyway.

Davina also cites masculine role models, such as Einstein (Y6 interview) and the male physicists in the popular US television show *The Big Bang Theory* (Y9 interview):

Interviewer: And um . . . is there anyone that you particularly look up to or would like to be like in the future?

Davina: Okay this is going to sound really strange actually. But um . . . you know *The Big Bang Theory*, the programme . . . I kind of want to be like the people in that, like I kind of want to do the sorts of jobs that they do.

Across her interviews, Davina repeatedly engages in masculine performances of 'muscular intellect' (Mac an Ghaill, 1994; Mac an Ghaill and Redman, 1997; Francis et al., 2010). That is, she engages in confident public assertions of her intelligence. Interestingly, despite asserting herself as a 'normal' girl in her Y8 interview, by her Y9 interview Davina seems highly aware that she is, in reality, quite exceptional (as per her above descriptions of herself as 'strange' and 'a bit of an exception'). Given the alignment of science with masculinity, we might hypothesise that Davina's performances of popular femininity might come under increasing pressure over time as they jar with her performances of science identity. In this respect, we suggest that she may follow Hailey (White British, middle-class girl), who seemed to change her performances of femininity over the course of the project, shifting from 'feminine scientist' (Y6) to more 'bluestocking' performances (by Y9), which – as discussed next – aligned more comfortably with performances of science identity.

'Bluestocking' girls: trying to make science possible

As detailed earlier, the majority of girls who expressed science and STEM-related aspirations over the 10–14 age period were those who performed what we termed 'bluestocking' femininity. The term 'bluestocking' was originally a derisory term applied in eighteenth-century England to denote women with scholarly and intellectual interests, but is currently popularly used in the UK to denote academic women. We employ the term as a (non-derisory) shorthand to capture and foreground the academic and 'non-girly' nature of these girls' identity performances and their lack of interest in performing more 'popular' hetero-normative femininities. Like Renold's (2005, p. 64) 'square girls' who are 'high-achieving, hard-working, rule-following and lacked any interest in popular fashion or "boys" either as friends or boyfriends', the 'bluestocking' girls in our study were high attaining, expressed strongly academic identities and constructed themselves (and were described by their parents) as 'clever', 'not girly' and 'really into science'.

In Y6 there were 16 girls who fitted this classification (11 with science aspirations and a further five with science-related aspirations). In Year 9 we categorised 13 girls as performing 'bluestocking' identity (four with science aspirations, and nine with STEM-related aspirations).

'Bluestocking' girls foregrounded the academic aspect of their identities. They tended to be quiet, articulate, studious girls who, when asked to introduce themselves at the start of the interview, tended to say things like 'I'm very interested in science and science lessons in school and er I get some high grades in my science test' (Preeti, British Asian, middle-class girl, who also added 'I'm quite quiet in class'). Or as Joanne (White British, middle-class girl) put it in her Year 9 interview:

> I think that I'm more different from them [other girls] because I'm not very sporty, I'm more academicy . . . I'm considered geekish . . . I'm not a very popular person.

The second defining feature of these girls' identities was that they described themselves as 'not girly' – which many felt distinguished them from their female peers. Instead, these girls enacted what might be termed a 'demure' and academic femininity. As Georgia explained, 'I don't really do girly things'. Joanne concurred, 'I'm not really that girly'. Like the 'square girls' in Renold's (2005) study and the 'nice girls' in Reay's (2001) research, these girls tended to perform 'asexual', less 'popular' or fashionable academic identities. Parents tended to describe their daughters as 'nice girls' and 'good girls' (see also Renold, 2005). For instance, Isobel, mother of Georgia, recounted:

But now she's found a lovely group and, you know, they're like her, they're quite studious and want to do well in life and they're not into boys and make up and . . . do you know what I mean. They're just normal down to earth girls and that's what's nice.

(Isobel, White British, middle-class mother)

These performances of 'not girly' sat comfortably with the girls' studious identities. As Walkerdine (1990) explains, female academic achievement has long been associated with asexuality, and various studies have drawn attention to girls who do not attempt to balance academic achievement with performances of hetero-femininity (e.g. Renold, 2005; Skelton et al., 2010). Indeed, the discursive association of female academic achievement with asexuality is such that research indicates that those girls (often from White or Black working-class backgrounds) who do perform sexualised hetero-femininity in school are often regarded by teachers as 'not academic' and counter to the idealised notion of the 'good schoolgirl' (e.g. Archer, 2008). Rather, 'good girls' are expected to suppress or balance their sexuality in order to be seen as 'good students'.

It was also notable that all the girls from minority ethnic backgrounds who expressed science and/or science-related aspirations in our study were categorised as performing 'bluestocking' femininity. For instance, three South Asian girls and one mixed South Asian/White girl expressed science-related aspirations to enter the medical profession – all of whom were classified as performing 'bluestocking' femininity. Across the three surveys we also found that South Asian students (i.e. students of Indian, Pakistani, Bangladeshi or other South Asian heritage) had stronger aspirations in science compared with White students and tended to express more positive attitudes towards school science. Other research, although not focused specifically on science, has also found more positive attitudes towards school and higher educational aspirations among at least some Asian subgroups, relative to White students (e.g. Elias et al., 2006; Strand, 2007, 2009; Strand and Winston, 2008).We suggest that, within some cultural discourses, science may be not only configured as a 'safe' route (Archer and Francis, 2007), leading to well-paid, high-status, socially recognised and familiar professions (such as within medicine) for which some groups may possess useful and relevant social capital, but also seen as a sexually appropriate (e.g. 'respectable') and desirable career route for girls.

Moreover, analysis of the girls' and their parents' interview data suggests that Mienie, Preeti and Isabel were performing versions of femininity that echo the South Asian 'good girls' in Shain's (2003) study (termed 'Survivors'), who are obedient, hard working and high achieving at school. Their families espoused cultural discourses that value science as an appropriate and desirable career route (for girls and boys), which renders careers in and from science as highly 'thinkable'. In particular, science-related careers are seen as 'respectable' (being associated with both social prestige and 'restrained' sexuality) and hence are strongly encouraged within families, providing an important source of capital and motivation for children to see careers from science as desirable and 'for me'.

Although these girls seemed to be able to draw on a culturally recognisable discourse of an intelligible 'bluestocking' female science identity, this was also a potentially precarious identification and many girls recognised that they were a bit 'different' from their female peers. As Preeti put it, 'most girls are interested in other subjects' (not science). Like the square girls in Renold's (2005) study, their resistance to performing 'girly' femininity and their maintenance of 'clever' identities at the cost of 'doing girl' opened them up to potential social ostracism through the threat of slippage into 'geek' identity. Indeed, parents of the 'bluestocking' girls tended to describe their daughters as 'shy', 'quiet' and 'sensitive', and several discussed their daughters' experiences of being bullied at school.

Against the 'chilly' and sometimes hostile climate that girls encountered in their pursuit of science, 'bluestocking' girls reported benefiting from strong motivation and encouragement from their families to continue with science. This compared starkly with the lack of any specific family encouragement and motivation to pursue science that was reported by the majority of non-STEM aspirant girls, as discussed earlier in the chapter. It took the form of both encouragement to continue with science post-16 and also the provision of science-related resources (see also Chapter 3):

> My mum wants me to do physics but I'm sure you already know, there's like this thing where more boys do physics than girls . . . But I'm not really sure whether I should do it or not, my mum wants me to.
>
> *(Preeti, Y9)*

> We have . . . we have *Focus* magazine and dad's recently signed me up to the *Physics World*.
>
> *(Joanne, Y9)*

Embracing 'geekiness'

By largely eschewing performances of popular femininity, the 'bluestocking' girls did not have to engage in such extensive balancing acts as the girls who attempted to perform feminine scientist identity. That is, on the whole they 'opted out' of socially competitive performances of 'popularity' and concentrated instead on performances of 'cleverness', which meant either embracing or resigning themselves to performances of (or being positioned by others as performing) 'geek' identity. Although, as Francis et al. (2012) discuss, the parameters and boundaries of 'cool' versus 'geek' identity will be drawn differently in different schools and social contexts, in general highly academic identities that were not balanced by performances of sports prowess and/or physical attractiveness were designated as 'geek' identities.

Well the popular people are usually kind of nice but dim really . . . they're usually really sporty . . . Well my mum always envisions me working in a lab somewhere so that's kind of stereotypical, what do you expect?

(Joanne)

Interviewer: And is there a particular you know image or way that you'd describe the kids who are . . . you know like you really into science at this school?

Caitlin: Well it's kind of a stereotype of people being really geeky.

(Caitlin, White British/European mixed, middle-class girl)

As one mother, Debbie, explained, a student's decision as to whether or not to continue with science can involve an identity negotiation, namely whether to embrace or resist the 'geeky' image of scientists. In Debbie's experience, this meant that her daughter had wrestled with the dilemma of whether to drop science (in order for her performances of popular femininity to remain intelligible) or to pursue it and risk social ostracism. As Debbie explains, her daughter resolved this identity dilemma by deciding to actively embrace the 'geeky image' of science and to valorise performances of geekiness, as exemplified by the contemporary public discourse of 'geek chic'.[6]

I know my daughter . . . she's got through the stage of not wanting to do science. And it wasn't that she wasn't interested in it, but she knew it had sort of a geeky image or whatever, and she's sort of gone through the . . . um, you know being put off by that, to actually thinking that's a really good thing. So her and her friends you know revel in the fact that they can be geeky and you know they can impress other people with their scientific knowledge and those sort of things . . . and she sees it as quite a positive thing now. I don't think it's ever put my son off, I think he's always just been so interested that none of that would even enter his head . . . I think girls are more sensitive to that sort of thing, cos they're . . . they're more perceptive . . . I mean generalising hugely here, but I think so. And I also . . . I mean she's lucky in that she goes to an all girls school and I actually think that really helps. I think had she gone to a mixed school I think she'd be struggling a lot more at this stage, she'd have to be a lot more convinced that that's what she wanted to do.

(Debbie, White British, upper-middle-class mother, Y9 interview)

As Debbie recounts, although her daughter never lost her intrinsic interest in science, for a while she was put off pursuing it further because of the 'geeky image'. However, over time she came to reconcile her concerns by taking up the discourse of 'geek chic' ('[they] revel in the fact that they can be geeky'), which, Debbie suggests, is enacted by the girls through (masculine) performances of muscular intellect ('they can impress other people with their scientific knowledge'). Interestingly, Debbie notes that this dilemma has been more salient for her daughter than her son ('I don't think it's ever put my son off . . . none of that would even enter his head'). We suggest that the alignment of popular femininity with the body and sociability (and the relational alignment of cleverness and science with masculinity) may make this a particularly pivotal identity negotiation for girls. Indeed, as we discuss elsewhere (Archer et al., 2014a), the alignment of science and masculinity seemed to cause fewer identity issues for boys – in that performances of science identity and popular masculinity are inherently more congruent.

The salience of these identity negotiations for girls was also underlined by the case of 'bluestocking' girls who dropped their science/STEM aspirations over the 10–14 age period, with Demi providing a case in point. Demi is a White British, middle-class girl who lives on the south coast of England. In Y6 she aspired to be a scientist (ideally wanting to do something involving chemistry). In Y8 she aspired to be an astronomer or journalist. But by Y9 she had dropped her science aspirations and wanted to be an accountant. In her younger years, she was somewhat dismissive of her female peers' performances of girly femininity ('they just like . . . all like girly stuff, like singing and hairdressers'). However, as she reached the age of 14, she confessed that she had 'gone off' science, which she related to various factors but which included her resistance to the 'geeky' image of science:

> I've just really, I've just sort of gone off of it, like not being, I don't think I'm as interested in science as I was a few years ago, so I've sort of gone off the idea of having a career in science . . . I don't want to offend them, but like [doing science is] a bit, um, nerdy maybe, geeky . . . Like that they're obsessed with it and they [students who are really into science] just relate to it all the time and go to the club every single week. It's just one of them like stereotypes everyone seems to follow, that like people who go to maths club or science club are like automatically branded as nerds and geeks. That's sort of worn onto what I think, so I sort of think that as well.
>
> *(Demi, Y9)*

Summary

In this chapter we have argued that the strong association of science with masculinity and 'braininess' (which is also dominantly configured as masculine) means that science aspirations are simply not thinkable for most girls as they do not fit with their 'normal' sense of self. Moreover, science aspirations are seen to offer little space for, or valuing of, performances of popular femininity. Girls who do aspire to continue with science are required to perform (and be recognised by others as performing) 'clever' student identities. Yet the performance of 'cleverness' can be problematic for girls in that it is based on performances of masculinity. Indeed, research shows that girls' high attainment in science may be 'explained away' through a discourse of 'hard work' rather than 'natural brilliance' (Carlone, 2004). Thus, girls who wish to continue with science are faced with a dilemma – they must either try to 'balance' their (masculine) performances of 'cleverness' and science identity with performances of popular femininity (a balancing act that is 'impossible' in Butlerian terms), or they must eschew popular femininity and embrace 'geeky' (bluestocking) femininity (which is also 'unintelligible' as a performance of femininity, in Butlerian terms).

Consequently, we suggest that it is perhaps unsurprising – given the excessive identity work required – that many girls who are interested in science either drop their science aspirations over time or shift to more 'caring' and 'creative' STEM-related aspirations (predominantly in the field of medicine), which align more easily with key dimensions of femininity. In other words, by aspiring to STEM-related careers that are more closely aligned with key dimensions of femininity (such as 'caring'), girls are better able to 'possibilise' their identities, in terms of both their performances of femininity and their performances of science identity.

Our analyses suggest that although the 'brainy' and 'geeky' image of science can be a potential barrier for any student, it is disproportionately problematic for girls and working-class students (see also Archer et al., 2012a). As we shall discuss more in our final chapter, we believe that these findings pose a substantial problem for efforts to widen science participation – namely, that unless the culture and image of science can change dramatically in order to valorise and possibilise performances of popular femininity, there would appear to be little scope for recruiting substantial new numbers or proportions of girls into the physical sciences and engineering within the existing conditions.

Notes

1 We do not have the space in this chapter also to present in detail our analyses of the data relating to boys' performances of masculinity and their science/STEM aspirations – for these, please refer to Archer et al. (2014a), in which the analyses are discussed in depth.
2 Of these 25 girls, nine were categorised as working class, eight as middle class, six as on the borders of working/middle class and two were unassigned due to lack of data.
3 http://www.bbc.co.uk/news/education-30136921 (accessed 21/12/15).
4 'Kiss up' means to falsely flatter or, in this case, to express a false opinion in order to curry favour with the interviewer.
5 In the Y9 survey, there was no significant difference between boys' and girls' reports of their parents' attitudes to science (that is, boys and girls both reported similar levels of parental interest in science), but a significant gender difference was noted in the Y8 survey. However, these differences in the mean scores were complicated by the MLM analyses, which showed that being female has a small positive effect on parental attitudes to science (.10).
6 For a definition, see http://www.oxforddictionaries.com/definition/english/geek-chic (accessed 21/12/15).

7

ETHNICITY AND SCIENCE ASPIRATIONS

British Asian and British Black students

In this chapter, we bring attention to bear on two key groups of students – British Asian students (whose families had migrated from the South Asian subcontinent), who tend to be well represented in post-16 science participation, and British Black students (those with African and/or Caribbean heritage), who tend to be under-represented in post-16 science participation. We explore the factors that combine to produce these patterns, arguing that the differences are not due to a lack of aspiration or home/family encouragement. Indeed, British Asian and Black students appear to report higher levels of interest, aspiration and family encouragement than their White peers.

In the first part of this chapter we consider the factors that combine to produce a strong valuing of and identification with science (the sense that 'science is who we are and what we do') among British Asian families. We suggest that these families tend to possess high levels of science capital and generate a science-rich family habitus which involves strongly motivating children to study science. This science-rich family habitus provides children with inspiring family role models and practical help and support and fosters a desire to follow family trajectories and achieve 'success'. This combines with a strategic/pragmatic approach to children's aspirations and their futures (in which studying science is seen as maximising the chances of success) and is premised upon identification with 'clever'/brainy identity.

In the second part of the chapter we discuss the factors that combine to make science participation 'not for us' among British Black students. First, we suggest that many of these students equate science with becoming a scientist – a career which is strongly aligned with White, middle-class masculinity. Second, we explore how the 'brainy' image of science (and the need to be 'clever' to continue with science post-16) negatively impacts disproportionately on Black students due to historic, dominant discursive associations of 'cleverness' with White, male, middle-class students. Third, we suggest that Black students and their families are disproportionately likely to possess low levels of science capital, which can impede both the formation and the realisation of their science aspirations. Finally, we conclude the chapter by noting that there were two British Black girls who did aspire to careers in science – although, as we discuss, these aspirations were also potentially precarious.

Not an issue of aspiration? Ethnicity patterns in the survey data

Across the surveys, a pattern emerged in which British Asian and Black students expressed stronger science aspirations than their White peers. For instance, the Y6 survey showed that Black and Asian students expressed stronger science aspirations than White students, as reflected by their mean scores on a composite variable comprising items related to aspirations in science (i.e. 'I would like to study more science in the future', 'I would like to have a job that uses science', 'I would like to work in science', 'I would like to become a scientist' and 'I think I could become a good scientist one day').[1]

Similar patterns emerged in the data from the Year 8 and Year 9 surveys, suggesting an overall picture in which Asian students expressed consistently stronger aspirations in science than White students. Black students also tended to hold stronger science aspirations than White students (yet not as strong as Asian students) – although we would caution that, in general, ethnicity did not emerge as a strong factor within multi-level modelling, so we present these findings as indicative rather than definitive.

Yet, despite the relatively high science aspirations of British Asian and Black students, post-16 participation figures would suggest that Black students' early science aspirations are not translating into their later participation. Various UK government policy texts foreground a 'poverty of aspiration' as an explanatory factor for minority ethnic underachievement and participation (e.g. DfES, 2005). Yet analysis of our survey data suggested that, on the whole, both British Asian and Black students reported high levels of parental support and ambition. For instance, on the Y9 survey, ANOVA analyses indicated that the differences among ethnic groups on a parental-ambition/aspirations[2] composite variable were significant ($F(4, 4595) = 103.008$, $p < .0001$), with post-hoc comparisons indicating that Black and Asian students scored significantly higher than White students. In other words, Asian and Black students would not appear to suffer from low levels of parental ambition. Moreover, analysis of the Y9 survey data showed that British Asian and Black students are more likely than White students to say they want to go to university 'very much'. In other words, it is difficult to attribute differential patterns of science participation between British Asian and Black students to a 'poverty of aspiration'.

We now turn to the qualitative data to see if a more in-depth understanding of the views and aspirations of British Asian and British Black students and parents can further advance our knowledge of ethnic patterns in science participation. In particular, we seek to explore why these aspirations and ambitions translate into participation for some but not others. We first consider what promotes high levels of post-16 science participation among British Asian students. We then consider what hinders science participation among British Black students.

British Asian students: 'science is what we do'

There were 11 students with South Asian cultural backgrounds in our interview sample, whom we tracked from age 10 to 14. These comprised six boys and five girls. The students came from a variety of South Asian backgrounds (mostly Indian, Pakistani, Sri Lankan) and included two mixed Asian/White students. Most of the students had been born in Britain (some were third generation) and so we use the term 'British Asian' to refer to them collectively.

By Y9, only two British Asian students did not express science/STEM-related aspirations (Raza and Mienie), although both said that they were still planning on taking at least one science at A level. Only Raza was not taking Triple Science.

All the British Asian students exhibited high levels of interest in science, with all students naming science and/or maths among their favourite school subjects in Y9. As Kaka put it in his Y9 interview, 'I love physics, and biology is probably my best one . . . and chemistry I love as well.'

In the interview sample, we found that the majority of British Asian students aspired to STEM-related careers, notably in *medicine* (for instance, seven of these students aspired to be a doctor between the ages of 10 and 14, and four of these were consistent aspirations across time points). Technology and engineering were also popular aspirations among British Asian boys (notably Colin, Bob and Yogi). The British Asian students also seemed to express more consistent science and STEM-related aspirations over the course of the study, particularly compared to their British Black interviewee counterparts.

> Well I am still into science so much. The one thing that I have not dropped ever in thinking what I want to be when I grow up – from Year 6 I've always wanted to be something with science – a scientist, like something to do with chemistry – I'd love to go into stuff like that. I'd love to be a surgeon with like biology, I'd like to go into stuff like that.
>
> *(Kaka, British Asian, middle-class boy, Y9)*

As we discuss next, we suggest that there were several key factors promoting this pervasive feeling that 'science is for us' among British Asian students: their relatively high levels of science capital and strong cultural discourses promoting science participation produce a science-rich family habitus which emphasises the notion that science is 'who we are and what we do'. This is underpinned by a strategic/pragmatic engagement with aspirations and high self-confidence in their academic ability.

High levels of science capital and the production of a science-rich family habitus ('a whole family of doctors')

Generally, the British Asian students in our sample came from more middle-class (e.g. professional) social backgrounds compared to the British Black students. They also possessed relatively high levels of family science capital. For instance, eight of the British Asian students had parents or family members who worked in STEM-related jobs and/or held degree-level science qualifications – and all of these students had at least one parent with a post-compulsory STEM qualification.

We suggest that high levels of science capital were mobilised within these families to produce a science-rich family habitus, in which science was woven into the daily fabric and identity of the families. In other words, for many of our British Asian families, science is both 'who we are' and 'what we do'. For instance, Bob (a British Asian/White middle-class boy) describes how his long-standing aspiration to become an electronics engineer is underpinned by a wide range of family science capital and is embedded within his family's everyday practices and sense of identity. His mother is a chemist, his father works in IT, his uncle is an electronics engineer and his older sister is studying biochemistry at university. Bob has always had lots of science kits and exposure to science at home, and he has always engaged in lots of engineering activities in his leisure time. In common with other high-science-capital students, Bob and his parents read the family copy of *New Scientist* magazine ('My parents get it, but we all read it'). Similarly, other British Asian students described how science was a familiar part of their family leisure time and discussions:

> My mum, she loves seeing natural programmes and she's very sciencey as well so she always has new ideas on how the modern world should be. And so we . . . we . . . she just . . . we like discuss when we get a family moment.
>
> *(Mienie, British Asian, middle-class girl, Y9)*

> Yes, so I don't just work in science, I am actually interested in it as well . . . So I do things with the children that are science related. So for example I'm a member of the Royal Society of Chemistry . . . so we took both kids in to London cos it was half term along to one of these talks – so they could get a different sense of what's out there. And it wasn't an academic talk particularly . . . but the point was they were going into a sort of scientific institution and they were meeting other people that were you know not in their circle of friends and whatever. So you know I will do things like that and I'll take them to you know a science museum and that sort of thing . . . I also do things like careers fairs at their school, they have like scientists and things to come in . . . we have *New Scientist* and he'll sit there over dinner reading that and telling me all about it and everything, yeah, he's fascinated by some of the things in that.
>
> *(Debbie, White British, upper middle class, mother of Bob)*

In particular, British Asian students seemed to benefit from high levels of science-related social capital that was distributed across extended family networks. Even when family networks were geographically distributed, strong social bonds and a familial discourse of identification with these job areas meant that students were able to mobilise the science capital within them, fostering, sustaining and materially helping the development of their own science-related aspirations. For instance, Colin (British Asian, middle-class boy) explained that his aspiration to become a doctor was inspired by his older cousin (who had personally overcome cancer and was now a qualified doctor). His aspiration was also fostered by a family 'tradition' of working in medicine:

> I think like especially after seeing my cousin, she's going to become a doctor soon, so I've seen her sort of work and say she needs to like practise for a practical exam or something she usually takes me as a patient, so it feels like I want to do it as well one day sort of thing . . . I think on my mum's family there's like a whole family of doctors, so like all the children are doctors and I don't see them often, but my mum always sort of talks about like how they study and how they've got like this far sort of thing.
>
> *(Colin, Y9)*

The presence of an inspirational family member and a family discourse of 'science is what we do' was found across most of the British Asian students. For instance, Samantha (British Asian/White, upper-middle-class girl) explained: 'My grandma was a GP and she always used to tell me about it and things, so my grandma definitely inspired me to want to become a doctor.' Samantha's mother, Claire, concurred, adding that Samantha's grandfather had also been a university researcher. Other British Asian students recounted similar science-related social capital from family members:

> My mum's really good at physics . . . My dad's side – they're doctors . . . some of them are doctors, others are like scientists to research and stuff.
>
> *(Preeti, British Asian, middle-class girl, Y9)*

> My dad is the only doctor in the family. My brother's going to go into medicine . . . My other, my family, my other family members they're accountants and they're into, they're more engineering as well . . . I probably look, I look up to my dad, but as well as my uncle, because he's just phenomenal with maths.
>
> *(Tom4, British Asian, middle-class boy, Y9).*

> And I want to be a paediatrician, that's like work with children. Cos my mum works with children and my dad's a doctor and I like children.
>
> *(Isabel, British Asian, middle-class girl, Y9)*

My cousin's just passed and she's become a pharmacist now . . . So that seems quite good because she said she enjoys it, and she's just passed her pre-reg there as well . . . So now she's a professional pharmacist . . . [Another] cousin just finished her GCSEs and she just got six A★s and three As and stuff. And my dad was like you've got to try and aim to get that as well.

(Rachel, British Asian, middle-class girl, Y9)

As the latter quote from Rachel and the above quote from Colin exemplify, the notion of inspirational family members and a family 'tradition' of going into STEM areas ran alongside a cultural discourse of social competition, in which children were encouraged to match or exceed the high attainment of close family members in order to maintain 'face'. As discussed by Archer and Francis (2007), this practice of family/community social competition has been found to be very effective in terms of promoting academic achievement among minority ethnic young people. The discourse of 'keeping up' with (or exceeding) the attainment of key others is both explicit and also an ingrained part of the everyday family habitus ('my mum always talks about like how they study and how they've got this far'), rendering it 'natural' to aspire to attain highly.

The science capital that students were able to mobilise from within their extended family networks not only was motivating and inspiring, but also provided the students with practical/material help to achieve their aspirations. For instance, Kaka was able to get help from his father, who holds a maths degree, and also his aunt, who holds a science degree:

My auntie, she teaches science, older science – Year 11s, Year 12s – in science. So she helps me a lot if I have trouble in science. So if I ask her she'll explain to me.

(Kaka, British Asian, middle-class boy, Y9)

My dad took a maths degree, so whenever I'm stuck like he can help me and then I get it.

(Rachel, British Asian, middle-class girl, Y9)

Yogi (British Asian, middle-class boy) also described how his father had inspired a love of engineering in him and had taught him about engineering from an early age ('My dad used to always teach me about it as well, cos he's quite a mechanic, he's quite a good grease monkey as he said', Y9).

This kind of support was also mobilised to help realise the students' aspirations. For instance, Tom4 described how his father was drawing on his social capital to explore options for Tom4 and to identify strategic areas of medicine for him to go into. Isabel also described having met lots of doctors through her father, a social network that might help her to realise her own medical ambitions. As discussed in Chapter 5, Debbie, mother of Bob, explained how their own family social network (capital) provided Bob with both inspiration and useful knowledge/information to help him develop his electronic engineer aspirations.

The encouragement that students received from their families was also explicit, with many of the British Asian students in our interview sample describing the strong parental push and motivation that they received to continue studying science (and particularly physics) post-16:

> Um, my dad would quite like me to go into something that keeps maths as a strong point, but also uses science.
>
> *(Tom4, British Asian, middle-class boy, Y9)*

> I think my parents would like me to be like a doctor or an accountant or like something to do with science, a scientist or something.
>
> *(Colin, British Asian, middle-class boy, Y9)*

> Yeah I have a lot of books about science. My dad really wants to push me on physics, because he says physics is just one of the greatest subjects ever, it will teach you so much about life. He just wants me to really go into physics.
>
> *(Kaka, British Asian, middle-class boy, Y9)*

Kaka's father Jack reflected on how he felt that his efforts over the years to instil in his son an interest in physics were now paying off:

> It's funny because I've always enjoyed physics, the best of the three [sciences], so I've pushed Kaka from the start. I bought him his own book before he even started physics, so he kind of went through that. I think Kaka is slowly starting to like physics quite a lot now as well.
>
> *(Y9 interview)*

Indeed, by the time of their Year 9 interviews, a number of students were starting to reflect on how their family and parents' practices were helpful in developing their own interest in the sciences:

> I didn't really like science when I was little, I used to tell my dad that I didn't like it, and he was like 'When I was little like maths and science were my two favourite subjects, if you like maths you kind of have to like science'. So then I was like thinking about it and I was like 'Well science is a bit like maths' so then I thought about it and . . . I do enjoy science a bit more now.
>
> *(Rachel, British Asian, middle-class girl, Y9)*

> It started off when I was quite young – my dad forced me to watch it [science television programmes]. And then eventually it started getting more interesting, and then I just started watching it on my own . . . you

know with every decision you make, your parents always have an influence in it. Specially with your hobbies and things like that, they always have an infl- . . . it's always back to your parents really.

(Yogi, British Asian, middle-class boy, Y9)

The parents who held science degrees themselves were the most enthusiastic to instil a love of science and an ambition to study it further in their children. For instance, as Geeta (Preeti's mum) explained, her own degree in physics and IT meant that not only did she strongly value these areas, but she also wanted Preeti to pursue them further. However, she was also aware of the potential barriers that Preeti might face (such as the gender imbalance in post-16 physics) and recounted how she tried to provide her daughter with support and motivation accordingly.

We suggest that the combination of high science capital, a science-rich family habitus and sustained, specific motivation over time to continue with science seemed to be effective, with most British Asian students maintaining science and STEM-related aspirations over time, in line with family expectations. In the case of Rachel, who at age 10 aspired to be an actress or fashion designer, her aspirations seemed to align better with her family's preferences over time, such that by age 14 she aspired to pharmacy.

A strong family motivation for science also seemed to override some students' potential reticence or resistance. For instance, despite citing an aspiration to become a doctor at each of her interviews, Preeti (British Asian, middle-class girl) had never seemed to show much interest in science and always cited another aspiration alongside doctor at each interview (e.g. teacher, actress). We had classified her early aspirations as predominantly 'pragmatic', given her stated lack of interest in science generally (see Archer et al., 2012a). Even at her Y9 interview, Preeti seemed unsure of her chosen career path, admitting that 'My dad's actually really wanting me to get into medicine', confessing that she was not totally sure herself because she felt that medicine would require too much 'hard work'. However, despite her own ambivalence, Preeti admitted: 'I'm probably most likely to be a doctor when I grow up though.' When asked why, by the interviewer, Preeti replied, 'I don't know, probably family history or something', continuing:

> They just force me to do what they want me to do and stuff. They don't force me, they just persuade me.

Overwhelmingly, the British Asian students we interviewed displayed a high level of alignment between the hopes and aspirations of both child and parents. Indeed, only Raza (British Asian, middle-class boy) remained resistant to his parents' wishes for him to pursue science and medicine:

> They want . . . like my mum wants to be . . . wants me to be a doctor which I'm not really . . . I think I could do it but I don't . . . I wouldn't

enjoy it really, I don't like that sort of stuff . . . yeah, my mum says 'Oh, be a doctor' but then I go 'But I don't want to be a doctor' but that's what she wants me to do.

(Y9 interview)

Analysis of the Y9 survey data suggested that Asian students were more likely than White students to agree that it was important that their future job choices pleased their families, but the interview analysis seemed to suggest that, more than this, students valued their parents' views. The students emphasised the high level of respect that they held for their parents' and family's opinions and experiences. They felt that their parents were best placed to advise on their futures, knowing their child's strengths and weaknesses and holding their best interests at heart:

I think friends and family is a lot better to talk to [than teachers or careers advisers], because it's a bit more personal, yeah, you have to talk to them about it. They know what you're good at and what you're not good at a lot better than most others.

(Yogi, British Asian, middle-class boy, Y9)

Yeah I go to my dad to decide . . . my family definitely. Because they are so supportive, they know what my weakness is, my strength, so they'd help me along the way.

(Kaka, British Asian, middle-class boy, Y9)

Strategic and pragmatic engagement with aspirations/future

The British Asian students and their parents seemed to espouse a highly strategic and pragmatic engagement with aspirations and choices regarding the future. In the survey, students of all ethnicities rated 'usefulness for a future job or career' as the most important factor influencing their subject choices at A level. This theme was reiterated in the interviews with Asian students, in which students and parents placed a high value on the perceived 'utility' of subjects such as science. Indeed, irrespective of whether they personally held post-16 science qualifications or not, all the British Asian parents strongly valued science as an 'enabling' subject that would help their children, whatever their future career trajectory. For instance, Geeta (mother of Preeti, Y9) asserted that 'without science you won't understand life itself in some way'. Similarly, Dawn (Mienie's mother), a financial administrator, reflected in the Y9 interview:

So I think it's good for her to do it [science], even if she you know does choose not to go into the science in the future, but at least she has a certain background and understanding of the science you know? Yeah, physics and anyway you need your physics in your maths and yeah and chemistry if you want to see what kind of compounds are in a certain product, you have a certain basic knowledge about it isn't it?

(Dawn, Malaysian, middle-class mother)

Dawn and a number of other parents also reflected that the sciences can be strategic qualifications with a strong extrinsic benefit, opening up additional career options, particularly within economic growth areas:

Now there is a lot of companies involved in bioscience, so it depends what choices are there and what offers are given to her and if, this is the reason I'm telling you, if her foundation is good then she has more choice for her I mean to get herself involved in.

(Dawn, mother of Mienie, Y9)

I really believe if you pick core subjects and if he doesn't want to do something that is even anything to do with science-related, you know, do science or, you know, have a science degree . . . and at least you've got . . . you can do absolutely anything then, yeah.

(Jack, British Asian, middle-class male, father of Kaka, Y9)

Family negotiations were underpinned by pragmatic strategies to promote their children's 'success'. For instance, while several students identified a particular 'dream' job, they also identified alternative 'safe'/known routes as being more realistic and as having better 'odds' of being realised. For instance, in his Y9 interview Colin explained:

Colin: I would say it would be a sort of 50/50 chance of me getting that [his dream job in sports medicine] as I would have to get the right grades and right A levels and the right university as well for the certain like career I'm choosing.
Interviewer: And how likely is kind of becoming a doctor?
Colin: I would say that's around like 65 to 75, 80%.

These processes of negotiation were voiced during family discussions, with parents seeming to provide guidance as to what might constitute more (or less) feasible career routes:

I saw people going into space and I told my mum I wanted to be an astronaut and she told me it wasn't really realistic as like there's only a couple of astronauts in the world and then not every day you go to space as well, so it wasn't realistic . . . I would like to be a footballer, but that's highly unlikely [Interviewer: How come?] Because I'm Asian . . . I think like I've seen programmes where they've said stuff, but like if you're Asian you can't do this.

(Colin, British Asian, middle-class boy, Y9)

As indicated by this quote, some parental concerns about particular aspirations were not simply that they would be unrealistic or hard to attain for anyone; they may also reflect a recognition that racism may present an additional hurdle for minority ethnic communities (Archer and Francis, 2007). Experiences of migration also produced other barriers, such as when qualifications or expertise gained in the country of origin are not recognised in the UK. For instance, as Preeti explained, 'My mum wanted to be a maths teacher, she's applied for so many schools and she hasn't got a job because she's done her GCSE out of the country.'

The students also suggested that their parents strongly encouraged them to pursue STEM careers, notably in medicine, because these were 'safer' (stable, well paid, highly respected, and families had specific capital to help realise these ambitions). Where students expressed non-STEM aspirations, parents tried to strategically insert a STEM angle into them:

> My mum really likes . . . she's quite keen on the doctor one but she said, with journalism though, it's quite a hard market to get into so you have to be really kind of strong and persuasive and you have to know you definitely want to do it.
> *(Samantha, British Asian/White, middle-class girl, Y8)*

Samantha's mum Claire agreed that she favoured medicine as a route for Samantha. She and her husband recognised, though, that Samantha was also creative and loved writing. Indeed, Samantha expressed a consistent aspiration to be a journalist, alongside her doctor aspiration, over the course of all three interviews. As Claire explained, she had suggested that Samantha consider a combination of the two ('she's very creative, writing . . . but she likes sciences as well. My husband suggested medical journalism'). Other students provided similar examples, in which their parents suggested science-related options for a particular non-science aspiration:

> I think my mum, she likes me to do science and I want to do sport, so like she gave me the idea of like maybe doing something linked with sports and science at the same time.
> *(Colin, British Asian, middle-class boy, Y9)*

> I think only last year my mum said to me what about a paediatrician. I was like oh yeah . . . Cos I didn't really want to be an anaesthetist cos it just . . . it was just too hard.
> *(Isabel, British Asian, middle-class girl, Y8)*

We interpret these examples as reflecting how, despite their relatively economically and socially advantaged positions, these British Asian families are still acutely aware that their children will be entering a highly competitive work market and may also be subject to ethnic and other inequalities such that the re/production of 'success' is not guaranteed and must be hard won. While racism and other social inequalities may close down certain options for British Asian students, the students also perceived that their diasporic positioning might also open up some strategic possibilities. For instance, as Yogi (British Asian, middle-class boy, Y9) explained:

> But I think the whole engineering industry . . . and India as well, that's coming quite big on industry . . . Yeah. So I think that's more the place I'll be going. Specially cos there's quite a shortage in engineering at the moment. Cos I've been looking into it like lately.

Self-confidence and 'brainy' identity

As we discussed in Chapter 4, identification with science requires students to negotiate the 'brainy' image of science. Across both the surveys and interviews, British Asian students reported a greater confidence in their academic science abilities. In the interview sample, while most British Asian students reported feeling fairly confident in their abilities, this was more marked for the boys than for the girls. Indeed, apart from Raza, all the boys confidently remarked on their 'intelligence' and science/STEM aptitudes. For instance, Kaka described himself as 'very intelligent in maths' and Tom4 asserted 'I'm academic'. At each interview, Tom4 spent considerable time outlining his academic aptitudes and his designation as 'gifted and talented'. He was always confident that he could enter the competitive, high-status field of medicine and believed that he would be well placed to study at a top university:

> I either want to go into neurosurgery or genetics, which because I've got a strong point of maths, so in genetics you have a lot of maths, so but I think I'd probably take either three sciences or two sciences and a maths at A level, then go to Cambridge and then from there med school and go on to junior doctor . . . I think I could, I think that's likely because Cambridge is quite a tough university to get into, but I think I could get into it.
>
> *(Tom4, British Asian, middle-class boy, Y9)*

Likewise, Yogi felt that 'Physics is sort of my thing . . . I just naturally do it'.

The British Asian girls were also confident that they would get to university, including the 'top' universities, but they were more likely to differentiate their aptitude between different areas of science. For instance, when asked if she could think of anything that might prevent her from going to university, Isabel replied 'I don't think so'. Likewise, Mienie (Y9) anticipated going to university but explained that her aptitudes lay more with maths, physics and chemistry than biology:

> I would like to do maths and I would like to do physics and chemistry, I'm not a biology girl because I don't like really biology but I love physics

because like all about the world and how things . . . and like chemistry. Because chemistry involves a lot of maths and equations and I like maths so it ties in . . . from small [a young age] I always wanted to go to Oxford but . . . because Oxford, if I do go, I'll be going more there for the science.

Her confidence also seemed to relate to her being one of only 20 students selected from her year group to study Triple Science ('there were a lot of people put in for it so at the end of the day they looked for who behaved well in lessons, their levels and everything. So luckily I got chosen which is good and yeah, we were all happy').

Parents tended to identify their children as 'clever', 'bright', 'intelligent' and being among the highest-attaining students in their year group/class. For instance, in the Y9 interviews, Nicola explained how '[Kaka] has always been, again, the top marks in his class year', and Claire explained that Samantha was 'too bright' not to continue her studies and pursue a challenging, high-status career. As Claire recounted, 'I said to her [Samantha] that she is clever, and that's why it's so important for her to do well.' Similarly, Geeta described her daughter Preeti as 'a very intelligent girl', and Victor spoke of his pride in how his daughter Rachel is currently 'over-achieving', attaining beyond age-expected grades.

Of the interviewees, only Raza (British Asian, middle-class boy) seemed unsure about his science ability and ended up taking the less prestigious Double Science award route at GCSE. As he recounted in his Y8 interview:

I can do Triple and I think I'm in a high enough set to do it, but I don't think I will because I don't want to do anything I'm not capable of doing . . . Yeah, I don't know if I'm up to it, I mean I could do it . . . well, maybe I could but I don't know that yet because I haven't tried it so I'm not really too sure.

It was also notable that while in Y6 he aspired to be a pilot or 'maybe a scientist', he later dropped any science aspirations and wanted instead to be an author (Y8) or a travel writer (Y9). We suggest that in this respect, even in the face of high home-science capital and strong cultural discourses and motivations to continue with science, the imperative also to perform 'clever/cleverest' student identity as a key component of science identity can contribute to rendering science aspirations 'not for me' for students like Raza.

Black British students: science is 'not for us'?

There were nine students (four boys and five girls) with 'Black' cultural backgrounds in our interview sample, whom we tracked from age 10 to 14. The students came from African and/or Caribbean backgrounds and included one mixed Black/White student. All the students had been born in Britain (some were third generation) and, reflecting this, we use the term 'Black British' to refer to them collectively.

In both the survey and the interviews Black British students expressed high levels of interest in pursuing a career in science. At age 14, almost half (4/9) of the Black British students in our interview sample aspired to science or science-related aspirations, although it was also notable that Black students were proportionally more likely than White or South Asian students to have 'never' held a science or STEM-related aspiration.

Of course, the interview numbers are small and should be treated with care, yet we still believe that our data have some valuable insights to offer – not least, as we discuss here, some insights into why many Black British young people may not continue into post-16 science and whether there are any particular reasons why many of these students may 'never' hold science-related aspirations.

Not low interest, low attainment or a poverty of aspirations

Some previous literature and education policy documents have suggested that the reasons why Black students tend to be under-represented in higher education, and particularly in fields such as science, can be attributed to their lower attainment, interest and/or aspirations. For instance, a report by the Royal Society (1998) highlights attainment differentials as a key reason for minority ethnic groups' under-representation in STEM subjects at degree level, and UK government education policy has consistently associated under-representation and lower levels of attainment among minority ethnic students with 'a poverty of aspirations' (e.g. DfES, 2005). There are also numerous initiatives aimed at encouraging a greater diversity of young people into STEM, which are based on attempts to increase young people's interest in science.[3] Yet none of these explanations were borne out by our data. For instance, only Tom2 was in lower school sets; the other Black British students we interviewed were in top sets or middle sets, with several reporting achieving high grades in their courses and being eligible to take the prestigious Triple Science option for GCSE. As Jake (Black British, working-class boy) said in his Y8 interview, 'my teacher's telling me to go for Science cos I'm really good at it'.

As set out at the beginning of this chapter, there was also no evidence of low family aspirations or lack of support in our sample. All Black British families aspired highly for their children, irrespective of social class (two families were lower middle class and seven were working class). All parents and children described strong parental support, pushing, and high expectations for children to continue into higher education and achieve a professional career. As John explained:

> I am satisfied, but still I still want them to do better . . . I still want them to do better. Just like . . . if you score 70%, that's a good mark. But still you want to score 80 or 90, that's all.
>
> (*John, Nigerian, working-class male, father of Kelsey and Cristiano, Y9*)

John felt he was typical of Nigerian families, as 'they rate education very highly'. He also felt that Nigerian families shared similarly high expectations to Asian families ('Seem as if the parents of Black and Asian – they want more from their children'). Likewise Robbie, another Nigerian father, explained:

> I mean I keep saying it . . . it's a very difficult world out there – you don't need anybody to tell you that. So the best you can give to yourself . . . it doesn't matter what the economy times are saying – education, you just need to have that. And the minimum you can get in today's world is just a degree – the minimum.
>
> *(Robbie, Nigerian, lower-middle-class male, father of Vanessa, Y9)*

These findings are echoed by other studies of minority ethnic students and their families in the UK (e.g. Archer, 2003; Archer et al., 2010b), and they reinforce observations from other work that Black students are strongly encouraged by their families to continue with science (e.g. Russell and Atwater, 2005).

From Year 6 to Year 9, the Black families in our study reported motivating their children frequently, almost daily, to work hard and aspire to higher education. Several parents also provided practical support, such as paying for private tutoring. Similarly, and echoing Lareau's (2003) conceptualisation of 'concerted cultivation', Gemma's mother V (Black British, lower middle class) described her parenting approach as 'I will say hands on, because I want her really to do well and I want to give her the encouragement because she is doing well, yeah'. However, unlike the middle-class parents in Lareau's sample, the Black families in our qualitative sample tended to enjoy less economic, cultural and social capital than some of the more privileged White and Asian middle-class families in the study. On the whole, the Black families tended to provide moral support, encouragement, guidance and motivation (e.g. Hanson, 2007) rather than subject expertise, social contacts or expensive extra-curricular activities.

There was no evidence of Black students lacking interest in science, with all students reporting liking science to some degree. For instance, Tom2, Gemma, Ali and Selena described themselves as 'really interested' in science and named it among their favourite subjects. Alan, Pamela, Kelsey, Jake and Cristiano described more of a moderate, or differentiated, interest, either not liking science as much as other subjects or liking some aspects of science but not others:

> It's basically all of it I love, I don't mind any of it.
>
> *(Tom2, Black British, working-class boy, Y9)*

Alan (mixed White/Black, lower middle class) also talked of wanting to 'take as much as I can' of science when it came to choosing his GCSE options. As his mum Tasha proudly reflected: 'He excels in maths and science.' These findings chime with research conducted in the US which shows that minority ethnic students, but particularly girls and women, tend to report strong interest in science (e.g. Brickhouse et al., 2000; Johnson, 2006). For instance, Hanson and Palmer-Johnson (2000) and Hanson (2004) found that African American women are very interested in science, sometimes more so than White American women. So if lack of interest is not the issue, what causes differential patterns in science aspirations?

We now explore three possible reasons why the Black British students we interviewed were proportionally less likely than British Asian or White British students to aspire to careers in science.

One: The 'science = scientist = White middle-class male' dilemma

As with the majority of students in the wider data-set (of all ethnic backgrounds), most Black students in the interview sample were only able to name a very narrow range of potential future careers that studying science might lead to, namely a scientist, science teacher or doctor. Pamela and Jake's views were typical:

> I think they [science subjects] don't lead to a lot of like jobs that are like around like today but I think they lead to . . . like you could be a microbiologist or stuff like that . . . an astronaut . . . a science teacher.
>
> *(Pamela, Black British, lower-middle-class girl, Y9)*

> Doctor, scientist . . . That's about it.
>
> *(Alan, mixed White/Black, lower-middle-class boy, Y9)*

In this respect, the Black students and their parents were typical of the majority of participants in the wider sample, in that they expressed fairly narrow views of the types of jobs that science qualifications might lead to. But they contrast with the British Asian students and parents discussed earlier, who tended to view science as an enabling qualification that is useful for 'everything'.

Overwhelmingly, the careers of scientist and science teacher were seen as 'not for me'. Indeed, Tom2, Gemma, Alan, Pamela, Kelsey and Jake were very clear that they had no interest in becoming a scientist and could not imagine themselves pursuing such a career.

> I'd find it boring. Wearing a white coat, walking around with glasses. I don't find that interesting, I find getting stuck in and making money is a much better job.
>
> *(Tom2, Black British, working-class boy, Y9)*

> I just don't like the thought of me being a scientist.
>
> *(Gemma, Black British, lower-middle-class girl, Y9)*

Gemma's resistance to the idea of 'being a scientist' was despite her doing well in science at school. Her mother V had even prompted her to consider a career in, or from, science when she realised that Gemma was attaining highly in science at school – a suggestion which Gemma refused.

> Well I was telling her [to consider] doctor or like if she's good in science, do something in this area even, forensic or things like that. But she likes to do her, she's talking about designer.
>
> *(V, Black British, middle-class mother, Y9)*

The students tended to evoke traditional, stereotypical images of scientists which, as Scantlebury et al. (2007) argue, were narrow and excluding of Others. Public and popular images of scientists tend to overwhelmingly represent scientists as White, middle-class men (Scantlebury et al., 2007), although, as discussed in Chapter 4, popular stereotypes expressed by students are also more complex than simply reproducing the traditional 'mad' or 'boffin' scientist stereotype (DeWitt et al., 2013a).

There is a substantial body of work critiquing the socio-historic exclusion of minority ethnic groups from scientific knowledge in Western societies (e.g. Baker, 1998; Harding, 1998; Losh, 2010). As Carlone and Johnson (2007, p. 1207) explain, 'the institutional and historical meaning of "being a scientist" actually means "being a White male", a message which is reinforced within many science classrooms (Atwater, 2000)'. The challenges experienced by minority ethnic students within the science classroom have also been powerfully documented within schools (e.g. Atwater, 2000; Brickhouse and Potter, 2001; Carlone and Johnson, 2007; Carlone et al., 2011; Rascoe and Atwater, 2005) and higher education (e.g. Atwater and Simpson, 1984; Malone and Barabino, 2009; Ong, 2005; Russell and Atwater, 2005; Seymour and Hewitt, 1997; Vining-Brown, 1994).

For instance, Atwater (2000) points to the symbolic violence experienced by Black girls within science classrooms in which 'White is the norm', and Malone and Barabino (2009) discuss how minority ethnic students report feeling isolated and marginalised within science classrooms. Black students have also been identified as being among those most likely to report finding it hard to position themselves, and to be seen by others, as 'properly' or authentically scientific (Carlone and Johnson, 2007).[4] Indeed, Hanson (2007, 2009) argues that the culture of science is particularly hostile to Black students.

The association of science and science careers with White masculinity creates a particularly 'chilly climate' for Black girls and women, who can experience both racism and sexism within science environments (Malcom et al., 1998). As we discussed in Chapter 6, 'girly' girls are generally less likely to express science aspirations than other girls, and they are more likely to drop aspirations for careers in science as they get older (see also Archer et al., 2012a, 2013). In light of this, it was perhaps unsurprising that the more 'girly' Black girls, like Gemma, had never expressed science aspirations, whereas Selena (Black British, working-class girl), who did aspire to a career in science and who is discussed further in the final section of this chapter, performed a more 'tomboy' gender identity. Drawing on an intersection of gender and class, through the notion of 'glamour' (Skeggs, 1997), Gemma's mother V concurs: 'Like she [Gemma] said [she aspires to] designer or hairdressing. You know all this glamour thing yeah . . . she likes her nails, her hair, drawing.' As exemplified by the discursive construction of Other students, outlined earlier in our theoretical framework, V's talk hints at the discursive association of middle-class femininity with demureness and academic achievement – which Gemma might be interpreted as resisting through her performance of 'glamorous' Black urban femininity. We suggest that these discursive associations may be amplified in the case of science (which is dominantly constructed as White, male and middle class) such that identifying with science may be particularly challenging (and require considerable identity work) for 'glamorous' Black girls.

As noted in a number of US studies, girls tend to be less likely to identify with science, and this impacts negatively on their progress and participation in post-compulsory science and science careers (Brickhouse et al., 2000; Brickhouse and Potter, 2001; Calabrese Barton et al., 2008; Carlone, 2004). As Gemma's performances of femininity are 'not brainy/swotty', we suggest that popular associations of science and science careers with both masculinity and 'cleverness' render such aspirations undesirable and incompatible in identity terms with her own production of self. Moreover, the dominant construction of science as aligned with *White* masculinity renders it even more 'unthinkable' in relation to Black femininity.

The association of science and science careers with White (middle-class) masculinity is also potentially problematic for Black boys, who are often demonised within popular discourse and excluded from dominant constructions of 'normal' masculinity. Numerous research studies have drawn attention to the ways in which Black masculinity is dominantly constructed as a 'risky' and 'dangerous' educational identity (e.g. Sewell, 1997), and the popular association of Black masculinity and low attainment, as discussed above, also contributed to rendering science aspirations less thinkable for Black boys in the study. In other words, popular associations of science and science careers with a particular version of masculinity (White and middle class) work to exclude *both* Black boys and Black girls from seeing science as a normal, conceivable and achievable potential aspiration.

As a result, we suggest that it was not surprising that half of the Black students we interviewed had little interest in continuing with science, given that they saw it as leading only to careers *in* science – jobs which are associated with White, middle-class masculinity. Brickhouse and Potter (2001) 'describe some of the difficulties students face who aspire to scientific or technological competence yet do not desire to take on aspects of the identities associated with membership in school science communities' (p. 965). The dilemmas faced by the Black students in our study may be exacerbated in this respect by the narrow, culturally limited, images of scientists discussed in the previous section, which, as other researchers have pointed out, 'don't look like me' (Scantlebury et al., 2007). Hence, although most liked science as a subject, and often did well in it at school, they did not feel it was 'for me' or personally relevant or necessary for their future working lives.

The perceived narrowness of pathways from school science into future careers seems to be an issue that affects science more than other core subjects. Indeed, we asked students about their perceptions of the usefulness of three core subjects, science, English and mathematics, and it was notable that Black students were much more likely to see English and mathematics as useful for 'most' jobs, but science as being of more limited or restricted utility. As Pamela put it:

> I think it's different because English and maths are used more widely but science is like a thing that you . . . like unless you want to be a scientist, isn't as relevant to you.
>
> *(Pamela, Black British, lower-middle-class girl, Y9)*

Only Selena and Cristiano (who expressed aspirations in and from science, respectively) talked explicitly about the value of science more broadly, for scientific literacy rather than just for jobs:

> Cos like science is like . . . you need a lot . . . like even for humans, like if there was no science there would be no humans . . . You know like trees yeah, how they give us oxygen like . . . if people didn't know that yeah, they'll be just cutting trees and then humans start dying and that.
>
> *(Selena, Black British, working-class girl, Y9)*

> Science like comes in everyday life when you're buying something and like it just gives you a little bit more information for when you're like going to the shops and you need to know where it's come from and stuff and you need to know what you need to look out for and stuff.
>
> *(Cristiano, Black British, working-class boy, Y9)*

Vanessa (Black British, lower-middle-class girl) was slightly more ambivalent in her Y6 interview, saying 'science doesn't help you quite a lot in life, but it does help a tiny bit so I do try to make an even chance of learning each thing'. But by Year 9 she also recognised the importance of science for everyday life and saw it as useful for careers both in and beyond science.

As we found in the wider student sample, young people who see science qualifications as transferable are (i) more likely to have close family members with science degrees and/or who have worked in science-related fields and (ii) more likely to plan to study science post-16 and/or aspire to careers in or from science. Some Black parents recognised that they personally lacked knowledge and awareness of where science can lead, and felt that this might be a disadvantage for themselves and their children.

> The problem is the lack of knowledge, the lack of awareness, where you know certain subjects like this can take them [children].
>
> *(Tasha, Black/White mixed race, lower-middle-class mother)*

For example, Bunmi (Black British, working-class mother of Jake) felt that she knew science could lead to a job as a scientist but did not actually have much of an idea what being a scientist involved, saying 'I don't know the jobs they do anyway when they're a scientist'. She wanted more career advice for children like her son.

Cristiano also commented in his Y9 interview that the government should 'introduce more jobs that include science. Cos like no one really . . . like understands like what job you can get like if you're going to take a subject.'

Two: Science and scientists as 'brainy': racialised discourses around 'cleverness'

Irrespective of their personal levels of attainment, interest and aspirations in science, Black students in the interview sample tended to construct science as a 'hard' and 'difficult' subject:

> I think it[science]'s like quite hard to like understand and like you have to remember all the theories and stuff like that and like your dates and things . . . like there's like more to remember and I'm like not very like good at remembering a lot of stuff.
>
> *(Pamela, Black British, lower-middle-class girl, Y9)*

> Physics, I still don't like though . . . it just seems too complicated and I just don't get it.
>
> *(Kelsey, Black British, working-class girl, Y9)*

> Sometimes science can be difficult because you don't really know what the answer is for sure . . . sometimes when you're doing science like you don't really understand what you're getting taught because when you're doing science, they have like lots of words that you don't understand.
>
> *(Cristiano, Black British, working-class boy, Y9)*

In this respect, they expressed similar views to the wider sample, in which approximately 80% of students on the Year 6, 8 and 9 surveys agreed that 'scientists are brainy'. However, in the interviews, Black students were more likely than students from other ethnic backgrounds to agree that someone needs to be clever to be really into science, and were less likely to describe scientists as 'normal' people (see DeWitt et al., 2013a).

The students tended to describe those who are really into science as 'really, really smart' (Kelsey, Y9):

> I think it's the clever people.
>
> *(Vanessa, Black British, lower-middle-class girl, Y9)*

> I think the clever people [are into science] . . . to be good at science . . . you kind of do need to be clever really.
>
> *(Cristiano, Black British, working-class boy, Y9)*

They were also less likely than the British Asian students to self-identify as 'clever'. For instance, Cristiano explained that he could not actually imagine himself becoming a scientist because he did not consider himself one of the 'smartest' in the class:

> Cos . . . there's many people in my science class who are smarter than me. People think like science, you need to like be really really smart like. Cos some people – they like science and they're good at it, but they don't think they're good enough like to pursue it.

Despite attaining reasonably well (e.g. reporting attaining A and B grades) and being in the top and middle sets at school, Cristiano still felt that he was not exceptional enough to contemplate a career in science, saying 'I'm not that good at science but I'm all right'.

This feeling of not being 'clever' enough to pursue science further was also voiced by Gemma, who was in the top set for science and was attaining good grades (levels):

> Like only clever people do Triple [Science] . . . I'm in the top set for science but I'll still love to do Double Science, [but] I wouldn't love to do Triple, no . . . I'm a high level 6, low level 7 in science and in top set.
>
> *(Gemma, Black British, lower-middle-class girl, Y9)*

Notably, this quite stereotypical view was less commonly expressed by students from other ethnic backgrounds in the wider sample (DeWitt et al., 2013b). Our theoretical lens leads us to see 'cleverness' as a racialised, gendered and classed discourse, such that the identity of the 'ideal' or 'clever' student is not equally open to all students as a viable and authentic identity. Black students have been socially and historically constructed as 'bad' students, with Blackness being aligned with intellectual inferiority within dominant racist discourse (e.g. Mama, 1995). As Bourdieu (1996, 2010) discusses, the working classes are also positioned by the middle classes as 'stupid', and feminists have drawn attention to the alignment of masculinity with 'natural, effortless' intelligence and the association of femininity with 'plodding diligence' (Carlone, 2004). Hence, we suggest that the Black students' discourse can be read as revealing traces of their positioning at the nexus of these intersecting inequalities of ethnicity and social class, with the upshot being that they find it difficult to authentically inhabit the identity of the 'clever science student' due to being positioned as Other in classed and racialised ways through pervasive and institutionalised forms of racism (e.g. Ball, 2003; Crozier, 2009; Crozier and Davies, 2008; Gillborn and Mirza, 2000; Gillborn et al., 2012; Wright et al., 2010). Indeed, as noted in research conducted with minority ethnic middle-class young people and parents, Archer (2011, 2012) found that the dominant conflation of 'Blackness' with 'working-classness' is such that minority ethnic middle-class participants found it difficult to inhabit (and articulate) a 'middle-class Black' identity. To use Butler's (1990) phrasing, for Black students in particular, cleverness is often an 'impossible' identity due to the intersection of ethnic and classed inequalities.

Three: Inequalities in the social distribution of (science) capital

As noted in the first half of the chapter, the Black British students were generally categorised as having lower levels of science capital than the British Asian students in our interview sample. For instance, working-class mothers like Saadiah and Bunmi explained bluntly, 'I don't know about the science' (Saadiah) and 'I don't like it [science]' (Bunmi). Despite her nursing background, V, Gemma's mother, still found science hard and uninteresting: 'I will say I'm not interested in science, but like in nursing you have to have some . . . because everything we do in nursing you have to have some bit of science beside it, so I don't know really . . . I see science as difficult.' In this respect, they exhibited some similarity to the small number of urban under-privileged mothers in Calabrese Barton et al.'s (2001) study, who regarded science as an 'untouchable domain' and whose accounts were characterised by views of science as 'hard' and disliked.

Out of all the Black students in our study, only the four with science/science-related aspirations reported doing any science-related activities in their spare time. For example, in her Y6 interview, Selena (Black British, working-class girl) described replicating school experiments at home. She also looked up science quizzes and information on the computer and watched science-related television programmes. She also spoke of considerable science interest among her siblings, saying of her twin brother, Tom2, 'he always talks about science' and her older sister: 'She loves things about science . . . cos she's got lots of books about science.' Vanessa (Black British, lower-middle-class girl) also talked about using science kits and resources (e.g. a microscope) provided by her father.

That those children who reported doing more STEM-related activities in their leisure time were also those who expressed STEM aspirations suggests the potential recursive relationship between behaviours, interest and aspirations.

Interest may prompt children to be more likely to want to engage in particular types of leisure activity, but their exposure to and practise of particular science-related behaviours may also reinforce and prompt further interest, not least due to the development of particular competencies. As Azevedo (2011) argues, hobbies and regular leisure activities are important for the reinforcement and development of particular lines of interest. Yet it was also notable that, apart from Vanessa, the Black students' out-of-school STEM activities were very much self-led/initiated and tended to use resources that the young people themselves had sourced or accessed. This compares starkly with the highly resourced, often adult-organised, science-related experiences that were reported by the science-aspirant, White middle-class students in the wider study (see Chapter 5 and Archer et al., 2010a, 2012b).

The importance of capital for facilitating young people's attainment of their aspirations was underlined by Alan's mother Tasha. She talked eloquently and poignantly about the effects that a lack of capital, and an impoverished, difficult upbringing, had had on her own life. She was highly motivated to ensure that Alan could have a better life and recognised his need for support:

> He definitely needs support. I never had that, so I found it really difficult to try and find my place within society. I never knew what I wanted to do, I never knew what I could be . . . I was always confused . . . cos certain things wasn't nurtured in me. So I think that is really important and that's something that I've taken from my own experience to my children.
>
> *(Tasha, Black/White mixed race, lower-middle-class mother)*

To this end, Tasha had already begun researching potential IT degree courses and had found one in a city where Alan's aunt lived, which would enable Alan to live with her while studying, in order to reduce costs.

Several of the Black families in the qualitative sample appeared to be disadvantaged not only by a lack of science capital but also by lower possession of other types of capital too, compared to other families in the sample. For example, they tended to be among the more economically disadvantaged families in the sample, and parents in particular talked about a lack of cultural capital that hindered their ability to navigate the education system effectively. It was notable that those families who did enjoy more cultural capital, such as John's (whose family was severely economically disadvantaged but who had educational cultural capital as the result of having been a secondary school teacher in Nigeria), talked about their greater confidence in navigating the educational system and supporting their children's education.

John talked about the effects of disadvantage on his own life and his subsequent commitment to motivating and supporting his children to achieve better. He described himself as 'not good at science' and recounted how he was put off science by a friend at school, but now regrets not learning science. As he explained, due to being uneducated themselves, his own parents never realised that he was not attending classes, nor thought to check:

> Unfortunately my parents were not educated. They can't say 'What did you do today?' Just go to school, come back home [say] 'Good morning', that's all. They don't check my record, they don't check. Whether I actually attended something.
>
> *(John, Nigerian, working-class father)*

John had trained and worked as a teacher in Nigeria, but his qualifications were not recognised in the UK and he could not afford to re-train. He now worked as a low-paid care worker. He had a profound belief in the importance of education and paid for private tutoring for all his children in maths and English throughout the course of the project.

All the Black parents in the interview sample described pushing their children to achieve 'better lives' through social mobility. For some, this contained echoes of children attempting to fulfil thwarted parental aspirations. As Bunmi explained about her son Jake's aspiration to become an accountant: 'I don't want to discourage him . . . because I wanted to be an accountant as well.' But Bunmi also felt disadvantaged by a lack of cultural capital, as she didn't know what subjects Jake would need to study in order to become an accountant, nor whether he would need to go to university. The family did not know anyone who was an accountant, and Bunmi described being at a loss to understand the UK system and dependent upon the school for advice and help:

> Well in this country I don't really know what are they doing . . . I know in my country if you want to be an accountant or banker you have to be very good in maths and English . . . I don't know about this country you know . . . So if he say he want to be an accountant, I think they should be tell him in school the kind of subjects, what he's got to be good, what you have to be good in.
>
> *(Bunmi, Black British, working-class mother)*

In sum, we suggest that the disadvantaged structural location of Black families means that they are disproportionately likely to be excluded from the possession of science capital, which will negatively impact on the likelihood of the children developing or sustaining science aspirations. This is potentially an issue for all working-class families but may be amplified by the intersection of racial and class inequalities.

Black, female, low SES . . . and aspiring to a science career: the case of Selena and Vanessa

So far we have argued that it is not unusual or unexpected that most Black students in our qualitative sample did *not* aspire to science, because they are situated at the nexus of intersecting inequalities which render science 'unthinkable'.

As discussed earlier, at age 14 three Black boys aspired to STEM-related careers: Cristiano and Ali aspired to become doctors (although Ali primarily aspired to a career in business) and Alan aspired to a career in IT. Two Black British girls of Nigerian heritage, Selena and Vanessa, aspired to a career in science as forensic scientists. As Gramsci (1971) notes, no hegemony is ever complete – there are always spaces of resistance, transgression (Butler, 1990) and hope (Apple, 2013). But what, specifically, makes it possible for Selena and Vanessa to overcome the odds to aspire to careers in science?

As we discuss more fully in Archer et al. (2014b), the cases of Selena and Vanessa provide an encouraging illustration of how the hegemonic impossibility of 'scientist' as a viable and desirable identity for Black students is not absolute but can be disrupted and transgressed. There appear to be several factors at work which help prompt and sustain their science aspirations. Common to both of the girls are their enjoyment of school science and their academic orientation and motivation to behave and attain well at school. Both their families possess educational cultural capital and both girls also perform 'non-girly' gendered performances of self which, as discussed in Chapter 6, align with dominant performances of science identity. Both girls are part of academically like-minded close friendship groups and attend single-sex schools. They also both identified desirable images of Black female forensic scientists in the popular media (notably on the US television show *CSI Miami*). Selena also identified with, and performed, 'clever' student identity, and Vanessa's family possessed considerable science capital (e.g. her father holds an overseas science degree and works as a technician in a secondary school).

Both girls seem motivated to pursue their ambitions and have supportive families (although their mothers feel that forensic science is risky and would prefer them to follow a 'safer', more 'known' medical route). Yet we also note a potential precariousness to the girls' aspirations and identity work. First, their structural positioning as urban, Black working-class/lower-middle-class girls suggests that they will need to work extra hard to prove themselves and maintain their aspirations. Accounts from women of colour who are successful scientists highlight the ongoing difficulties and inequalities that challenge such women in their trajectories, requiring considerable resilience and support:

> In reality, these women have to fight for their identities, performing, developing, and achieving them again and again in different contexts and across time.
>
> *(Carlone and Johnson, 2007, p. 1208)*

Second, neither is single-minded in their aspirations. Other research notes that multiple and provisional, or future outcome-dependent, aspirations are a common pragmatic risk-management strategy among disadvantaged urban young people

(Archer et al., 2010b), but expressing and pursuing a single, consistent aspiration over time is more likely to lead to a young person successfully attaining that aspiration (Yates, 2008). Third, their aspirations to work in forensic science may be potentially risky choices. Forensic science has grown in popularity at degree level, which has led to such courses becoming competitive and oversubscribed.[5] Research indicates students attracted to forensic science as a result of television representations are likely to have unrealistic expectations of the course and may be at greater risk of non-completion (e.g. Weaver et al., 2012). There has been widespread concern about the closure of the UK public sector forensic science service in 2010,[6] with associated uncertainty regarding job outcomes for these graduates. Moreover, because forensic science is one of the more popular and 'glamorous' areas of science (as portrayed by *CSI*-style popular programmes), it is not clear whether the girls' science aspirations would transfer to other potential careers in or from science – i.e. would their perception of forensic scientists as potentially 'like me' extend more generally to all, or other sorts of, scientists? Fourth, both mothers appear to have some concerns about their daughters' aspirations to careers in forensic science and may not fully support this ambition. This may be particularly important given the emphasis placed by wider studies on family support as a predictor of post-compulsory science participation (e.g. Hanson, 2007; Mujtaba and Reiss, 2014).

Summary

In this chapter we have argued that similar factors promote or constrain the development and realisation of science aspirations across different ethnic groups – notably the interaction of science capital, family habitus and the 'brainy', White, male, middle-class image of science/scientists. However, intersections of ethnicity, gender and social class mean that these factors play out differently between British Asian and Black families and students, producing different patterns of aspiration and progression. Moreover, we suggest that social inequalities mean that the 'success' of minority ethnic students within science is never guaranteed and that these students and families may have to work extra hard, and mobilise considerable resources, in order to achieve their ambitions.

Notes

1 On this variable, White students had a mean of 13.3, whereas the mean for Asian students was 15.8 and Black students 14.4. An ANOVA revealed that the difference among these groups was significant, $F(5, 9313) = 41.98$, $p < .001$, and post-hoc comparisons (Bonferroni) reflected that the score of Black students was significantly lower than that of Asian students but significantly higher than that of White students. At the same time, it should be mentioned that ethnic categories had very low effect sizes (if they appeared at all) in the multi-level model of the aspirations in science composite variable, suggesting that while there are differences among groups, ethnicity is not as closely related to aspirations in science as other factors.

2 This variable contained the items: 'They want me to make a lot of money when I grow up'; 'They want me to get a good job when I grow up'; 'It is important to them that I get good marks in school'; 'They expect me to go to university'.
3 http://tisme-scienceandmaths.org/wp-content/uploads/2012/06/Mapping-and-Classification-of-STEM-Interventions.pdf (accessed 25/5/16).
4 See also the literature on stereotype threat e.g. Steele and Aronson (1995).
5 E.g. see media coverage such as www.timeshighereducation.co.uk/176350.article (accessed 25/5/16).
6 E.g. see www.publicsectorexecutive.com/Crime-reduction/government-must-protect-forensic-science--mps (accessed 25/5/16).

8

CONCLUSIONS AND IMPLICATIONS FOR RESEARCH, POLICY AND PRACTICE

Working with this cohort of students and families over five years has been a pleasure and a privilege. We would like to reiterate our profound thanks to the schools and teachers who enabled us to collect the many thousands of survey responses across the three waves of the study. We are particularly grateful to our interviewees, who have kindly let us follow their lives and have allowed us rich glimpses into their developing identities and aspirations. We have observed with fondness and pride as the students have grown, over time, from children into young adults. Indeed, it was with some sadness that we said goodbye to them and their parents at the end of the five years, not knowing whether we would be able to continue to follow their lives.

In this chapter we want to take the opportunity to reflect back, asking: what did we want to achieve in this research, and have we done this? We also want to look forward, to consider what our findings tell us about what could, and should, be done to improve participation in science education and to move towards greater equity.

Reflections: What have we learned? What have we contributed?

We set out, at the beginning of the study, to try to make sense of the various influences that shape children's science and career aspirations. We believe that our work has shed new light on this complex process, drawing out the tangled interweaving of identities and inequalities of gender, ethnicity and social class and how these shape the possibility and desirability of science within children's lives – that is, the extent to which children will see it as being 'for me' (or not).

Our analyses have highlighted how *interest in science, alone, does not explain patterns of differential aspiration*. Indeed, we were somewhat surprised to see the relatively high levels of interest in science that young people reported across the three surveys. We expected interest to be high in primary school, but we anticipated that there would be more of a drop-off in interest in the Y8 and Y9 surveys, reflecting concerns expressed in the wider literature that secondary school science is failing to engage young people (Barmby et al., 2008; Lyons, 2006; Osborne et al., 2003). Although educational research rarely produces 'good news' stories, our survey analyses suggest that, on the whole, schools in England are currently doing a good job in maintaining student interest in science during Key Stage 3 (early secondary years, 11–14), and we believe that this should be acknowledged (and celebrated!).

Our research also shows that *most young people have high aspirations – just not for science*. As discussed in Chapter 2, this finding challenges some dominant UK education policy views; it has, to date, been assumed that 'problems' of post-16 participation – particularly among working-class and minority ethnic communities – may be attributable to cultures of low aspiration. Indeed, our research shows clearly that Asian and Black students actually aspire to science careers more than White students. The challenge is, therefore, how we might better support and translate these aspirations into participation (particularly among Black students).

We have also found that *negative views of school science and scientists are not the main barrier to science aspiration and participation*. This finding challenges the premise of many existing interventions, which seek to raise participation by making science more 'fun' and/or by attempting to introduce young people to more positive images of scientists and scientist role models. As we discuss in the next section, on implications, it is not that we consider there to be anything 'wrong' with such approaches, but rather that our findings indicate that they are not necessarily tackling the main drivers of aspiration and are therefore insufficient in and of themselves to positively influence science aspirations.

We consider a particular contribution of our work, in both academic and practical terms, to be our conceptualisation of science capital. As discussed throughout the book, we have found that *science capital is a key influence on science aspirations*. Children from families with high science capital are more likely to aspire to continue with science post-16 – a pattern that holds both within and across social boundaries. For instance, despite their different social class, gender and ethnic locations, Robert M (White, upper-middle-class boy) and Vanessa (Black, lower-middle-class girl) both held higher levels of science capital and aspired to careers in science. In contrast, Gus (White, upper-middle-class boy) and Gemma (Black, lower-middle-class girl) held lower levels of science capital and never aspired to continue with science. This is not to say that we see science capital as deterministic (indeed, some students with high science capital did not aspire to science careers, although almost all did intend to take at least one science at A level). Rather, we consider science capital to be a major influence on students' aspirations, in that families with high science capital strongly value and promote science to their children and, crucially, weave it into everyday family life in ways that foster interest and familiarity with science and also provide a practical 'feel' for and identification with science. Hence science becomes not just 'something we do' but also part of 'who we are'.

Another key theme within the book is our analysis that *the 'brainy' image of science/science careers puts many young people off*. We contend that this is a particular issue for girls, working-class and Black students, who have been traditionally excluded from dominant notions of 'cleverness', in that the dominant discursive construction of the 'ideal student' is configured in ways that are associated with being White, male and middle class (Archer and Francis, 2007).

Indeed, we argue strongly that the *White, male, middle-class image of science careers remains a barrier to students' science aspirations*. Depressingly, decades of efforts aimed at improving this association appear to have had little effect, as we found that both students and parents alike associate science careers with this narrow demographic. In the following section we discuss potential ideas for tackling this issue.

As discussed in Chapter 6, we found that *girls have to work harder to manage their identities and to balance these with their science aspirations*. That is, science aspirations require girls to engage in considerably more identity work than is the case for boys because they need to find ways to reconcile performances of femininity with the 'masculine' nature of science. In line with other studies, we also found that girls are less likely to report being 'pushed' towards science by others. Girls who are planning to continue with science post-16 must engage in intensive and extensive identity work, in order to render science aspirations 'possible'. We suggest that it is not surprising that relatively few girls maintain science aspirations over time (particularly in relation to the most masculinised areas of science, such as physics), given the extensive identity work 'marathon' that is required to maintain and possibilise such aspirations.

A key motivation driving our conceptual approach has been to avoid a deficit view that 'blames' young people, particularly those from less privileged back-grounds, for their 'choices' and their non-participation in science. In this respect, we have taken a position that (i) treats science participation as a social justice issue (rather than, say, a concern to service the science 'pipeline'), (ii) values and fore-grounds the young people's and their parents' accounts, (iii) pays attention to the interplay of identities and inequalities/social structures, and (iv) considers the issues within a holistic frame, taking into account societal, policy, institutional and family factors – treating aspirations as socially produced and located phenom-ena. As we discuss next, this approach leads us to consider the implications (for 'improving' participation) across a number of levels.

Looking ahead: implications and potential ways forward

We hope that our study will have relevance and value for a range of audiences, including policy-makers, practitioners and researchers. In short, we hope that our work makes a useful and valuable contribution to both knowledge and the goal of achieving more equitable science participation. Rather than attempting to separate out specific messages for specific audiences, we have chosen to discuss our ideas thematically. This is because we find that many of the messages cut across boundaries and that often the boundaries between audiences are blurred or overlapping.

We have also deliberately tried to include ideas and potential implications that operate at a range of levels. That is, we try to include both some 'big' and some 'smaller' messages. The 'big' messages may not be immediately achievable, but we believe that it is important to articulate these, to contribute to building a vision, and staking out orientation points, for where policy and the science-education field need to be heading in the future. The 'smaller' messages are more tangible ideas that might be implemented more or less immediately, given appropriate contextual and resourcing scenarios. These 'smaller' messages might not change the world overnight, but we hope that they will enable discernible potential improvements and constitute part of the multi-front, multi-level approach to improving science participation that we are advocating. In this sense, to build on the metaphor that we introduce next, they can be conceptualised as providing 'oil' to the STEM-participation system, as well as working to help 'unstick' some of the many drivers of science participation that we have been investigating in our study.

A complex system – no silver bullet

We start with the somewhat depressing, yet unsurprising, conclusion that the 'problem' of inequitable science participation is produced through a complex system of interrelating factors that operate across a range of levels. To borrow a metaphor from engineering, we might conceptualise a system of multiple interlocking and overlaying gears (representing, for instance, education policy, institutional factors, gender, social class, ethnicity, science capital, out-of-school science learning contexts, the culture of physics, the media, the student, the family, and so on). Acting only on one part of the system (e.g. on one specific gear) will not necessarily make the whole system 'work', particularly if another key gear is 'stuck'. For instance, improving (e.g. diversifying, broadening) young people's images of scientists may be useful and important for various reasons, but action on this front alone is unlikely to have much impact on the system as a whole (and participation outcomes) while other, perhaps bigger, drivers remain firmly 'stuck'.

For instance, even if we managed to dramatically increase the proportion of young people aspiring to continue with physics post-16, the structure of the education system in England is unlikely to allow the majority to progress. As discussed earlier in the book, most young people are currently 'streamed' into GCSE science qualification routes that are unlikely to enable access to science A levels. Moreover, access to A-level physics tends to be much more tightly constrained (to those achieving A/A★ at GCSE) compared to other subjects (such as English, which tends to accept students with a much broader range of attainment). Finally, analysis suggests that A-level physics is graded more severely than other subjects (e.g. Thomson, 2015), which raises the question as to whether it is reasonable or even 'fair' to try to encourage more students to pursue the subject in the first place.

Changing the discourse: from 'raising aspirations' to 'enabling equitable aspirations'

As we have discussed in earlier chapters, our findings challenge mainstream education policy rhetoric in that we found no evidence of a widespread poverty of aspiration among young people, and we are critical of the enduring policy preoccupation with 'raising' young people's aspirations as a means to improve science participation. Indeed, the imperative to 'raise aspirations' not only conveys a blaming of particular communities for their positions of disadvantage, but also fails to acknowledge that the odds of attaining 'high' aspirations are unfairly stacked against those who occupy positions of social disadvantage. Instead, we feel a more fruitful way forward would be for policy and practice to focus on 'levelling the playing field', providing greater support to disadvantaged young people to develop and scaffold their aspirations and addressing some of the systems which work to reproduce relations of privilege and disadvantage. Like others (e.g. St Clair and Benjamin, 2011), we advocate a shift away from 'raising' aspirations towards 'supporting and enabling equitable aspirations', recognising that different students will require different amounts of support to enable them to access and navigate routes to achieving interesting and fulfilling and well-paid jobs. Indeed, we suggest that, without such support, students are likely to continue to fall into particular racialised, classed and gendered patterns of aspiration.

Shifting the focus: from 'increasing interest' to 'building science capital'

As we have previously discussed, our interpretation of the main discourses to date that have been driving much of the intervention work aimed at improving science participation is that these have been organised around the premise that increasing student interest in science will result in increased participation. Yet our analyses suggest that student interest in science is higher than previously assumed – and, importantly, there are numerous barriers to interest being realised or 'translated' into participation. We thus suggest that interventions will need to go beyond trying to make science more 'fun' if they are to have any sort of meaningful effect on science participation. Instead, we suggest that emphasis might usefully be shifted towards a project aimed at building the science capital of students and families.

Our contention raises a thorny conceptual issue: namely, is it possible to build capital? As we have reflected elsewhere (Archer et al., 2015), from a more sociological point of view, capital might be seen as part of the 'problem' and thus – along with the system that ascribes differential value to it – needs to be dismantled. Yet, from a more educational point of view, capital might be a tool for change, such that if we can increase the resources of the disadvantaged, they might be able to 'compete' better within society.

The approach we are advocating falls some way between these two imagined positions. We are interested in exploring the possibilities for both (i) changing the field within which capital is ascribed value and deployed, so that more diverse forms of capital are valued and can be leveraged in the context of science learning, and (ii) increasing individual student and family capital by finding ways to increase their symbolic (exchange-value) forms of science-related cultural and social capital. At the time of writing, we are currently developing, implementing and researching ways to realise these two aspects within the Enterprising Science project (www. kcl.ac.uk/enterprisingscience). This project involves working with secondary school science teachers to develop a 'science capital approach' to teaching, which seeks to embed and address the various dimensions of science capital within a teacher's everyday classroom practice. For instance, adopting a science capital approach might involve an explicit valuing of the different forms of knowledge, interest and experience that diverse students bring with them and then seeking ways to elicit, value and link these to science learning as part of everyday teaching. A science capital approach would also seek both to value students' use-value capital and also to cultivate particular 'high-value' forms of science capital (i.e. those with the greatest exchange value, that is, the potential for generating value across different contexts, but notably within the sphere of formal education). This would include various forms of scientific literacy, science-related attitudes, dispositions, social capital (e.g. fostering regular science-based conversations with others outside of school) and practices (e.g. watching science-related television, reading science books/magazines, going to an after-school science club).

We will discuss our ideas further through reference to the potential for building science capital through just one specific aspect of science capital, which falls broadly within the arena of science-related attitudes and dispositions, namely: *understanding the transferability and usefulness of science*. We have chosen this aspect because, first, it clearly relates to the findings from ASPIRES, in that we found that many students who do not see science as being 'for me' tend to perceive science qualifications as only really useful for those who want to become a scientist, science teacher or doctor. In contrast, students who aspire to careers in science tend to see science as a highly transferable qualification that is useful for 'any job'. Second, we believe that it represents an area of attitude/disposition that is relatively amenable to intervention. Indeed, an early exploration with one London school suggested that it is easier to change student attitudes about the transferability of science than, say, their aspirations – and that these changes seem to persist over time (Archer et al., 2014b).

We suggest that schools and STEM organisations could usefully support young people to appreciate the potential transferability of science qualifications, as one concrete means of helping to build their science capital. In our view, it would be helpful in this respect to do more to convey how science does not just lead to jobs in science, and that science skills are useful in all areas of life and can be relevant for a young person whatever they aspire to. We suggest that currently the bulk of interventions and promotional materials that we have come across tend to prioritise providing young people with information about careers in STEM (e.g. different types of science or engineering careers). We believe that it could be more useful to attempt to break the 'science = scientist' link, so that a greater spectrum of young people might be supported to see the potential relevance of science for their own lives, and to open up spaces and ways for young people to identify with science.

To this end, we suggest that schools, STEM organisations and careers professionals might usefully, instead, promote the message that 'science keeps your options open'. This could involve conveying to young people the vast spectrum of possible careers *from* science, not just careers *in* science (like scientist and doctor). In this respect, we are not suggesting that teachers or STEM organisations should seek to try to provide definitive information on the entirety of careers that science might be useful for. Rather, we are suggesting a shift in emphasis such that, rather than placing the main focus of intervention work on showing the existence, interest or attractiveness of particular STEM careers, the driving message should be to convey how science skills are useful for all. Of course, this approach calls into question another dominant discourse, namely the primacy of the 'STEM pipeline', which we discuss in the next subsection.

But how best to build young people's awareness of the transferability of science in practice? We suggest that, in line with our complex system metaphor, this might be most usefully achieved by action on more than one front. For instance, as discussed above, we are interested in the potential for science teachers to embed this form of capital into everyday science teaching through the messages that they convey – for instance, finding regular moments and spaces for students to consider how the content and skills they are learning have resonance and meaning beyond the classroom, both generally and in relation to their own lives, as well as explicitly valuing students' attempts to connect their own lives and experiences to what they are learning in the science classroom. STEM organisations will also have an important role to play and could consider how to promote key transferability messages within their outreach work and promotional materials.

We also suggest that students in England would benefit from more, better and earlier careers education. Indeed, our data suggest that the view of a career in science as being 'not for me' is already fairly solidified at primary school (despite students' enjoyment of science); hence we suggest that efforts to build science capital (and convey the transferability of science) need to start young and be threaded throughout all stages of education. There would thus seem to be a value in finding ways to stop the 'closing down' of aspirations that is evident even in primary-school-aged children, and supporting aspirations more equitably through the provision of high-quality careers education.

There are many different models for providing careers education, but the OECD (2012b) reports that high-performing countries usually have very good information, advice and guidance provision which is embedded in the school system. This can include not only the personalised support and guidance aspects but also more general forms of citizenship and cultural capital building (to help young people understand the wider system, the changing job market and how to navigate routes through education and employment).

Challenging the elitism of science: beyond the pipeline and the 'brainy' scientist

Our conceptual framework and our empirical findings lead us to believe that the 'elitism' of science constitutes a major block to more equitable science participation. Indeed, we suggest that the reproduction of science as a 'special' and powerful field sits in tension with efforts to diversify participation. As with any high-status area, entry to, and the boundaries of, the most prestigious aspects of science are tightly regulated and patrolled. For instance, as we have discussed earlier, entry to the most prestigious Triple Science route at GCSE and access to science A levels (particularly physics) are strictly controlled and limited to a small proportion of students. This regulation can also be observed at play within public and media debates, as exemplified, for instance, by the widespread media coverage in 2006 of leading figures (dubbed the 'science elite' by *The Times*) who condemned the introduction of a new science GCSE curriculum (21st Century Science) which was perceived to lack 'rigour' and be 'dumbing down' due to its focus on science and societal issues and discussion. Indeed, the curriculum was lambasted by Baroness Warnock for being 'more suitable for the pub than the schoolroom'. A central feature of the opposition to 21st Century Science was that it was perceived to be inadequate for servicing the STEM pipeline. We suggest that such practices are both symptomatic and constitutive of the elitism of science and illustrate the 'high stakes' nature of the field.

However, we find it difficult to conceive of how participation might be meaningfully widened (and made more equitable) while the elitism of science remains unchallenged. As discussed in various chapters throughout this book, the current dominant narrow culture and practices around science effectively work to 'weed out' those who do not, cannot or will not fit the White, male, middle-class, 'brainy' performance of science. For us, a more equitable vision of science participation will require science to give up its elitism – so that it is not just a case of demanding more square pegs to fit a square hole.

We consider that one important aspect of this task will be to *disrupt the dominance of the 'pipeline'* as the primary rationale for widening participation in science. Of course, our view reflects in no small part our own social-justice values and standpoint, which place goals of public scientific literacy, social mobility and the democratisation of science as being of greater importance than encouraging more young people to become scientists. However, we also see a pragmatic value in challenging the pipeline metaphor, not least given that the dominance of the pipeline (i.e. the view that studying science is primarily important for producing the next generation of scientists) is also part of the problem. In other words, as we have shown, it is part of the set of factors that are discouraging many students from continuing with science, even within the pipeline itself. The dominance of the pipeline has also had a profound effect on science education, shaping the nature and structure of what students encounter in their science classes – as exemplified by the existence of the Triple Science GCSE route in England. As Claussen and Osborne (2012) discuss, UK and US approaches to science education have tended to be orientated towards servicing the pipeline, which serves the few at the expense of the many.

Arguably, a science education system that is based on a pipeline model – of funnelling 'the best and the brightest' into science by erecting increasingly challenging barriers that students must overcome in order to continue their participation in the discipline – sits at odds with widening participation and equitable science participation. The pipeline of increasing selectivity (into Triple Science, onto A-level science) favours those with access to greater resources, thus contributing to the reproduction of privilege in the sciences. This pattern is also exacerbated by the image of science as being 'only for the clever' (see Chapter 4 in this book, as well as DeWitt et al., 2013a) – an image which is, of course, reinforced by the prerequisites of increasingly higher attainment needed to continue participation.

We suggest that a more useful metaphor is that of science education as a 'springboard', usefully preparing and equipping young people with skills and knowledge that will help them move through a multitude of pathways in life, including pathways within science. That is, conceiving of science as a springboard could serve multiple aims around science engagement and participation, encouraging increasing diversity among those working in occupations in and from STEM.

The second task that we want to consider is how we might challenge the prevalence of the *'brainy' image of science and scientists*. Instead, we suggest that a more equitable and useful image to organise science education around would be that of the 'everyday' scientist. That is, we would like to encourage schools and organisations to value and foreground how everyone is already scientific, highlighting the science skills that are deployed in everyday life, enabling students to bring a wide range of skills, competencies, interests and experiences to bear when doing science and valuing a greater spectrum of contexts within which science can be 'done' and more diverse ways of doing and being in science. This involves not only greater efforts to routinely represent the diversity of scientists (even a cursory glance at current popular science media reveals that the scientists represented on television and beyond are still predominantly White, male, middle class and 'brainy') but also greater valuing and prominence of 'lay' or 'non-professional' or 'becoming' scientists (e.g. young people) – in short, representations of the general public (in all their diversity) 'doing' science. Such reproductions or images could also be extended to highlight not only the diversity but also the 'everydayness' of practising scientists – as ordinary people with 'normal' lives (families, hobbies and so forth) who are motivated by interest in and curiosity to overcome the puzzles and challenges of science.

Third, we believe that more still needs to be done to *challenge and disrupt the White, male, middle-class image of science and scientist*. However, this is an inherently difficult project: undoubtedly there is value in making representations of science and scientists more diverse, but it needs to be accompanied by real improvements in the diversity of who actually does 'do' science (especially in areas like physics and engineering, post-16 and beyond). Efforts to broaden representations of science can also end up proverbially trapped between a rock and a hard place. For instance, a case might be made for the helpfulness of work that seeks to promote popular hetero-femininity as compatible with 'doing science' (e.g. as a way to help broaden possibilities for girls to identify with science). Yet such attempts can also meet with considerable resistance and derision (as in the case of the 'Science: It's a Girl Thing' video discussed in Chapter 4). For instance, they may be criticised for foregrounding narrow, stereotypical notions of femininity. Women scientists may also resist such representations as not reflecting their identities and/or for 'trivialising' their contributions to science and their authenticity as scientists. Indeed, as discussed by Francis et al. (forthcoming), the 'girly girl' is a particularly demonised and controversial discursive figure within the talk of parents and young people. Hence the task of how we deconstruct the association of science/scientists with masculinity remains challenging.

Foregrounding equity within schools

Our analyses highlight the urgent need to attend closely to what happens in the science classroom, in order to open up the space in which students can come to identify with science and to see themselves as 'science people'. But, in line with the Institute of Physics' *Opening doors* report (IOP, 2015), we feel that this might be most usefully achieved within the context of a whole-school equity approach. This is because science does not exist in a vacuum – a social-justice approach within the science classroom is much more likely to have a significant effect if it is also embedded and enacted within a wider school culture that shares these social-justice values and practices.

We do not have the space here to rehearse the wealth of literature (and the debates therein) on how schools might go about embedding a social-justice approach. However, we would provide the following pointers. The IOP (2015) report suggests a range of practical ways in which schools might usefully reflect on their 'gender climate' and practices in relation to science/physics. The work of Warrington and Younger (2000) is also highly instructive regarding how to adopt a general, whole-school gender-equity approach.

The work of Hayes and colleagues (2005) and Lingard (2005) on socially just, 'productive' pedagogies provides an excellent orientation for teachers wishing to ensure that their practice is beneficial to all students.

In terms of providing orientation points for science educators, we are particularly influenced by the exemplary work of Angela Calabrese Barton and colleagues in the US. This work reminds us of the central role that classroom experiences of science have in shaping the extent to which students identify – or not – with science (e.g. Basu and Calabrese Barton, 2007; Calabrese Barton and Tan, 2009; Carlone et al., 2014; Olitsky et al., 2010). Moreover, their work in informal science learning settings (e.g. after-school clubs, maker spaces) shows that it is possible to create and enact more empowering and democratised science learning spaces. Some of the most inspirational work to date has taken place in these settings, and we feel that the approaches and principles developed there could – and should – be applied to mainstream education. While doing so presents tremendous challenges, it also offers huge potential for enabling more equitable science participation. In particular, we advocate for approaches that support science educators to find ways to open up the possibilities for diverse students to be, and to be recognised as being, 'scientific'. While we are only beginning to explore these possibilities in our current work, we offer a preliminary set of questions for those, particularly teachers, working within mainstream education to use for reflection on the practices enacted in their own settings (see Appendix).

A dilemma for England: is early specialisation helpful?

We believe that our findings raise some fundamental questions for national education policy. For instance, is the current English system of early specialisation (through the Double/Triple Science routes at GCSE and A levels) really helpful for improving science participation? We suggest that the current arrangements seem to work against widened participation by restricting the pool of potential science students and by putting off the majority through the construction of science as 'only for the elite brainiest few'. Arguably, a more open, inclusive, less specialised system would result in greater, and broader, participation in science. Put differently, if the majority of students were allowed and encouraged – and even required – to continue with a greater number of subjects through to the end of compulsory schooling, more students would continue with science until that point and a greater diversity of those participating in science until the age of 18 would necessarily follow. We acknowledge that such a restructuring of the system carries with it tremendous costs – in terms of economic and human capital – but we feel it is critical to emphasise the systemic nature of the hurdles that must be overcome, including those created by early specialisation, in order for efforts to broaden participation in science to have a chance of success.

Conclusion: towards more equitable science participation

We hope that our study has shed some useful light on the complex web of factors that result in unequal patterns of participation in science. At the very least, we believe that our study has produced a substantial and valuable data-set that has the capacity to inform research, policy and practice. At the heart of this work are the views and experiences of young people. We hope that we have done some justice to the complexity of their lives. As Angela Calabrese Barton reminds us:

> When a child's worldview is left unvalued and expressionless in an educational setting, what should we expect in terms of engagement, investment and learning from that child?
>
> *(Barton et al., 2011, p. 4)*

We are now in the privileged position of being able to follow our cohort of young people for another five years, through the ASPIRES 2 project, from age 14 to 18. We look forward to continuing to track their experiences of, and views on, science and their future lives and the waxing and waning of their different identifications with (or dissociations from) science. We also hope that, in doing so, we might continue to produce insights that can contribute to creating a more inclusive and socially just science education that can positively transform the lives of all young people.

APPENDIX

Some starter reflection points for educators wanting to broaden science participation

The following are not meant to be exhaustive (!) but we hope that they provide some sort of starting point for discussion, either as an individual reflection tool or (even better) as potential questions to prompt peer reflection and talk within staff meetings.

Developing a better understanding of the issues in your setting

- What are the current patterns of participation in and engagement with science that you see in your setting? For example, who takes Triple/Double Science at GCSE? Who takes A-level physics/biology/chemistry? Who goes on to STEM apprenticeships? Who attends after-school STEM clubs? Are there patterns in terms of attainment? Are some groups 'under-participating' in some areas of science compared to their prior attainment? (E.g. the proportions of students gaining an A/A★ in different subjects at GCSE versus the proportion taking A levels in the same subjects)
- Who sees themselves (and is seen by others) as being a 'science person', and who does not? Are there patterns by gender, ethnicity, social class, etc.? Is it only the highest-attaining students who identify with science?
- How is science represented currently in your classes/school? E.g. what 'messages' about science are conveyed explicitly and implicitly (by the way staff and students talk about science, by curriculum materials, by visual displays, newsletters and by practices/procedures – e.g. entry criteria for subject options)? Is science seen as being 'hard'/difficult or is it seen as being open to all?
- What sort of visibility and profile does science currently have in your setting, compared to other subjects?

- What sort of science-capital profile do you think there might be among your students? How might this compare nationally? (See http://onlinelibrary. wiley.com/doi/10.1002/tea.21227/abstract, which shows about 5% of students aged 11–15 have high science capital and 27% have low science capital; the majority have medium levels of science capital.)

Thinking about practical changes

- How might lower-attaining students be better supported to see themselves as being scientific? (E.g. through the structure of working groups/pairs and tasks; by designing approaches that foreground the student as 'expert'; by using students' own diverse experiences and skills as the medium through which they 'do' science)
- How might science classes foreground a valuing of diverse identities and experiences within science? E.g. might there be scope for more eliciting and valuing of students' out-of-school experiences within science classes which can then be linked to the science content and skills being taught?
- How is the 'brainy' image of science/scientists reinforced or challenged in classes and in the school more generally? What sorts of materials and practices help challenge or reinforce these messages?
- To what extent is science learning represented and valued in terms of the pipeline or as a springboard for life? How might the springboard analogy be conveyed more effectively to students?
- How might you enable more girls to get sustained encouragement from a key adult over time to help motivate and support them to continue with physics/engineering?
- How might the message that 'science keeps your options open' (science is transferable and useful for life/any career) be embedded within everyday science teaching?
- Are there ways to help students to access earlier careers education? Is careers education conveying the message that science is transferable and a springboard? Are girls being encouraged into STEM apprenticeships as much as boys? If not, could this be addressed?
- How might students be supported (in science classes and beyond) to connect science with their own lives? For instance, how might classroom science teaching help students to make meaningful connections between their own current (and future) lives and what they encounter in the curriculum? If you would like to share the concept of science capital with colleagues, the following link provides an accessible two-minute animation summary: www. youtube.com/watch?v=A0t70bwPD6Y

BIBLIOGRAPHY

AAUW (American Association of University Women). (2010). *AAUW annual report.* Washington, DC: AAUW.

ACOLA (Australian Council of Learned Academies). (2013). *STEM: Country comparisons.* Melbourne: ACOLA.

Adler-Nissen, R., Hassing Nielsen, J., and Sørensen, C. (2012). *The Danish EU presidency 2012: A midterm report.* Stockholm: Swedish Institute for European Policy Studies (SIEPS).

Alldred, P., and Burman, E. (2005). Analysing children's accounts using discourse analysis. In S. M. Greene and D.M. Hogan (Eds.), *Researching children's experience: Approaches and methods.* London: Sage.

Anderson, B. (1992). *Imagined communities.* London: Verso.

Anthias, F. (2001). New hybridities, old concepts: The limits of 'culture'. *Ethnic and Racial Studies, 24*(4), 619–641.

Anthias, F., and Yuval-Davis, N. (1992). *Racialized boundaries: Race, nation, gender, colour and class and the anti-racist struggle.* London: Routledge.

Apple, M.W. (2013). *Can education change society?* New York: Routledge.

Archer, L. (2003). *Race, masculinity and schooling: Muslim boys and education.* Maidenhead: Open University Press.

Archer, L. (2008). The impossibility of minority ethnic educational 'success'? An examination of the discourses of teachers and pupils in British secondary schools. *European Educational Research Journal, 7*(1), 89–107.

Archer, L. (2010). 'We raised it with the Head': The educational practices of minority ethnic, middle-class families. *British Journal of Sociology of Education, 31*(4), 449–469.

Archer, L. (2011). Constructing minority ethnic middle-class identity: An exploratory study with parents, pupils and young professionals. *Sociology, 45*(1), 134–151.

Archer, L. (2012). 'Between authenticity and pretension': Parents', pupils' and young professionals' negotiations of minority ethnic middle-class identity. *Sociological Review, 60*(1), 129–148.

Archer, L. (2014). Conceptualising aspiration. In A. Mann, J. Williams and L. Archer (Eds.), *Understanding employer engagement in education: Theories and evidence.* London: Routledge.

Archer, L., and Yamashita, H. (2003). 'Knowing their limits'? Identities, inequalities and inner city school leavers' post-16 aspirations. *Journal of Education Policy, 18*(17), 53–69.

Archer, L., and Francis, B. (2007). *Understanding minority ethnic achievement.* London: Routledge.

Archer, L., Hutchings, M., and Ross, A. (2003). *Higher education and social class.* London: RoutledgeFalmer.

Archer, L., Hollingworth, S., and Halsall, A. (2007). 'University's not for me – I'm a Nike person': Urban, working class young people's negotiations of 'style', identity and educational engagement. *Sociology, 4*(2), 219–237.

Archer, L., DeWitt, J., Osborne, J., Dillon, J., Willis, B., and Wong, B. (2010a). 'Doing' science versus 'being' a scientist: Examining 10/11-year-old schoolchildren's constructions of science through the lens of identity. *Science Education, 94*(4), 617–639.

Archer, L., Hollingworth, S., and Mendick, H. (2010b). *Urban youth and schooling.* Maidenhead: Open University Press.

Archer, L., DeWitt, J., Osborne, J., Dillon, J., Willis, B., and Wong, B. (2012a). 'Balancing acts': Elementary school girls' negotiations of femininity, achievement, and science. *Science Education, 96*(6), 967–989.

Archer, L., DeWitt, J., Osborne, J., Dillon, J., Willis, B., and Wong, B. (2012b). Science aspirations, capital, and family habitus: How families shape children's engagement and identification with science. *American Educational Research Journal, 49*(5), 881–908.

Archer, L., DeWitt, J., Osborne, J., Dillon, J., Willis, B., and Wong, B. (2013). 'Not girly, not sexy, not glamorous': Primary school girls' and parents' constructions of science aspirations. *Pedagogy, Culture and Society, 21*(1), 171–194.

Archer, L., DeWitt, J., and Willis, B. (2014a). Adolescent boys' science aspirations: Masculinity, capital, and power. *Journal of Research in Science Teaching, 51*(1), 1–30.

Archer, L., DeWitt, J., and Osborne, J. (2014b). Is science for us? Black students' and parents' views of science and science careers. *Science Education, 99*(2), 199–237.

Archer, L., DeWitt, J., and Wong, B. (2014c). Spheres of influence: What shapes young people's aspirations at age 12/13 and what are the implications for education policy? *Journal of Education Policy, 29*(1), 58–85.

Archer, L., Dawson E., DeWitt, J., Seakins, A., and Wong, B. (2015). Science capital: A conceptual, methodological, and empirical argument for extending Bourdieusian notions of capital beyond the arts. *Journal of Research in Science Teaching,* buff. ly/1LNleLK.

Archer, L., Moote, J., Francis, B., DeWitt, J., and Yeomans, L. (forthcoming). The 'exceptional' physics/engineering girl: A sociological analysis of longitudinal data from girls aged 10–16 to explore gendered patterns of post-16 participation.

Aschbacher, P.R., Li, E., and Roth, E.J. (2010). Is science me? High school students' identities, participation and aspirations in science, engineering, and medicine. *Journal of Research in Science Teaching, 47*(5), 564–582.

Atherton, G., Cymbir, E., Roberts, K., Page, L., and Remedios, R. (2009). *How young people formulate their views about the future: Exploratory research.* London: Department for Children, Schools and Families.

Attwood, G., and Croll, P. (2011). Attitudes to school and intentions for educational participation: An analysis of data from the longitudinal survey of young people in England. *International Journal of Research and Method in Education, 34*(3), 269–287.

Atwater, M.M. (2000). Females in science education: White is the norm and class, language, lifestyle and religion are nonissues. *Journal of Research in Science Teaching, 37*(4), 386–387.

Atwater, M.M., and Simpson, R.D. (1984). Cognitive and affective variables affecting black freshmen in science and engineering at a predominately white university. *School Science and Mathematics, 84*(2), 100–112.

Avraamidou, L. (2013). Superheroes and supervillains: Reconstructing the mad scientist stereotype in school science. *Research in Science and Technological Education, 31*(1), 90–115.

Azevedo, F.S. (2011). Lines of practice: A practice-centered theory of interest relationships. *Cognition and Instruction, 29*(2), 147–184.

Baker, D. (1998). Equity issues in science education. In B.J. Fraser and K.G. Tobin (Eds.), *International handbook of science education* (pp. 869–896). Boston, MA: Kluwer.

Ball, S.J. (2003). *Class strategies and the education market.* London: RoutledgeFalmer.

Ball, S., Maguire, M., and Macrae, S. (2000). *Choices, transitions and pathways.* London: Falmer Press.

Barman, C.R. (1999). Students' views about scientists and school science: Engaging K-8 teachers in a national study. *Journal of Science Teacher Education, 10*(1), 43–54.

Barmby, P., Kind, P.M., and Jones, K. (2008). Examining changing attitudes in secondary school science. *International Journal of Science Education, 30*(8), 1075–1093.

Barton, A.C., Basu, J., Johnson, V., and Tan, E. (2011). Introduction. In J. Basu, A.C. Barton and E. Tan (Eds.), *Democractic Science Teaching.* Rotterdam: Sense Publishers.

Basu, S.J., and Calabrese Barton, A. (2007). Developing a sustained interest in science among urban minority youth. *Journal of Research in Science Teaching, 44*(3), 466–489.

Basu, S.J., Calabrese Barton, A., and Tan, E. (Eds.). (2011). *Democratic science teaching.* Rotterdam: Sense Publishers.

Bauman, Z. (2000). *Liquid modernity.* London: John Wiley & Sons.

Beck, U., and Beck-Gernsheim, E. (2004). Families in a runaway world. In J. Scott, J. Treas and M. Richards (Eds.), *The Blackwell companion to the sociology of families* (pp. 419–554). Oxford: Blackwell Publishing.

Bell, J., Donnelly, J., Homer, M., and Pell, G. (2009a). Using the National Pupil Database to evaluate curriculum innovation in science. *British Educational Research Journal, 35*(1), 119–136.

Bell, P., Lewenstein, B., Shouse, A.W., and Feder, M.A. (Eds.). (2009b). *Learning science in informal environments: People, places, pursuits.* Washington, DC: National Academies Press.

Bennett, J., and Hogarth, S. (2009). Would you want to talk to a scientist at a party? High school students' attitudes to school science and to science. *International Journal of Science Education, 31*(14), 1975–1998.

BIS (Department for Business, Innovation and Skills). (2009). *The demand for science, technology, engineering and mathematics (STEM) skills.* London: BIS.

Boaler, J., and Sengupta-Irving, T. (2006). Nature, neglect and nuance: Changing accounts of sex, gender and mathematics. In C. Skelton and L. Smulyan (Eds.), *Gender and education: International handbook* (pp. 207–220). London: Sage.

Bøe, M.V. (2011). Science choices in Norwegian upper secondary school: What matters? *Science Education, 96*(1), 1–20.

Bourdieu, P. (1984). *Distinction: A social critique of the judgement of taste.* Cambridge, MA: Harvard University Press.

Bourdieu, P. (1990). *In other words: Essays toward a reflexive sociology.* Cambridge: Polity Press.

Bourdieu, P. (2001). *Masculine domination.* Cambridge: Polity Press.

Bourdieu, P. (1996/2010). The myth of 'globalization' and the European welfare state. In G. Sapiro (Ed.), *Sociology is a martial art.* New York: New Press.

Bourdieu, P. (2010). *Sociology is a martial art*. New York: New Press.

Bourdieu, P., and Passeron, J.C. (1990). *Reproduction in education, society and culture*. London: Sage.

Bourdieu, P., and Wacquant, L. (1992). *An invitation to reflexive sociology*. Chicago, IL: University of Chicago Press.

Brannen, J., and Nilsen, A. (2007). Young people, time horizons and planning: A response to Anderson et al. *Sociology, 41*(1), 153–160.

Brickhouse, N.W., and Potter, J.T. (2001). Young women's scientific identity formation in an urban context. *Journal of Research in Science Teaching, 38*(8), 965–980.

Brickhouse, N.W., Lowery, P., and Schultz, K. (2000). What kind of a girl does science? The construction of school science identities. *Journal of Research in Science Teaching, 37*(5), 441–458.

Brown, P., and Hesketh, A. (2004). *The mismanagement of talent employability and jobs in the knowledge economy*. Oxford: Oxford University Press.

Buck, G.A., Leslie-Pelecky, D., and Kirby, S.K. (2002). Bringing female scientists into the elementary classroom: Confronting the strength of elementary students' stereotypical images of scientists. *Journal of Elementary Science Education, 14*(2), 1–9.

Buck, G.A., Plano Clark, V.L., Leslie-Pelecky, D., Lu, Y., and Cerda-Lizarraga, P. (2008). Examining the cognitive processes used by adolescent girls and women in identifying science role models: A feminist approach. *Science Education, 92*(4), 688–707.

Burman, E., and Parker, I. (Eds.). (1993). *Discourse analytic research: Repertoires and readings of texts in action*. London: Routledge.

Burns, J. (2014). Embrace engineering's creative side to fix skills crisis. BBC News, www.bbc.co.uk/news/education-30136921 (accessed 21 December 2015).

Butler, J. (1990). *Gender trouble: Feminism and the subversion of identity*. London: Routledge.

Butler, J. (1993). *Bodies that matter: On the discursive limits of sex*. London: Routledge.

Cakmakci, G., Tosun, O., Turgut, S., Orenler, S., Sengul, K., and Top, G. (2011). Promoting an inclusive image of scientists among students: Towards research evidence-based practice. *International Journal of Science and Mathematics Education, 9*(3), 627–655.

Calabrese Barton, A., and Brickhouse, N.W. (2006). Engaging girls in science. In C. Skelton, B. Francis and L. Smulyan (Eds.), *Handbook of gender and education* (pp. 221–235). Thousand Oaks, CA: Sage.

Calabrese Barton, A., and Tan, E. (2009). Funds of knowledge and discourses and hybrid space. *Journal of Research in Science Teaching, 46*(1), 50–73.

Calabrese Barton, A., and Tan, E. (2010). We Be Burnin'! Agency, identity, and science learning. *Journal of the Learning Sciences, 19*(2), 187–229.

Calabrese Barton, A., Hinden, T., Contento, I., Treadeau, M., Hagiwara, S., and Yang, K. (2001). Underprivileged mothers' views on science. *Journal of Research in Science Teaching, 38*(6), 688–711.

Calabrese Barton, A., Tan, E., and Rivet, A. (2008). Creating hybrid spaces for engaging school science among urban middle school girls. *American Educational Research Journal, 45*(1), 68–103.

Carlone, H.B. (2003). (Re)producing good science students: Girls' participation in high school physics. *Journal of Women and Minorities in Science and Engineering, 9*(1), 17–34.

Carlone, H.B. (2004). The cultural production of science in reform-based physics: Girls' access, participation, and resistance. *Journal of Research in Science Teaching, 41*(4), 392–414.

Carlone, H.B., and Johnson, A. (2007). Understanding the science experiences of successful women of color: Science identity as an analytic lens. *Journal of Research in Science Teaching, 44*(8), 1187–1218.

Carlone, H.B., Cook, M., Wong, J., Sandoval, W.A., Barton, A.C., and Tan, E. (2008). Seeing and supporting identity development in science education. *Proceedings of the 8th International Conference on the Learning Sciences: Volume 3* (pp. 214–220). Utrecht: International Society of the Learning Sciences.

Carlone, H.B., Haun-Frank, J., and Webb, A. (2011). Assessing equity beyond knowledge- and skills-based outcomes: A comparative ethnography of two fourth-grade reform-based science classrooms. *Journal of Research in Science Teaching, 48*(5), 459–485.

Carlone, H.B., Scott, C.M., and Lowder, C. (2014). Becoming (less) scientific: A longitudinal study of students' identity work from elementary to middle school science. *Journal of Research in Science Teaching, 51*(7), 836–869.

CBI (Confederation of British Industry). (2010). *Ready to grow: Business priorities for education and skills. Education and skills survey.* London: CBI.

CBI (Confederation of British Industry). (2011). *Ready to grow: Business priorities for education and skills. Education and skills survey.* London: CBI.

CBI (Confederation of British Industry). (2012). *Learning to grow: What employers need from education and skills. Education and skills survey.* London: CBI.

Chambers, D.W. (1983). Stereotypic images of the scientist: The draw-a-scientist test. *Science Education, 67*(2), 255–265.

Charlesworth, S. (2000). *Bourdieu, social suffering and working-class life.* Oxford: Blackwell Publishing.

CIHE (Council for Industry and Higher Education). (2009). *The demand for STEM graduates and post-graduates.* London: CIHE.

Claussen, S., and Osborne, J. (2012). Bourdieu's notion of cultural capital and its implications for the science curriculum. *Science Education, 97*(1), 58–79.

Cleaves, A. (2005). The formation of science choices in secondary school. *International Journal of Science Education, 27*(4), 471–486.

Collins, P.H. (2000). *Black feminist thought: Knowledge, consciousness, and the politics of empowerment.* New York and London: Routledge.

Congressional Commission on the Advancement of Women and Minorities in Science, Engineering and Technology Development (CAWMSET). (2000). *Land of plenty: Diversity as America's competitive edge in science, engineering and technology.* Arlington, VA: National Science Foundation.

Crenshaw, K. (1989). Demarginalizing the intersection of race and sex: A Black feminist critique of antidiscrimination doctrine, feminist theory and antiracist politics. *The University of Chicago Legal Forum, 140*, 139–167.

Croll, P. (2008). Occupational choice, socio-economic status and educational attainment: A study of the occupational choices and destinations of young people in the British Household Panel Survey. *Research Papers in Education, 23*(3), 243–268.

Croll, P., Attwood, G., and Fuller, C. (2011). *Children's lives, children's futures.* London: Continuum.

Crowley, K. (1999). Parent explanations during museum visits: Gender differences in how children hear informal science. *Visitor Studies Today, 3*(3), 21–28.

Crowley, K., Callanan, M.A., Tenenbaum, H.R., and Allen, E. (2001). Parents explain more often to boys than to girls during shared scientific thinking. *Psychological Science, 12*(3), 258–261.

Crozier, G. (2009). 'The girls will get married and the lads will go to the restaurants': Teacher expectations or parent aspirations? Exploding the myths about Asian parents' expectations of their children. *Theory into Practice (TIP), 48*(4), 290–296.

Crozier, G., and Davies, J. (2008). 'The trouble is they don't mix': Self-segregation or enforced exclusion? Teachers' constructions of South Asian students. *Race, Ethnicity and Education, 11*(3), 285–301.

Delamont, S., Benyon, J., and Atkinson, P. (1988). In the beginning was the Bunsen: The foundations of secondary school science. *Qualitative Studies in Education, 1*(4), 315–328.

DeWitt, J., and Archer, L. (2015). Who aspires to a science career? A comparison of survey responses from primary and secondary school students. *International Journal of Science Education, 37*(13), 2170–2192.

DeWitt, J., Osborne, J., Dillon, J., Willis, B., and Wong, B. (2010). High aspirations but low progression: The science aspirations–career paradox amongst minority ethnic students. *International Journal of Science and Mathematics Education, 9*(2), 243–271.

DeWitt, J., Archer, L., Osborne, J., Dillon, J., Willis, B., and Wong, B. (2011). High aspirations but low progression: The science aspirations–careers paradox among minority ethnic students. *International Journal of Science and Mathematics Education, 9*(2), 243–271.

DeWitt, J., Archer, L., and Osborne, J. (2013a). Nerdy, brainy and normal: Children's and parents' constructions of those who are highly engaged with science. *Research in Science Education, 43*(4), 1455–1476.

DeWitt, J., Osborne, J., Archer, L., Dillon, J., Willis, B., and Wong, B. (2013b). Young children's aspirations in science: The unequivocal, the uncertain and the unthinkable. *International Journal of Science Education, 35*(6), 1037–1063.

DeWitt, J., Archer, L., and Osborne, J. (2014). Science-related aspirations across the primary–secondary divide: Evidence from two surveys in England. *International Journal of Science Education, 36*(10), 1609–1629.

DfE (Department for Education). (2010). *The importance of teaching: The schools white paper 2010.* London: Her Majesty's Stationery Office.

DfE (Department for Education). (2012). *Subject progression from GCSE to AS level and continuation to A level.* Research Report DFE-RR195. London: DfE.

DfE (Department for Education). (2014). *Statistical first release: GCSE and equivalent attainment by pupil characteristics in England, 2012/2013.* London: DfE.

DfES (Department for Education and Skills). (2003). *Using the national healthy school standard to raise boys' achievement.* Wetherby: Health Development Agency.

DfES (Department for Education and Skills). (2004). *Schools race equality policies: From issues to outcomes.* London: Her Majesty's Stationery Office.

DfES (Department for Education and Skills). (2005). *Higher standards, better schools for all: More choice for parents and pupils.* London: Her Majesty's Government.

Dick, T.P., and Rallis, S.F. (1991). Factors and influences on high school students' career choices. *Journal for Research in Mathematics Education, 22*(4), 281–292.

Dorr, A., and Lesser, G.S. (1980). Career awareness in young children. *Communication Research and Broadcasting, 3*, 36–75.

Driver, R., Leach, J., Millar, R., and Scott, P. (1996). *Young people's images of science.* Buckingham: Open University Press.

Durant, J. (1993). What is scientific literacy? In J. Durant and J. Gregory (Eds.), *Science and culture in Europe.* London: Science Museum.

Eccles, J.S. (1993, March). *Parents as gender-role socializers during middle childhood and adolescence.* Paper presented at the Society for Research on Child Development Biennial Meeting, New Orleans, LA.

Edgar, D. (2004). Globalization and Western bias in family sociology. In J. Scott, J. Treas and M. Richards (Eds.), *The Blackwell companion to the sociology of families* (pp. 3–16). Oxford: Blackwell Publishing.

Elias, P., Jones, P., and McWhinnie, S. (2006). *Representation of ethnicity groups in chemistry and physics*. London: Royal Society of Chemistry and Institute of Physics.

Elliot, S., and Umberson, D. (2004). Recent demographic trends in the US and implications for well-being. In J. Scott, J. Treas and M. Richards (Eds.), *The Blackwell companion to the sociology of families* (pp. 34–53). Oxford: Blackwell Publishing.

Epstein, D., Mendick, H., and Moreau, M.P. (2010). Imagining the mathematician: Young people talking about popular representations of maths. *Discourse Studies in the Cultural Politics of Education, 31*(1), 45–60.

Ferry, T.R., Fouad, N.A., and Smith, P.L. (2000). The role of family context in a social cognitive model for career-related choice behavior: A math and science perspective. *Journal of Vocational Behavior, 57*(3), 348–364.

Finson, K.D. (2002). Drawing a scientist: What we do and do not know after fifty years of drawings. *School Science and Mathematics, 102*(7), 335–345.

Flick, L. (1990). Scientist in residence program improving children's image of science and scientists. *School Science and Mathematics, 90*(3), 204–214.

Flouri, E., and Panourgia, C. (2012). *Do primary school children's career aspirations matter? The relationship between family poverty, career aspirations, and emotional and behavioural problems*. London: Centre for Longitudinal Studies, Institute of Education.

Faucault, M. (1978). *The history of sexuality*. London: Penguin.

Francis, B. (2000a). *Boys, girls and achievement: Addressing the classroom issues*. London: Routledge.

Francis, B. (2000b). The gendered subject: Students' subject preferences and discussions of gender and subject ability. *Oxford Review of Education, 26*(1), 35–48.

Francis, B. (2005). Not/knowing their place: Girls' classroom behaviour. In G. Lloyd (Ed.), *'Problem' girls: Understanding and supporting troubled and troublesome girls* (pp. 9–21). London: RoutledgeFalmer.

Francis, B. (2009). The role of the boffin as abject other in gendered performances of school achievement. *Sociological Review, 57*(4), 645–669.

Francis, B. (2010). Re/theorising gender: Female masculinity and male femininity in the classroom? *Gender and Education, 22*(6), 477–490.

Francis, B., Skelton, C., and Read, B. (2010). The simultaneous production of educational achievement and popularity: How do some pupils accomplish it? *British Educational Research Journal, 36*(2), 317–340.

Francis, B., Skelton, C., and Read, B. (2012). *The identities and practices of high achieving pupils: Negotiating achievement and peer cultures*. London: Continuum.

Francis, B., Archer, L., and Moote, J. (forthcoming). Femininity, science, and the denigration of the girly girl.

Frome, P.M., and Eccles, J.S. (1998). Parents' influence on children's achievement-related perceptions. *Journal of Personality and Social Psychology, 74*(2), 435–452.

Frosh, S., Phoenix, A., and Pattman, R. (2002). *Young masculinities: Understanding boys in contemporary society*. Basingstoke: Palgrave Macmillan.

Fuller, C. (2009). *Sociology, gender and educational aspirations: Girls and their ambitions*. London: Continuum.

Furman, M., and Calabrese Barton, A. (2006). Capturing urban student voices in the creation of a science mini-documentary. *Journal of Research in Science Teaching, 43*(7), 667–694.

Gartland, C. (2015). Student ambassadors: 'Role models', learning practices and identities. *British Journal of Sociology of Education, 36*(8), 1192–1211.

Gee, J.P. (1996). *Social linguistics and literacies*. London: Taylor & Francis.

George, R. (2006). A cross-domain analysis of change in students' attitudes toward science and attitudes about the utility of science. *International Journal of Science Education, 28*(6), 571–589.

Gillborn, D., and Mirza, H.S. (2000). *Educational inequality: Mapping race, class and gender.* London: Office for Standards in Education (Ofsted).

Gillborn, D., Rollock, N., Vincent, C., and Ball, S.J. (2012). 'You got a pass, so what more do you want?' Race, class and gender intersections in the educational experiences of the Black middle class. *Race Ethnicity and Education, 15*(1), 121–139.

Gilmartin, S.K., Li, E., and Aschbacher, P. (2006). The relationship between secondary students' interest in physical science or engineering, science class experiences, and family contexts: Variations by gender and race/ethnicity. *Journal of Women and Minorities in Science and Engineering, 12*(2–3), 179–207.

Goldthorpe, J. (1996). Class analysis and the reorientation of class theory: The case of persisting differentials in educational attainment. *British Journal of Sociology of Education, 47*(3), 481–505.

Gorard, S., and See, B.H. (2009). The impact of socio-economic status on participation and attainment in science. *Studies in Science Education, 45*(1), 93–129.

Gorard, S., See, B.H., and Davies, P. (2012). *The impact of attitudes and aspirations on educational attainment and participation.* University of Birmingham: Joseph Rowntree Foundation.

Gramsci, A. (1971). *Selections from the prison notebooks.* London: Lawrence & Wishart.

Greenwood, C., Harrison, M., and Vignoles, A. (2011). *The labour market value of STEM qualifications and occupations.* London: Royal Academy of Engineering.

Griffin, C. (1985). *Typical girls.* London: Routledge.

Gutman, L.M., and Schoon, I. (2012). Correlates and consequences of uncertainty in career aspirations: Gender differences among adolescents in England. *Journal of Vocational Behavior, 80*(3), 608–618.

Hall, S. (1990). Cultural identity and diaspora. In J. Rutherford (Ed.), *Identity: Community, culture, difference* (pp. 392–403). London: Lawrence & Wishart.

Hall, S. (1992). New ethnicities. In J. Donald and A. Rattansi (Eds.), *Race, culture and difference* (pp. 252–259). London: Sage.

Hall, S. (1996). Introduction: Who needs 'identity'? In S. Hall and P. du Gay (Eds.), *Questions of cultural identity* (pp. 1–17). London: Sage.

Hannover, B., and Kessels, U. (2004). Self-to-prototype matching as a strategy for making academic choices: Why high school students do not like math and science. *Learning and Instruction, 14*(1), 51–67.

Hanson, S. (2004). African American women in science: Experiences from high school through the postsecondary years and beyond. *National Women's Studies Association Journal, 16*, 96–115.

Hanson, S. (2007). Success in science among young African American women: The role of minority families. *Journal of Family Issues, 28*(1), 3–33.

Hanson, S. (2009). *Swimming against the tide: African American girls and science education.* Philadelphia, PA: Temple University Press.

Hanson, S.L., and Palmer-Johnson, E. (2000). Expecting the unexpected: A comparative study of African American women's experiences in science during the high school years. *Journal of Women and Minorities in Science and Engineering, 6*, 265–294.

Harding, S. (1986). *The science question in feminism.* Ithaca, NY, and London: Cornell University Press.

Harding, S. (1998). Women, science, and society. *Science, 281*(5383), 1599–1600.

Haworth, C., Dale, P., and Plomin, R. (2008). A twin study into the genetic and environmental influences on academic performance in science in nine-year-old boys and girls. *International Journal of Science Education, 30*(8), 1003–25.

Hayes, D., Mills, M., Christie, P., and Lingard, B. (2005). *Teachers and schooling making a difference.* New South Wales: Allen & Unwin.

Helwig, A.A. (1998a). Developmental and sex differences in workers' functions of occupational aspirations of a longitudinal sample of elementary school children. *Psychological Reports, 82,* 915–921.

Helwig, A.A. (1998b). Occupational aspirations of a longitudinal sample from second to sixth grade. *Journal of Career Development, 24,* 247–265.

Hey, V. (1997). *The company she keeps: An ethnography of girls' friendship.* Buckingham: Open University Press.

Hidi, S., and Renninger, K.A. (2006). The four-phase model of interest development. *Educational Psychologist, 41*(2), 111–127.

HM Treasury. (2011). *The plan for growth.* London: BIS.

Hoskins, K. (2012). *Women and success: Professors in the UK academy.* Staffordshire: Trentham Books.

House of Lords, Select Committee on Science and Technology. (2012). *Higher education in science, technology, engineering and mathematics (STEM) subjects.* London: The Stationery Office Limited.

Huang, G., Taddese, N., and Walter, E. (2000). *Research and development report: Entry and persistence of women and minorities in college science and engineering education.* Washington, DC: National Center for Education Statistics, US Department of Education.

Huber, R.A., and Burton, G.M. (1995). What do students think scientists look like? *School Science and Mathematics, 95*(7), 371–376.

Hulleman, C.S., and Harackiewicz, J.M. (2009). Promoting interest and performance in high school science classes. *Science, 326,* 1410–1412.

IOP (Institute of Physics). (2012). *It's different for girls: The influence of schools.* London: IOP.

IOP (Institute of Physics). (2015). *Opening doors: A guide to good practice in countering gender stereotyping in schools.* London: IOP, www.iop.org/publications/iop/2015/file_66429. pdf (accessed 15 April 2016).

Jenkins, E.W., and Nelson, N.W. (2005). Important but not for me: Students' attitudes towards secondary school science in England. *Research in Science and Technological Education, 23*(1), 41–57.

Johnson, A. (2006). Policy implications of supporting women of color in the sciences. *Journal of Women, Politics, and Policy, 27*(3–4), 135–150.

Johnson, A., Brown, J., Carlone, H., and Cuevas, A.K. (2011). Authoring identity amidst the treacherous terrain of science: A multiracial feminist examination of the journeys of three women of color in science. *Journal of Research in Science Teaching, 48*(4), 339–366.

Jones, P., and Elias, P. (2005). *Science, engineering and technology and the UK's ethnic minority population: A report for the Royal Society.* Coventry: University of Warwick.

Kane, J.M. (2012). Young African American children constructing academic and disciplinary identities in an urban science classroom. *Science Education, 96*(3), 457–487.

Kenway, J., and Bullen, E. (2001). *Consuming Children.* Maidenhead: Open University Press.

Kiernan, K. (2004). Changing European families: Trends and issues. In J. Scott, J. Treas and M. Richards (Eds.), *The Blackwell companion to the sociology of families* (pp. 17–33). Oxford: Blackwell Publishing.

Kintrea, K., St Clair, R., and Houston, M. (2011). *The influence of parents, places and poverty on educational attitudes and aspirations.* London: Joseph Rowntree Foundation.

Koren, P., and Bar, V. (2009). Pupils' image of 'the scientist' among two communities in Israel: A comparative study. *International Journal of Science Education, 31*(18), 2485–2509.

Kristeva, J. (1982). *Powers of horror: An essay on abjection.* New York: Columbia University Press.

Lareau, A. (2003). *Unequal childhoods: Class, race and family life.* Berkeley: University of California Press.

Lareau, A. (2007). Race, class and the transmission of advantage. In L. Weis (Ed.), *The way class works: Readings on school, family, and the economy* (pp. 117–133). New York: Routledge.

Lingard, B. (2005). Socially just pedagogies in changing times. *International Studies in Sociology of Education, 15*(2), 165–186.

Logan, M.R., and Skamp, K.R. (2013). The impact of teachers and their science teaching on students' 'science interest': A four-year study. *International Journal of Science Education, 35*(17), 2879–2904.

Losh, S.C. (2010). Stereotypes about scientists over time among US adults: 1983 and 2001. *Public Understanding of Science, 19*(3), 372–382.

Losh, S.C., Wilke, R., and Pop, M. (2008). Some methodological issues with 'Draw a Scientist Tests' among young children. *International Journal of Science Education, 30*(6), 773–792.

Lowell, B.L., Salzman, H., Bernstein, H., and Henderson, E. (2009). *Steady as she goes? Three generations of students through the science and engineering pipeline,* www.ewa.org/ sites/main/files/steadyasshegoes.pdf (accessed 13 January 2016).

Lyons, T. (2006). Different countries, same science classes: Students' experiences of school science in their own words. *International Journal of Science Education, 28*(6), 591–613.

Lyons, T., Quinn, F., Rizk, N., Anderson, N., Hubber, P., Kenny, J., Sparrow, L., West, J., and Wilson, S. (2012). *Starting out in STEM: A study of young men and women in first year science, technology, engineering and mathematics courses.* Armidale: University of New England.

Mac an Ghaill, M. (1994). *The making of men.* Buckingham: Open University Press.

Mac an Ghaill, M., and Redman P. (1997). Educating Peter: The making of a History Man. Cited in Francis et al. (2009), *The gendered subjectivities of high-achieving pupils.* Full ESRC End of Award Research Report, RES-062-23-0462. Swindon: ESRC.

McMahon, M., Carroll, J., and Gillies, R.M. (2001). Career dreams: Occupational aspirations of year six children. *Australian Journal of Career Development, 10,* 25–31.

McRobbie, A. (1978*). Jackie: An ideology of adolescent femininity.* Birmingham: University of Birmingham.

Maguire, M. (2005). Textures of class in the context of schooling: The perceptions of a 'class-crossing' teacher. *Sociology, 39*(3), 427–443.

Malcom, S.M., Van Horne, V.V., Gaddy, C.D., and George, Y.S. (1998). *Losing ground: Science and engineering graduate education of Black and Hispanic Americans.* Washington, DC: American Association for the Advancement of Science.

Malone, K.R., and Barabino, G. (2009). Narrations of race in STEM research settings: Identity formation and its discontents. *Science Education, 93,* 485–510.

Mama, A. (1995). *Behind the masks: Race, gender and subjectivity.* London: Routledge.

Manis, J.D. (1989). *Factors affecting choices of majors in science, mathematics, and engineering at the University of Michigan.* Ann Arbor: University of Michigan, Center for the Education of Women.

Matthews, B. (1996). Drawing scientists. *Gender and Education, 8*(2), 231–244.

Mead, M., and Metraux, R. (1957). Image of the scientist among high-school students. *Science, 126*(3270), 384–390.

Mendick, H. (2005). A beautiful myth? The gendering of being/doing 'good at maths'. *Gender and Education, 17*(2), 203–219.

Mendick, H., and Epstein, D. (2010). Constructions of mathematicians in popular culture and learners' narratives: A study of mathematical and non-mathematical subjectivities. *Cambridge Journal of Education, 40*(1), 25–38.

Mendick, H., and Francis, B. (2012) Boffin and geek identities – abject or privileged? *Gender and Education, 24*(1), 15–24.

Mendick, H., Allen, K., and Harvey, L. (2015). 'We can get everything we want if we try hard': Young people, celebrity, hard work. *British Journal of Educational Studies, 63*(2), 161–178.

Miles, M.B., and Huberman, A.M. (1994). *Qualitative data analysis: An expanded sourcebook.* Newbury Park, CA: Sage.

Millar, R. (1996). Towards a science curriculum for public understanding. *School Science Review, 77*(280), 7–18.

Millar, R., and Osborne, J.F. (Eds.). (1998). *Beyond 2000: Science education for the future.* London: King's College London.

Mujtaba, T., and Reiss, M.J. (2012). What sort of girl wants to study physics after the age of 16? Findings from a large-scale UK survey. *International Journal of Science Education.* doi:10.1080/09500693.2012.681076.

Mujtaba, T., and Reiss, M.J. (2014). A survey of psychological, motivational, family perceptions of physics education factors that explain 15-year-old students' aspirations to study physics in post-compulsory English schools. *International Journal of Science and Mathematics Education, 12*(2), 371–393.

Murphy, C., and Beggs, J. (2005). *Primary science in the UK: A scoping study. Final report to the Wellcome Trust.* London: Wellcome Trust.

Murphy, C., Varley, J., and Veale, O. (2012). I'd rather they did experiments with us . . . than just talking: Irish children's views of primary school science. *Research in Science Education, 42*(3), 415–438.

Newton, L.D., and Newton, D.P. (1998). Primary children's conceptions of science and the scientist: Is the impact of a National Curriculum breaking down the stereotype? *International Journal of Science Education, 20*(9), 1137–1149.

OECD (Organisation for Economic Co-operation and Development). (2012a). *Better skills, better jobs, better lives: A strategic approach to skills policies.* Paris: OECD.

OECD (Organisation for Economic Co-operation and Development). (2012b). *PISA in focus 18: Are students more engaged when schools offer extracurricular activities?* Paris: OECD.

Ofsted (Office for Standards in Education). (2011). *The annual report of Her Majesty's chief inspector of education, children's services and skills.* Norwich: Ofsted.

Olitsky, S., Flohr, L.L., Gardner, J., and Billups, M. (2010). Coherence, contradiction, and the development of school science identities. *Journal of Research in Science Teaching, 47*(10), 1209–1228.

Ong, M. (2005). Body projects of young women of color in physics: Intersections of gender, race, and science. *Social Problems, 52*, 593–617.

ONS (Office for National Statistics). (2001). *National Statistics Socio-Economic Classification (NS-SEC).* London: Office for National Statistics.

Osborne, J.F. (2007). Science education for the twenty first century. *Eurasia Journal of Mathematics, Science and Technology Education, 3*(3), 173–184.

Osborne, J.F., and Collins, S. (2001). Pupils' views of the role and value of the science curriculum: A focus-group study. *International Journal of Science Education, 23*(5), 441–468.

Osborne, J.F., and Patterson, A. (2011). Scientific argument and explanation: A necessary distinction? *Science Education, 95*(4), 627–638.

Osborne, J., Simon, S., and Collins, S. (2003). Attitudes towards science: A review of the literature and its implications. *International Journal of Science Education, 25*(9), 1049–1079.

Paechter, C. (2000). *Changing school subjects: Power, gender and curriculum.* Buckingham: Open University Press.

Painter, J., Jones, M.G., Tretter, T.R., and Kubasko, D. (2006). Pulling back the curtain: Uncovering and changing students' perceptions of scientists. *School Science and Mathematics, 106*(4), 181–190.

Pakulski, J., and Waters, M. (1996). *The death of class.* London: Sage.

Palmer, D.H. (1997). Investigating students' private perceptions of scientists and their work. *Research in Science and Technological Education, 15*(2), 173–183.

Perkins, J. (2013). *Professor John Perkins' Review of Engineering Skills.* London: Department of Business, Innovation and Skills.

Phipps, A. (2008). *Women in science, engineering and technology: Three decades of UK initiatives.* Stoke-on-Trent: Trentham Books.

Rascoe, B., and Atwater, M.M. (2005). Black males' self-perceptions of academic ability and gifted potential in advanced science classes. *Journal of Research in Science Teaching, 42*(8), 888–911.

Reay, D. (2001). Finding or losing yourself? Working-class relationships to education. *Journal of Education Policy, 16*(4), 333–346.

Reay, D. (2004). 'It's all becoming a habitus': Beyond the habitual use of habitus in educational research. *British Journal of Sociology of Education, 25*(4), 431–444.

Reay, D., David, M., and Ball, S. (2001). Making a difference? Institutional habituses and higher education choice. *Sociological Research Online, 5*(4).

Reay, D., David, M., and Ball, S. (2005). *Degrees of choice: Social class, race and gender in higher education.* Stoke-on-Trent: Trentham Books.

Reiss, M.J. (2001). How to ensure that pupils don't lose interest in science. *Education Today, 51*(2), 34–40.

Renold, E. (2005). *Girls, boys and junior sexualities: Exploring children's gender and sexual relations in the primary school.* London: Routledge.

Robb, N., Dunkley, L., Boynton, P., and Greenhalgh, T. (2007). Looking for a better future: Identity construction in socio-economically deprived 16 year olds considering a career in medicine. *Social Science and Medicine, 65*(4), 738–754.

Royal Academy of Engineering. (2012). *Jobs and growth: The importance of engineering skills to the UK economy – Royal Academy of Engineering econometrics of engineering skills project. Final report.* London: Royal Academy of Engineering.

Royal Society. (1998). *Science and the revision of the National Curriculum.* London: The Royal Society.

Royal Society. (2008a). *Exploring the relationship between socioeconomic status and participation and attainment in science education.* London: The Royal Society.

Royal Society. (2008b). *Science and mathematics education, 14–19: A 'state of the nation' report on the participation and attainment of 14–19 year olds in science and mathematics in the UK, 1996–2007.* London: The Royal Society.

Russell, M.L., and Atwater, M.M. (2005). Traveling the road to success: A discourse on persistence throughout the science pipeline with African American students at a predominantly white institution. *Journal of Research in Science Teaching, 42*(6), 691–715.

Savage, M. (2000). *Class analysis and social transformation.* Buckingham: Open University Press.

Savage, M., Devine, F., Cunningham, N., Taylor, M., Li, Y., Hjellbrekke, J., Le Roux, B., Friedman, S., and Miles, A. (2013). A new model of social class? Findings from the BBC's Great British Class Survey experiment. *Sociology, 47*(2), 219–250.

Scantlebury, K., and Baker, D. (2007). Gender issues in science education research: Remembering where the difference lies. In S. Abell and N. Lederman (Eds.), *Handbook of research on science education* (pp. 257–286). Mahwah, NJ: Erlbaum.

Scantlebury, K., Tai, T., and Rahm, J. (2007). 'That don't look like me.' Stereotypic images of science: Where do they come from and what can we do with them? *Cultural Studies of Science Education, 1*(3), 545–558.

Scherz, Z., and Oren, M. (2006). How to change students' images of science and technology. *Science Education, 90*(6), 965–985.

Schneider, B., and Stevenson, D. (1999). *The ambitious generation: America's teenagers, motivated but directionless.* Yale, CT: Yale University Press.

Schoon, I. (2001). Teenage job aspirations and career attainment in adulthood: A 17 year follow-up study of teenagers who aspired to become scientists, health professionals, or engineers. *International Journal of Behavioral Development, 25*(2), 124–132.

Schoon, I., Parsons, S., and Sacker, A. (2004). Socioeconomic adversity, educational resilience, and subsequent levels of adult adaptation. *Journal of Adolescent Research, 19*, 383–404.

Schreiner, C., and Sjøberg, S. (2004). *Sowing the seeds of ROSE: Background, rationale, questionnaire development and data collection for ROSE (the Relevance of Science Education). A comparative study of students' views of science and science education.* Oslo: University of Oslo.

Schummer, J., and Spector, T.I. (2008). Popular images versus self-images of science. In B. Huppauf and P. Weingart (Eds.), *Science images and popular images of the sciences* (pp. 69–95). London: Routledge.

Scott, J., Treas, J., and Richards, M. (Eds.). (2004). *The Blackwell companion to the sociology of families.* Oxford: Blackwell Publishing.

Sewell, T. (1997). *Black masculinities and schooling.* Stoke-on-Trent: Trentham Books.

Seymour, E., and Hewitt, N. (1997). *Talking about leaving: Why undergraduates leave the sciences.* Boulder, CO: Westview Press.

Shain, F. (2003). *The schooling and identity of Asian girls.* Stoke-on-Trent: Trentham Books.

Shanahan, M.-C., and Nieswandt, M. (2011). Science student role: Evidence of social structural norms specific to school science. *Journal of Research in Science Teaching, 48*(4), 367–395.

Simon, S., Hoyles, C., Mujtaba, T., Farzad, B.R., Reiss, M., Rodd, M., and Stylianidou, F. (2012, April). *Understanding participation rates in post-16 mathematics and physics (UPMAP).* Paper presented at the annual meeting of the American Educational Research Association (AERA), Vancouver.

Sjaastad, J. (2012). Sources of inspiration: The role of significant persons in young people's choice of science in higher education. *International Journal of Science Education, 34*(10), 1615–1636.

Sjøberg, S., and Schreiner, C. (2005). How do learners in different cultures relate to science and technology? Results and perspectives from the project ROSE (the Relevance of Science Education). *Asia-Pacific Forum on Science Learning and Teaching, 6*(2), 1–17.

Skeggs, B. (1997). *Formations of class and gender: Becoming respectable*. Thousand Oaks, CA: Sage.

Skeggs, B. (2004). *The re-branding of class: Propertising culture*. Basingstoke: Palgrave Macmillan.

Skelton, C., Francis, B., and Read, B. (2010). "Brains before 'beauty'?" High achieving girls, school and gender identities. *Educational Studies, 36*(2), 185–194.

Smith, E. (2010a). Do we need more scientists? A long-term view of patterns of participation in UK undergraduate science programmes. *Cambridge Journal of Education, 40*(3), 281–298.

Smith, E. (2010b). Is there a crisis in school science education in the UK? *Educational Review, 62*(2), 189–202.

Smith, E. (2011). Women into science and engineering? Gendered participation in higher education STEM subjects. *British Educational Research Journal, 37*(6), 993–1014.

Smith, E., and Gorard, S. (2011). Is there a shortage of scientists? A re-analysis of supply for the UK. *British Journal of Educational Studies, 59*(2), 159–177.

Smith, W.S., and Erb, T.O. (1986). Effect of women science career role models on early adolescents' attitudes toward scientists and women in science. *Journal of Research in Science Teaching, 23*(8), 667–676.

Snow, C.P. (1959). *The two cultures*. Cambridge: Cambridge University Press.

Solomon, J., Duveen, J., and Scott, L. (1994). Pupils' images of scientific epistemology. *International Journal of Science Education, 16*(3), 361–373.

Song, J., and Kim, K.-S. (1999). How Korean students see scientists: The images of the scientist. *International Journal of Science Education, 21*(9), 957–977.

Spivak, G.A. (1988). Can the subaltern speak? In C. Nelson and L. Grossberg (Eds.), *Marxism and the interpretation of culture* (pp. 271–313). Urbana: University of Illinois.

Springate, I., Harland, J., Lord, P., and Wilkin, A. (2008). *Why choose physics and chemistry? The influences on physics and chemistry subject choices of BME students*. London: Institute of Physics and Royal Society of Chemistry.

Stake, J.E. (2006). The critical mediating role of social encouragement for science motivation and confidence among high school girls and boys. *Journal of Applied Social Psychology, 36*(4), 1017–1045.

St Clair, R., and Benjamin, A. (2011). Performing desires: The dilemma of aspirations and educational attainment. *British Educational Research Journal, 37*(3), 501–517.

Steele, C.M., and Aronson, J. (1995). Stereotype threat and the intellectual test performance of African-Americans. *Journal of Personality and Social Psychology, 69*, 797–811.

Steinke, J., Knight Lapinski, M., Crocker, N., Zietsman-Thomas, A., Williams, Y., Higdon Evergreen, S., and Kuchibhotla, S. (2007). Assessing media influences on middle school aged children's perceptions of women in science using the Draw-a-Scientist Test (DAST). *Science Communication, 29*(1), 35–64.

Strand, S. (2007). *Minority ethnic pupils in the longitudinal study of young people in England (LSYPE)*. London: Department for Children, Schools and Families.

Strand, S. (2009, April). *In-school factors and the White British–Black Caribbean attainment gap: Test, tiers and unintended consequences of assessment practice*. Paper presented at the annual meeting of the American Educational Research Association (AERA), San Diego.

Strand, S., and Winston, J. (2008). Educational aspirations in inner city schools. *Educational Studies, 34*(4), 249–267.

Taconis, R., and Kessels, U. (2009). How choosing science depends on students' individual fit to 'science culture'. *International Journal of Science Education, 31*(8), 1115–1132.

Tai, R.H., Liu, C.Q., Maltese, A.V., and Fan, X. (2006). Planning early for careers in science. *Science, 312*, 1143–1144.

Taylor, F., and Marsden, E. (2012). *Influencing the perceived relevance of Modern Foreign Languages in Year 9: An experimental intervention (Research report)* (No. 30). York: Centre for Language Learning Research, University of York, www.york.ac.uk/depts/educ/research/ResearchPaperSeries/index.htm (accessed 15 January 2016).

Tenenbaum, H.R., and Leaper, C. (2003). Parent–child conversations about science: The socialization of gender inequities? *Developmental Psychology, 39*(1), 34–47.

Thomas, L. (2002). Student retention in higher education: The role of institutional habitus. *Journal of Education Policy, 17*(4), 423–442.

Thomson, D. (2015). *Is A-level physics too hard (and media studies too easy)?* www.educationdatalab.org.uk/Blog/October-2015/Is-A-level-physics-too-hard-and-media-studies.aspx#.VqX4QpqLQ-W (accessed 15 January 2016).

Tomanovic, S. (2004). Family habitus as the cultural context for childhood. *Childhood, 11*(3), 339–360.

Toplis, R. (2012). Students' views about secondary school science lessons: The role of practical work. *Research in Science Education, 42*(3), 531–549.

Trice, A.D. (1991a). A retrospective study of career development: 1. Relationship among first aspirations, parental occupations, and current occupations. *Psychological Reports, 68*, 287–290.

Trice, A.D. (1991b). Stability of children's career aspirations. *Journal of Genetic Psychology, 152*, 137–139.

Trice, A.D., and McClellan, N. (1993). Do children's career aspirations predict adult occupations? An answer from a secondary analysis of a longitudinal study. *Psychological Reports, 72*, 368–370.

Truss, L. (2014). *Speech: Elizabeth Truss on support for maths and science teaching*, www.gov.uk/government/speeches/elizabeth-truss-on-support-for-maths-and-science-teaching (accessed 7 July 2014).

UKCES (UK Commission for Employment and Skills). (2012). *Working futures 2010–2020: Main report.* London: UK Commission for Employment and Skills.

UKCES (UK Commission for Employment and Skills). (2013). *UK commission's employer perspectives survey 2012.* London: UKCES.

UK Science and Innovation Network. (2013). *UK science and innovation network report.* London: UK Science and Innovation Network.

US President's Council of Advisors on Science and Technology. (2010). *Report to the President and Congress. Designing a digital future: Federally funded research and development in networking and information technology.* Washington, DC: Executive Office of the President – President's Council of Advisors on Science and Technology.

Varelas, M., Kane, J.M., and Wylie, C.D. (2011). Young African American children's representations of self, science, and school: Making sense of difference. *Science Education, 95*(5), 824–851.

Vining-Brown, S. (1994). *Minority women in science and engineering education: Final report.* Princeton, NJ: Educational Testing Service.

Walkerdine, V. (1990). *Schoolgirl fictions.* London: Verso Books.

Warrington, M., and Younger, M. (2000). The other side of the gender gap. *Gender and Education, 12*, 493–507.

Weaver, R., Salamonson, Y., Koch, J., and Porter, G. (2012). The CSI effect at university: Forensic science students' television viewing and perceptions of ethical issues. *Australian Journal of Forensic Sciences, 44*(4), 381–391.

Whitelegg, E., Holliman, R., Carr, J., Scanlon, E., and Hodgson, B. (2008). *(In)visible witnesses: Investigating gendered representations of scientists, technologists, engineers and mathematicians on UK children's television. Research report series for UKRC.* Milton Keynes: Open University.

Wilkinson, S., and Kitzinger, C. (Eds.). (1995). *Feminism and discourse: Psychological perspectives.* London: Sage.

Wong, B. (2012). Identifying with science: A case study of two 13-year-old 'high achieving working class' British Asian girls. *International Journal of Science Education, 34*(1), 43–65.

Wright, C., Standen, P.J., and Patel, T. (2010). *Black youth matters: Transitions from school to success.* London: Routledge.

Xie, Y., and Killewald, A.A. (2012). *Is American science in decline?* Cambridge, MA: Harvard University Press.

Yates, S. (2008). *Youth's career aspirations and socio-economic outcomes in adulthood.* Discussion paper published on The Wider Benefits of Learning website, www.learningbenefits. net/Publications/DiscussionPaperIntros/Youthcareerintro.htm (accessed 15 June 2014).

Yates, S., Harris, A., Sabates, R., and Staff, J. (2011). Early occupational aspirations and NEETs: A study of the impact of uncertain and misaligned aspirations and social background on young people's entry into NEET status. *Journal of Social Policy, 40,* 513–534.

INDEX

Page numbers in *italic* refer to figures and tables